YOUR BABY
MONTH BY MONTH

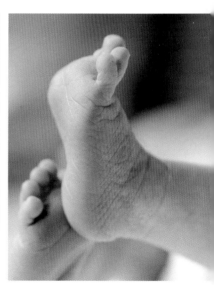

YOUR BABY
MONTH BY MONTH

WHAT TO EXPECT FROM BIRTH TO 2 YEARS

SU LAURENT Consultant Paediatrician
and **PETER READER** GP

London, New York, Munich,
Melbourne, Delhi

Writer Maya Isaaks
Produced for DK by
Dawn Bates and Emma Forge
Senior art editor Glenda Fisher
Senior editor Esther Ripley
Managing editor Penny Warren
Managing art editor Marianne Markham
DTP designer Sonia Charbonnier
Production controller Mandy Inness
Art director Peter Luff
Category publisher Peggy Vance
Publishing director Corinne Roberts
Photography by Vanessa Davies
Picture research Sarah Smithies
Jacket design by Emma Forge
Jacket editor Adam Powley

Every effort has been made to ensure that the information contained in this book is complete and accurate. However, neither the publisher nor the authors are engaged in rendering professional advice or services to the individual reader. The ideas, procedures, and suggestions contained in this book are not intended as a substitute for consultation with your healthcare provider. All matters regarding the health of you and your baby require medical supervision. Neither the publisher nor the author accept any legal responsibility for any personal injury or other damage or loss arising from the use or misuse of the information and advice in this book.

First published in Great Britain in 2007
by Dorling Kindersley Limited,
80 Strand, London WC2R 0RL

A Penguin Company

2 4 6 8 10 9 7 5 3 1

A CIP catalogue record for this book is available from the British Library.
ISBN: 978-1-4053-1808-2
Reproduced in Singapore by Colourscan

Printed and bound in Singapore by Star Standard

Discover more at
www.dk.com

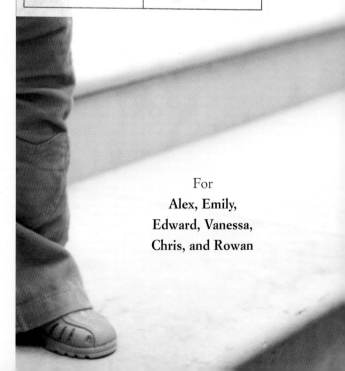

For
**Alex, Emily,
Edward, Vanessa,
Chris, and Rowan**

Contents

"You'll discover that there is no relationship like that between a parent and child."

"Struggling with your defiant toddler? Take a deep breath and remember which one of you is the child."

Health concerns

Foreword

However much time parents-to-be may spend contemplating what life might be like with their first baby, pregnancy does little to prepare them. The majority find themselves going it alone within hours of the birth in the ultimate hands-on learning experience. It gets easier but it gets more complicated, too, because at no other time in life does a human being change and develop as fast as in the first two years.

If I were to suggest some ideal sources of advice and information for new parents, I would look for a person with extensive first-hand experience of the needs of young babies. I would also want someone who could offer medical advice because nothing is more worrying than a sick baby. Lastly, I would want to hear from experienced parents – people who have seen their own children grow and learn and can separate the real anxieties from the stages that pass. In this book you'll find all three: Su Laurent, a paediatrician and colleague, responsible for the day-to-day care of newborn and premature babies, is writing with her husband Peter Reader, a GP with long experience of family health, and together they have three children.

What I like about this book is that the authors have no designs on being baby gurus with a fixed dogma. Instead, they offer the essentials for responding to the changing needs of babies and toddlers, neatly packaged in sections for each age and stage of development, and delivered with licence for parents to do it in their own way, trusting their own instincts. Similarly, Peter and Su emphasize the wide range of what is normal in child development and counsel against unhelpful and unrealistic comparisons between babies, and with the aspirations of more pushy parenting manuals. Here is permission to relax and enjoy your baby, give him or her the freedom to grow and develop – and look after yourselves, too.

Dr Tanya Byron
CLINICAL PSYCHOLOGIST

"Here is permission to relax and enjoy your baby, give him or her the freedom to grow and develop – and look after yourselves, too."

Introduction

Becoming a parent is probably the most exciting, uplifting, and emotional event we'll experience in our lives. With all the highs, however, there are worries and fears. Will I be a good enough parent? How can I take on the responsibility of a helpless baby, let alone a strong-willed toddler? Am I selfless enough to give up the freedom I cherish?

Su Laurent and Peter Reader

From the moment they discover they are pregnant, most mothers-to-be feel a mixture of anticipation and anxiety. This extends throughout childhood and beyond. We adore our babies and cherish every development, but we also worry about whether they are feeding too much or too little, sleeping too much or too little, and even pooing too much or too little. Are we playing with them enough? Are they over- or under-stimulated? What nursery or school should they go to?

As doctors (a paediatrician and a GP) and as parents, we have heard and felt these anxieties many times and realize that it's impossible to take all the guilt and anxiety out of parenting. All parents, however wonderful, will find something to blame themselves for or worry about – it goes with the job.

Every baby is born with a unique temperament. However, as parents we impose our values and concerns on our children. This means that both nature and nurture play key roles in the development of a child's personality and, like it or not, our own upbringing and values are those we impart to our children. The good news is that, although many of us worry about our style of parenting, most of us are good enough parents and do the best we can by our children.

Once you have a baby, everyone will offer parenting tips that they have found invaluable. Inevitably, these are conflicting: should you leave your baby to cry or pick him up straight away? Should you follow a routine or go with the flow? Should you go out to work or stay at home? Whatever views you hold, your baby will flourish if he is loved and cherished, and if you try to see things from his point of view. With this in mind, there are some key themes that we return to throughout this book.

■ **Behaviour:** it will be a long time before your baby understands the concept of "good" or "bad" behaviour. However, he craves your attention and will repeat behaviour that gets a response. If you consistently praise desirable behaviour and ignore the undesirable, he is more likely to behave as you would like and will delight in your approval. The opposite is also true. If you ignore him when he's playing happily, and give him attention when he empties the cat's bowl, he will be encouraged to do it again.

■ **Play:** this is essential to your child's development. Through play, children discover the world around them, develop their motor skills, and learn how to communicate. Early play with your child is also a strong way of bonding, and is a vital part of making your child feel secure and loved.

■ **Sleep:** this will play a huge part in your new life as a parent. At birth babies generally sleep as much in the day as at night, but by his first birthday your baby will probably have his main sleep at night. However, night waking is common, so we help you understand how to promote a good sleep pattern and offer advice on what to do if things don't go to plan.

■ **Food:** this is tackled head on with tips on avoiding fussy eaters and what to do if, despite your best efforts, your toddler refuses all fruit and vegetables and eats only white bread and crisps. The heart of this advice

FROM 0–2 YEARS

YOUR BABY'S DEVELOPMENT
In each section, we describe key areas of development, baby and toddler care essentials, and toys and games your baby might respond to.

His new world

First smile

Physical skills

About to crawl

| MONTHS | 1 | 2 and 3 | 4, 5, and 6 | 7, 8, and 9 |

▶ The 1st Year

is understanding what a powerful weapon food can be. By converting the food battleground into an enjoyable family experience, feeding your toddler can become a pleasure for you all.

In this book, we have blended our experience as parents with our knowledge as doctors to give you straightforward guidance. We explain what you can expect at each age and stage; what support is on offer from the health services; and how to address common problems and illnesses. We encourage a relaxed approach by minimizing the rules and highlighting important areas. By gaining insight into these essentials, we hope you will feel confident about developing your own style of parenting. Just remember these five golden rules:

■ The best environment for a child to grow up in is one that is high in warmth and low in criticism.

■ Never compare your parenting skills with those of your friends.

■ Never compare your child's abilities with those of his friends.

■ When your child is displaying challenging behaviour, always remember which one of you is the parent.

■ Enjoy the experience – childhood is a magical time and is gone so quickly. Remember, too, that most children turn out fine. That is because most of us follow our instincts, providing our children with unconditional love and an environment in which they can grow and develop to reach their full potential. Good luck and happy parenting!

| On her feet | On the move | New toys | New skills | Having fun |

| 0, 11, and 12 | 13, 14, and 15 | 16, 17, and 18 | 19, 20, and 21 | 22, 23, and 24 |

▶ The 2nd Year

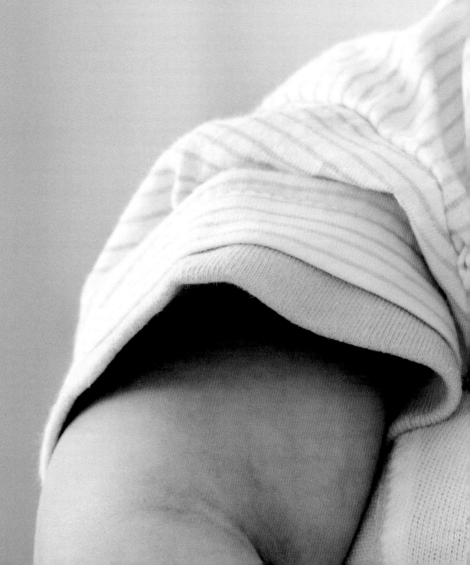

THE 1ST YEAR

From a tiny scrunched-up newborn to a feisty, mobile little person, the first year of life is an exciting journey. Never again will your child go through such rapid changes in growth and development – it is a time of joy and discovery for you all.

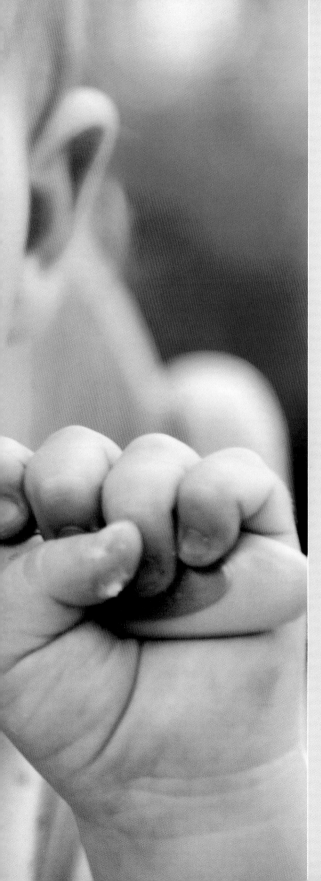

Contents

YOUR NEWBORN BABY

WEEK 0–1

HEALTH CHECKS YOUR BABY WILL BE GIVEN A THOROUGH MEDICAL EXAMINATION IN THE FIRST 24 HOURS

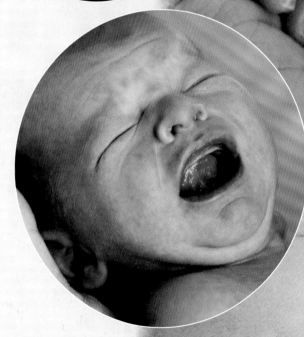

ADAPTING TO HIS WORLD
CRYING IS A NATURAL RESPONSE TO HIS NEW ENVIRONMENT, BUT YOU WILL SOON LEARN WHAT HIS CRIES MEAN

YOUR AMAZING NEWBORN TINY FINGERS AND TINY TOES – YOU'LL NEVER TIRE OF LOOKING AT YOUR BABY

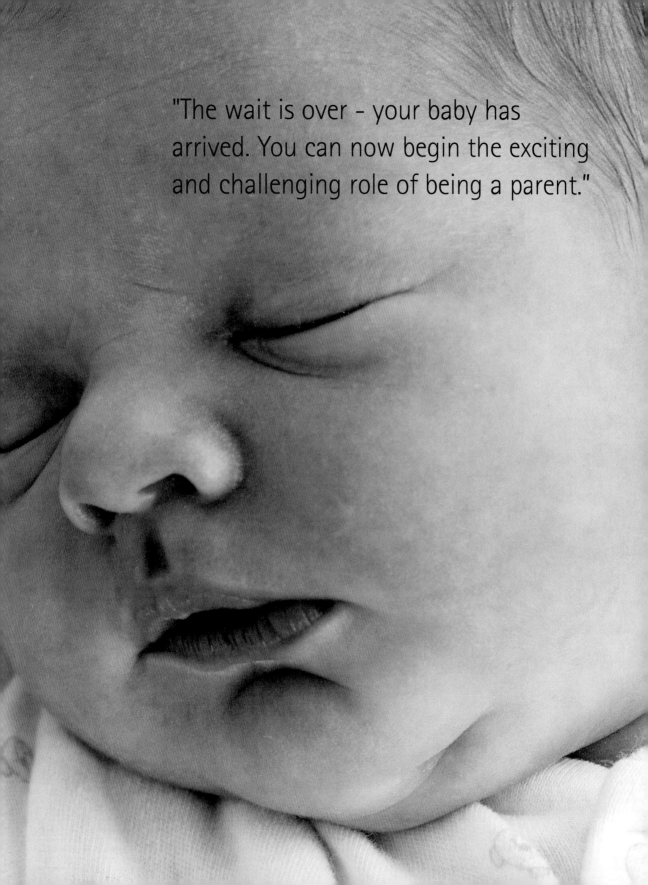

"The wait is over – your baby has arrived. You can now begin the exciting and challenging role of being a parent."

In the beginning

Meeting your newborn baby is without doubt one of life's most amazing experiences. You are likely to feel a combination of exhaustion, elation, and shock, but there is no right or wrong way to respond – just let the moment unfold and greet your baby in the way that feels right for you.

What your baby may look like

Be prepared for your baby to look rather odd immediately after the delivery, and probably nothing like you imagined. As she emerges, she will be a bluish-purple colour, but don't be alarmed – when she takes her first breath she will turn reddish-pink. Her extremities might stay blue for a while as her circulation is immature.

If you have had a vaginal delivery, your baby's head will have been moulded by the birth canal and may look elongated and even rather pointed. She will look less like a little alien after a few days as her head returns to a more normal shape. If she was helped out with a ventouse (suction cap), she will have a baggy, swollen circle on her scalp where it was attached. If you had a forceps delivery, she may have bruising and swelling on the sides of her head, but this will soon heal.

Your baby's genitals may seem swollen and baby girls sometimes have vaginal spotting. Both sexes may have swollen breasts and might even leak milk from their nipples. These physical characteristics are nothing to worry about – they are caused by your hormones circulating around your baby's body and will soon settle down. She may be covered with vernix, a white, greasy substance that protected her skin while she was surrounded by amniotic fluid. Without it, her skin would have reacted pretty much as yours does if you stay in the bath for too long. If your baby was overdue, you'll probably notice that her skin is rather dry as the vernix will have been absorbed. Some babies are born with soft hair on their bodies, called lanugo, which will soon rub off. The earlier a baby is born, the more lanugo she may have. When you look into her eyes, don't be surprised if they are blue, even if your whole family has brown eyes. Most Caucasian babies start life with

FIRST HOURS *Blemishes and soft, downy hair are common characteristics of newborn babies, and his face and eyes are likely to appear slightly swollen.*

dark blue eyes, while Asian and Afro-Caribbean babies often have dark grey or brown eyes. By 12 weeks your baby's eyes will have changed colour if they're going to, but you might not see the final shade until she's a year old.

Your feelings for your baby

This small person has been squirming, kicking, and maybe even getting hiccups inside you, for months and you're bound to have formed some ideas about her character. But what if you were expecting a girl and it's a boy? Or your baby doesn't look the way you expected she would? You may feel overwhelmingly emotional or you may not feel very much at all. While there are parents who fall in love with their newborn instantly and

Minor newborn oddities

It is common for babies to have minor blemishes or problems at birth.

▶ **Stork marks** (capillary naevi) are little red blemishes, usually on the eyelids, forehead, and nape of the neck. They are made up of dilated capillaries, or very small blood vessels. They are of no significance and will disappear naturally, often within the first two years and almost always by the age of five.

▶ **Port wine stains** (capillary angioma) are due to an abnormal development of the blood vessels in a patch of skin and, unfortunately, do not fade with time. Laser treatment, however, which takes place over 2–4 years, can be very effective, especially if it is started early. Laser technology is improving

all the time, leading to a reduced risk of scarring.

▶ **Mongolian blue spots** (dermal melanocytosis) look like bruises and are commonly seen in Afro-Caribbean or Asian babies. They are generally found on the base of the spine and backs of the legs, but may also appear on the arms and hands. They are of no significance, usually disappearing by around three years.

▶ **Strawberry marks** (haemangiomas) are often not visible immediately after birth, but gradually appear in the first few days or weeks. They are raised and bright red because they are made up of lots of small blood vessels. Although they continue to grow, they usually vanish leaving no scar by the time a child is five.

▶ **Positional talipes** is where a baby is born with feet that appear to turn in, or occasionally out, at the ankle. It is usually the result of the feet being squashed in the womb towards the end of pregnancy. This condition can appear alarming, but is not normally of any great significance. It can be differentiated from the more serious fixed talipes (club foot) by the fact that the baby's foot can be returned back to a normal position by pressure on the sole. The treatment for positional talipes is regular, gentle massage to encourage the foot back into the correct position. A physiotherapist may show you how to do this. As the foot grows and the baby begins to stand up, the foot will adopt a normal position by itself.

talk about "recognizing" their baby as soon as
she's born, many others take longer. This is
entirely normal – she is someone you have never
met before and it may feel as though she is a
stranger. Relax and let things take their course,
and you will find that the bond between you
will gradually develop.

Developing a bond

There is no set time for bonding, but there are
ways to help it along. If you can hold your baby
against your chest immediately after she is born,
it will give your relationship a great start, and
research shows that a leisurely period of skin-to-
skin contact between you as soon as possible
contributes to breastfeeding success. If you
can't hold her at first, perhaps because you have
had a Caesarean, you can gently stroke her hand
and cuddle her once you are able. Breastfeeding
is possible immediately after your baby is born and, as many babies are
very alert straight after delivery, this is a great way to bond with her.
Having said that, don't worry if she is too sleepy or you don't feel up to it.
What is most important is that there is someone around to help you get
your baby latched on properly when you are ready (see page 31). It can
take a while to get this right – if she is your first baby, breastfeeding will
be a learning experience for both of you.

CLOSE CONTACT
Holding your baby
against you – skin to
skin – can promote
bonding and will help
your newborn baby
to thrive.

Have skin-to-skin contact whenever you can – as well as being a lovely
experience, it is beneficial to your baby and will help you feel close to her.
Make sure she is dry and the room is warm. Don't worry about her getting
chilly: if your baby is held against your skin she will maintain her body
temperature well, but if you are concerned you can wrap a towel or light
blanket around the two of you.

During pregnancy your baby will have become used to hearing your
voice and will find it soothing, so don't feel shy about talking to her. She
will naturally take an interest in faces from birth, and if you hold her facing
you and slowly poke out your tongue, she might even attempt to copy you.

Dad's-eye view

A baby can seem a bewildering prospect, especially as this new "bit of kit" doesn't come with an instruction manual. Today's quick hospital discharges mean that the transition from "couple" to "family" seems to take place in the twinkling of an eye.

When our daughter was born, I remember arriving at the delivery suite at 5 pm and joking that we had to be back in time to watch ER at 10 pm. To my amazement, by 10 pm I was sitting on the sofa with a take-out pizza and my new daughter asleep beside me. In a curious way it felt almost as if we'd popped out to pick the baby up from the hospital, in a similar way to the pizza. (Though Su probably felt a little differently about the ease of popping out for the baby!) It seemed such a short step and yet we now had a whole new person in our lives.

I appreciate that not every birth is as simple (with our second baby, Su ended up having an emergency Caesarean), but the change from being a couple to being a family will be just as sudden and real, however the birth goes. It can take weeks or even months to adjust and bond with your baby, and emotions such as jealousy, frustration, and anxiety are normal, so don't be too hard on yourself. Talk with your partner – it's important to understand and support each other through this transition. For most, though, it's a magical time. I was a bit anxious about the impact of a new baby in our lives, but fell in love straight away.

If you have had a Caesarean

A Caesarean section is major surgery so you'll need even more time to recover and shouldn't expect too much of yourself too soon. I remember finding it difficult to reach for a glass of water, let alone my baby! There can be a silver lining to this, though, as the first hours and days after a Caesarean delivery are a great time for new dads to become acquainted with their babies and all the attendant chores.

Your scar will be sore initially so ask for pain relief when you need it. However livid it looks, it will eventually fade to a pale line, which is hardly noticeable. Moving around may be difficult, but you will be encouraged to get out of bed soon after to speed up your recovery. Do ask for help with breastfeeding. There are ways to hold your baby so that she is not resting on your abdomen, such as lying her down beside you or in a "rugby ball hold" (see page 53). If you had an emergency Caesarean, you may feel upset, disappointed, or even a failure. To help you come to terms with it, talk to the midwives and obstetrician. Remember, it is no-one's fault – what is most important is that your baby has been delivered safely.

First checks

Your baby will be given a number of health checks in the first 24 hours. Straight after the birth she will be given a score on what is known as the Apgar scale and, later, a complete top-to-toe examination. She will also be weighed and measured – the starting points for her growth charts (see pages 62–63).

The Apgar scale

Apgar tests are used to check a newborn baby's health so that any medical treatment can be given as quickly as possible. Breathing, heart rate, colour, muscle tone, and response to stimuli are measured as soon as a baby is born, and again five and 10 minutes later to ensure that she is adjusting to life outside the womb. The tests are carried out so quickly and efficiently by the midwife that you might not even be aware of them.

Apgar scoring

Each of the five factors that are taken into consideration are given scores of between 0 and 2 and these are added together. Most babies score between 7 and 10. A baby who scores lower than 7 is likely to need some sort of medical help.

WHAT IS MEASURED	0	1	2
▶ Breathing	Baby not breathing	Slow, irregular, or laboured breathing	Breathing normally, without effort
▶ Heart rate	Absent	Less than 100 beats per minute	More than 100 beats per minute
▶ Colour	Bluish-grey	Pink, but with blue extremities (hands and feet)	Pink all over, including extremities
▶ Muscle tone	Floppy and not moving	A little movement of extremities	Active spontaneous movements
▶ Response to stimuli	No response to stimulation, such as a gentle pinch	Grimaces in response to stimuli	Active response to stimuli – pulls away, possibly sneezes, coughs, or cries

Top-to-toe examination

At some point during these first 24 hours your baby will have a thorough medical examination to make sure she is healthy and to detect any problems or abnormalities. A paediatrician, a midwife, or your GP will check her heart and lungs, head, mouth, hands, feet, hips, and spine (see below). Her eyes will be checked for obvious abnormalities or discharge and a light will be shone into them to check for cataracts. Her abdomen will be examined to see whether her tummy feels as it should and whether the cord stump looks healthy. After counting the number of toes, her feet will be checked for talipes, where the feet are turned in (or sometimes out) at the ankle (see page 22). The pulses at the top of your baby's legs will be felt, and her skin will be checked for any birthmarks (see page 22).

The genitals and anus are examined to ensure they are formed normally. A boy will be checked to see whether his testicles have descended into the scrotum and that the opening in his penis is at the tip, rather than underneath. On rare occasions, it may be difficult to be certain whether the baby is a girl or boy. If this is the case, doctors will need to do some tests to establish the baby's gender.

You will be asked whether your baby has had a wee and a poo during the first 24 hours. Some babies pass urine containing reddish crystals that look like brick dust. This is normal but tell the doctor or midwife as it may be a sign that your baby is slightly dehydrated and not getting enough milk and, if this is the case, you may need extra help with feeding.

HEALTH CHECKS

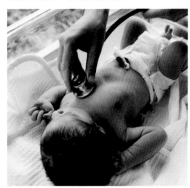 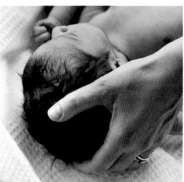 

HEART AND LUNGS *are checked to ensure they sound normal.*

HEAD SHAPE *and fontanelles (soft spots between the skull bones) are examined.*

MOUTH AND PALATE – *the separate sections should have fused together.*

Your baby's reflexes

Your newborn has several "primitive" reflexes, including sucking, grasping, and rooting – when her cheek or lips are stroked she should turn her head and open her mouth. These responses indicate that her nervous system is in good working order.

Her startle – or "moro" – reflex occurs when she is gently (and safely) dropped back into a waiting hand.

She will throw her arms outwards to save herself. If she is held upright with her feet touching a flat surface, she will make stepping movements. I convinced my mother-in-law that her grandson could walk at birth by demonstrating this!

The evolutionary purpose of these reflexes is to allow baby mammals to survive. Some, such as the stepping reflex, are not important to human babies but are vital to baby animals that need to walk immediately after birth. Others, such as the sucking and rooting reflexes, are essential for all babies.

These primitive reflexes need to disappear to allow normal development to take place and this happens over the first few months.

Newborn hearing check

A simple test is used to check your baby's hearing in the first few days or weeks. She may be given one of two kinds:

■ **Oto-acoustic emission (OAE) screen:** a soft earpiece with a microphone is placed in the outer part of your baby's ear, and quiet clicking sounds are played. If she hears normally, the earpiece will pick this up.

■ **Automated auditory brainstem response (AABR) screen:** if she is less than a day old, or the OAE test doesn't give a clear result, sounds are played through headphones and her brain's responses are monitored via sensors.

HANDS AND FEET *are checked for numbers of fingers and toes.*

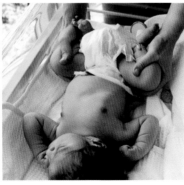

HIPS *are examined to ensure they are properly in their sockets.*

SPINE *is checked to ensure it is straight and free from abnormalities.*

Heel-prick test

This is a screening test in which blood is taken from a newborn baby's heel to check for rare but treatable problems. The result is usually negative, but for the few babies who have one of these conditions, the screening is essential; early treatment can prevent severe disabilities and be life saving. Your baby may be checked for –

■ **Phenylketonuria (PKU):** this inherited condition affects the ability to metabolize, or process, a type of amino acid in food. Babies with PKU are treated with a special diet, which allows them to lead a normal life. However, if untreated, PKU can cause irreversible mental disability.

■ **Congenital hypothyroidism (CHT):** in this condition, reduced levels of the hormone thyroxine cause impaired growth and brain development. Once identified, babies with CHT are given thyroxine and develop normally.

■ **Sickle cell disorders (SCD):** these inherited disorders cause the red blood cells to change to a sickle shape that does not pass easily through small blood vessels, causing severe pain, infection, and sometimes even death. Early treatment can help reduce the severity of SCD.

■ **Cystic fibrosis (CF):** this genetic condition affects the lungs and digestive system. To help them lead longer, healthier lives, babies with CF need a special diet, physiotherapy to help remove accumulated secretions from their lungs, and medication.

■ **Medium chain acyl-coA dehydrogenase deficiency (MCADD):** this condition prevents a baby metabolizing fats properly, which can lead to serious illness and may be linked to cot death. If identified early, it is treatable through medication and diet.

Vitamin K injection

Because newborn babies don't have a very good supply of vitamin K, which is essential for blood clotting, there is a small risk of spontaneous bleeding, so they are offered an injection shortly after birth. Some years ago there was a controversy about this injection because it was thought to be linked to an increased risk of leukaemia, but this has now been disproved.

If you would prefer your newborn baby not to have the injection, it is usually possible for her to be given oral vitamin K drops instead – the dose will need repeating after a few days, and then again after a few weeks, in order for it to be effective.

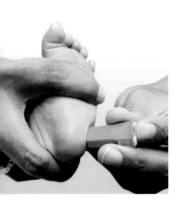

SCREENING *Before your baby is a week old, a drop of blood will be taken from her heel and tested for specific, although rare, medical conditions.*

Your baby's first feed

Feeding your baby from the breast in the first few days is very important to her health. Before your breast milk comes in (around three days after the birth), you will be giving her colostrum. This yellow fluid contains essential antibodies and nutrients that are of tremendous benefit to your baby.

Getting support

When my first child was born I was totally unprepared for the physical and emotional turmoil of discovering that breastfeeding didn't come naturally to me. My breasts became sore and I soon succumbed to bottles. Second time around I was determined that things would be different, so I attended a breastfeeding workshop during pregnancy, then asked a midwife to help me position my baby on the breast after the birth. I soon became a confident breastfeeding mum.

Breastfeeding is a natural process, but it doesn't always come easily and I sympathize with women who struggle with it. However, I know that getting good support and giving yourself time to get the hang of breastfeeding can help you succeed and enjoy it. You may find you get hooked on the closeness of breastfeeding, and even if you don't, you will have given your baby a fantastic start to life. My best tip came from a nurse who said: "Stuff as much of your areola as you can into your baby's mouth and hold her firmly to the breast until she gets the hang of it." It worked for me.

At first, you may feel contractions when you feed because the hormone that causes your milk ducts to squeeze the milk out also makes your womb contract. This only lasts a few days.

THE BEST START *Breast milk is extremely beneficial to your baby. Even if you are unsure about breastfeeding, try giving it a go in the first few days – it may be easier than you thought.*

Why breastfeed?

There are many advantages to breastfeeding your baby. It is –

■ **Nutritious:** breast milk contains all the nutrients your baby needs and is easily digestible, so there is less chance of her becoming constipated and more chance of her producing sweeter-smelling nappies.

■ **Protective:** your baby will receive antibodies through breast milk, which help protect her from illnesses such as ear infections, vomiting and diarrhoea, urinary tract infections (UTIs), coughs, and colds. Research has found that there is a lower risk of cot death (see page 39) among breastfed babies. It will also help her growth and development and make her less likely to develop allergies, such as asthma and eczema.

■ **Convenient:** once you and your baby have mastered breastfeeding, it is very easy, as well as practical. How much simpler it is to pop out with your baby if all you need is a nappy in your pocket rather than all the paraphernalia that goes with bottle-feeding.

■ **Good for you:** breastfeeding helps your womb contract after the birth and helps you lose weight (as long as you resist eating too many cakes and biscuits). Research has found that the longer a woman breastfeeds, and the more babies she breastfeeds, the more her chances of developing breast cancer are reduced.

EXPERT HELP Don't be afraid to seek support. Getting the technique right from the start increases the chance of you succeeding at, and enjoying, breastfeeding.

Although there are some downsides to breastfeeding, it is possible to overcome most of these. The disadvantages are –

■ **It requires patience:** without advice and support, breastfeeding can be difficult and make you feel anxious and inadequate, so do ask for help from your midwife or find a breastfeeding counsellor (see page 312).

■ **It may be sore at first:** you will almost inevitably have some tenderness for a week or so as you get used to breastfeeding While this is a common side-effect, the risk of it happening is reduced if your baby is latched on to the breast correctly (see opposite).

■ **It is time-consuming:** if you bottle-feed, you can share feeds and have a break.

Feeding your baby

I hope with the information I have given you so far you will feel that you can at least give breastfeeding a go. The following section will help to get you started by showing you how to get your baby latched onto the breast, and how to deal with some common breastfeeding problems. On pages 52–55 you will find a guide to breastfeeding positions, plus advice on what to eat and drink during the months you are breastfeeding.

See the sequence below for how to get your baby latched on and remove her from the breast. To ensure she is feeding properly and to prevent problems such as sore nipples (see page 32), make sure she has the whole of your nipple, and most of the dark areola that surrounds it, in her mouth. Your baby's lower jaw does most of the work, "stripping" out the milk, but she can only use it effectively if she is latched on. In the correct position, she will feed rhythmically and you will see her jaw move steadily as she swallows. If she is not latched on correctly, she won't be able to feed properly and your nipple is likely to get sore. If this is the case, slide your finger into her mouth to break the suction (see below) and try again. In the first few days your baby will breastfeed very frequently to increase your milk supply; by feeding often she stimulates your breasts to make more.

GETTING STARTED

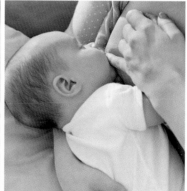

1 PUTTING HER ON THE BREAST *Make sure your baby's face and entire body are turned towards the breast. Hold her level with the breast with your nipple pointing towards her nose.*

2 LATCHED ON *If your baby is latched on to the breast correctly, her lower lip should be curled back underneath your nipple and her ears should move as she sucks.*

3 TAKING HER OFF THE BREAST *Once your baby has finished feeding, slide your little finger into the corner of her mouth. This will break the seal it forms around the breast.*

Breastfeeding concerns

▶ **My breasts are swollen and painful. What can I do?**

Swollen, hard, engorged breasts are common when you start breastfeeding. You can relieve them by putting a couple of cold cabbage leaves (from the fridge) inside your bra. Expressing a little milk before feeding (see page 89) will help your baby latch on to engorged breasts. An easy way to do this is to stand under a warm shower and gently massage your breasts from the top or sides towards the nipple to get the milk flowing.

▶ **Why has my week-old baby lost weight?**

It is usual for babies to lose as much as 10 per cent of their birth weight during the first few days. This often happens before your milk comes in around three or four days after the birth, but the weight is regained once your baby settles into feeding. The community midwife will weigh your baby as part of her regular checks and will keep an eye on how much weight she loses. If your baby loses more than 10 per cent of her birth weight, you will be offered feeding advice and her progress will be closely monitored, although this is usually a minor glitch rather than anything serious.

▶ **My baby has a blister on her lip. Should I be concerned?**

This is called a sucking blister, and is caused by rubbing on the lip while feeding. It may come and go in the first few weeks, but it won't bother your baby and will disappear without treatment.

▶ **Is it normal for a new baby to keep bringing up milk?**

Yes – this is called possetting and is nothing to worry about. Your baby may seem to bring up copious quantities, but this is unlikely to affect her nutritionally and she'll probably continue to gain weight. If you're worried about the amount, ask your health visitor for advice.

If the vomiting worsens or becomes projectile (where your baby is sick with such force that it shoots across the room), she'll need to see a doctor to rule out conditions such as gastro-oesophageal reflux or pyloric stenosis (see page 275). During this first week, if your baby has yellow or green vomit, contact your doctor immediately as she may have a bowel obstruction. In older babies, vomit this colour is probably a sign of a tummy upset, but this is not the case in a newborn.

▶ **How can I soothe sore nipples?**

Ask your midwife or health visitor to check your baby's position on the breast because this is a prime cause of sore nipples. After breastfeeding use a small amount of nipple cream, such as a lanolin or calendula-based ointment. To ease the pain, take paracetamol every 4–6 hours or ibuprofen every 6–8 hours (don't exceed the recommended dose). Prevent your nipples becoming sore by letting them air-dry after feeding. Also check that your nursing bra fits correctly and avoid using plastic-backed breast pads, which can keep your nipples damp. You can buy nipple shields, which allow your baby to suckle without touching the nipple, but these can be difficult to position correctly. Special moist dressings can help cracked nipples. If sore nipples persist, you may have thrush (see page 283) so ask your GP to check for this fungal infection.

Bottle-feeding your baby

If you have decided you would prefer not to breastfeed your baby or, for some reason, you have been unable to establish breastfeeding, see the box below for how to get started on bottle-feeding. If you have had breastfeeding difficulties, you might first want to seek advice from your midwife or breastfeeding counsellor who can offer help and advice. But if breastfeeding just hasn't worked out, don't feel guilty. It is better for your baby to have relaxed, happy parents who give bottles with love and care.

The good news is that formula milk is designed to be nutritionally as close as possible to breast milk so your baby will still have a good start in life. Bottle-feeding has the advantage of being something you can share, so you can have a break while dad or grandma takes a turn. The downside to bottle-feeding your baby is that you will have to be that bit more organized. Make sure you have bought everything you need – bottles, teats, and formula milk – and that you are fully equipped when you are out and about with your baby. See pages 58–59 for advice on sterilization.

Getting started

Bacteria can multiply once the feed is mixed so make up each bottle as you need it, rather than keeping made-up formula in the fridge.

If she hasn't finished the bottle, throw away any leftover formula after half an hour, to minimize the risk of tummy upsets.

1 Wash your hands and fill a bottle with as much cooled, boiled water as you need.

2 Add the correct amount of milk powder (the container will have full instructions) by using the scoop provided and levelling it off with a knife (see below). Stick strictly to the correct amount of powder, as adding extra can lead to problems such as constipation.

3 Put the cap on the bottle, give it a thorough shake and add a teat.

4 You don't need to warm the bottle but if you want to, stand it in a jug of hot water for a few minutes, then test the temperature on the inside of your wrist (it should be around body heat). Microwaves aren't ideal for warming bottles as the intense heat can create hot spots that could scald your baby. If you do warm her milk in the microwave, give it a really good shake and then test the temperature carefully.

5 Tip the bottle so that milk fills the teat before you feed your baby so that she doesn't take in too much air.

Early concerns

It is natural to be concerned about your newborn baby's health – you are, after all, totally responsible for this tiny person. As you care for your baby, it helps to know what is normal and what is not, but remember your midwife is on hand in the early days, and your health visitor after that.

Baby poo

Your baby's first stools will be sticky, tarry, and dark green. This early poo is called meconium, and has built up in your baby's intestine during pregnancy. For the first couple of days, it is a good idea to smooth petroleum jelly over your baby's bottom before putting on her nappy so that when she passes meconium, it will be easier to clean off. If she doesn't pass meconium in the first 24 hours, she may have an obstruction, so tell your doctor or midwife.

The cord stump

When your baby's umbilical cord is cut, it resembles a white, rubbery tube, around 4cm (1.5in) long, hanging from what will be her tummy button. At birth it is clamped with a plastic clip, which is removed when the cord is completely dry. Over the next 7–10 days, the stump will dry out, turn brown, and drop off. Occasionally, the cord stump can become sticky and, rarely, a little infected. Usually, this is of no significance and all you will need to do is wash it with cooled boiled water and cotton wool. Show it to your midwife when she visits – in very rare cases, your baby may need antibiotics.

As the cord dries, your baby's tummy button will heal up beneath it, leaving a normal-looking navel. Occasionally the skin under the cord stump will be very moist and pink and, if this happens, your GP will treat it with a silver nitrate stick. This will do your baby no harm at all.

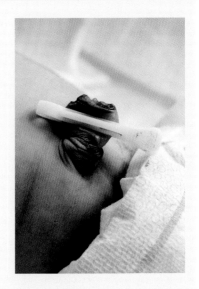

Once your breast milk has come in, or your baby is having bottles, her poos will change. They can vary considerably in colour and consistency: from yellow or orange to brown, liquid to semi-solid, all of which are normal. While breastfed babies' poo smells rather mild and sweet – a bit like toffee yoghurt – bottle-fed babies' poo is much whiffier.

Jaundice

It is not unusual for babies to become jaundiced (look slightly yellow) on the third or fourth day of life. This happens in around half of all full-term babies, and is due to their immature liver being unable to cope with some of the body's waste products. Mild jaundice won't need treatment, but some babies will need to spend time under a UV phototherapy light to help break down the waste products. Unfortunately, this means a short spell back in hospital, although it is usually for only 48 hours.

Newborn babies who are jaundiced within 24 hours of their birth, or who remain jaundiced for more than 10 days, will require further tests to check for other rare causes. These include liver disease, infection, hypothyroidism, and blood disorders.

PHOTOTHERAPY *With treatment, jaundice won't cause your baby any health problems.*

Common concerns

▶ **Is it normal for a new baby to have spots?**

Yes – lots of newborns have harmless white spots (milia), which may come and go in the first few weeks. The only damage they can do is to your baby photos! Clean your baby's face normally and don't squeeze the spots. Another common rash is erythaema toxicum, in which the spots have a yellow raised centre and a red ring around them. They don't need treatment either.

▶ **My newborn baby's eyes are gooey. Is this serious?**

Sticky eyes are common and are usually caused by contact with bacteria in the vagina during the birth. Clean the discharge with cooled boiled water and cotton wool (use a separate piece for each eye). The problem should clear up in a few days, but get your GP to check your baby's eyes just in case there is an infection. Sticky eyes are sometimes due to blocked tear ducts. These normally correct themselves without treatment.

▶ **My baby is always snuffling. Could she have a cold?**

Your baby can't breathe through her mouth yet, so if she has mucus in her nose she will snuffle when she breathes. This is common and as long as she is otherwise well don't worry. If, however, your baby is having difficulty with feeding or breathing, see your GP.

QUESTION&ANSWER

Babies in special care

Some newborns need extra medical help and will spend some time in a special unit. This may be a neonatal unit (NNU), which provides intensive care, or a special care baby unit (SCBU), which is for babies with less complex needs.

REASONS FOR SPECIAL CARE

Babies need to be cared for in the NNU or SCBU for a variety of reasons:

▶ If your baby is born before 35-36 weeks, she will probably need to be in special care as she will be more prone to infection and her immature lungs could cause breathing difficulties.

▶ If she was born at the right time but is smaller than expected, she is likely to spend time in special care to make sure that her body is coping with life outside the womb.

▶ If you have diabetes, your baby may need special care. She may be very large because she will have received too much of the glucose you were unable to metabolize during pregnancy.

▶ If your baby is severely jaundiced, she may be given phototherapy (see page 35) in the SCBU.

▶ Babies who need an operation after delivery will go to the SCBU or NNU.

▶ If you have had twins or more, there is a higher chance they will need special care as they are more likely to have been born prematurely.

WHAT IS A NNU LIKE?

It can be deeply distressing to see your tiny baby in such an alien environment full of high-tech equipment, and emotional upsets are very common in any NNU.

Although it may seem hard to believe, all the technology and terminology will become second-nature to you if your baby is in the unit for any length of time. Meanwhile, it may help to know what some of the equipment is for –

▶ **Incubator:** your baby may be cared for in an incubator, which is an enclosed cot where the temperature and humidity can be controlled and where she can be given oxygen if necessary. The incubator has portholes at the sides so the medical staff can look after your baby, and you will also be able to reach in and touch her.

▶ **Ventilator:** this machine supports your baby's breathing. A tube is passed into the trachea (windpipe) and oxygen is puffed into her lungs until she is able to breathe on her own.

▶ **Continuous positive air pressure:** this device is a way of supporting a baby's breathing without putting a tube into her windpipe. Oxygen is puffed into her nose under pressure, which helps her lungs to remain inflated and often enables babies to come off the ventilator earlier, or even avoid going on one at all.

CARING FOR YOUR BABY

Although your baby needs special care, the staff will encourage you to talk to her if she is not too tired, and hold her if she is well enough. Even tiny babies on ventilators can be cuddled, and she will soon recognize your voice.

If she is too sick or small to feed, your baby may be given milk through a soft tube that goes up her nose and down into her tummy. You will be encouraged to express breast milk, which has the advantage of stimulating your milk production for when she is able to suckle. Very pre-term or sick babies will be fed by a drip. This is called parenteral nutrition.

"It was an incredibly difficult time when my baby was in the neonatal unit, but it helped to get involved in her care."

If she is strong enough, your baby will benefit from being close to you, cuddled up against your chest, tucked inside a shirt or cardigan. This is known as "kangaroo care" and it is a lovely way to get used to handling her. As she gets stronger, you will be able to take over more of her care.

Parents often wonder what to do while sitting next to their baby in the NNU or SCBU. My advice is that it is never too early to start reading to her. She will be soothed by your voice and you will get to relive some of your favourite children's stories. If you are not too embarrassed, singing lullabies can be soothing for both of you.

LOOKING AFTER YOURSELF

If you discover during your pregnancy that your baby is likely to be born prematurely, or with a condition that will need special care, you will be given the opportunity to look around the neonatal unit and prepare yourselves. For many parents, though, the need for their newborn baby to have special care will come as a shock.

A NNU is nearly always a rollercoaster of ups and downs, and the staff will be with you all the way to explain everything and support you. It can be a very worrying and stressful time so do make sure you ask any questions you need to and don't worry about asking several times. If you feel you need a more detailed discussion about your baby's condition, don't hesitate to ask for an appointment with the consultant.

Try to be gentle with yourself – and that goes for dads, too. You will want to be with your baby, but take breaks so you are not overwhelmed. If there is an emergency and you are not on the ward, the staff will make sure you are contacted straight away.

TUMMY TIME *Pre-term babies often cope better on their tummies, but must be taught to lie on their backs before they go home.*

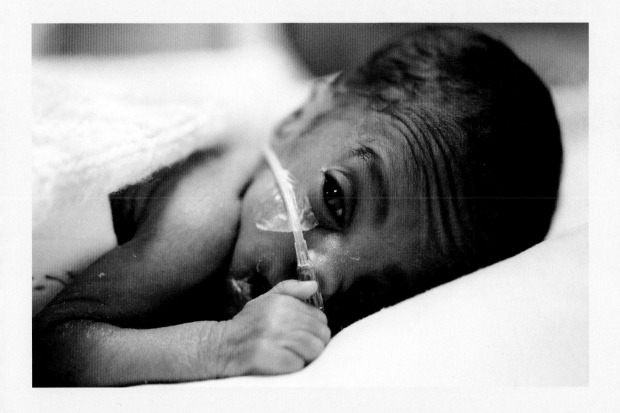

FIRST JOURNEY *To take your baby home in the car, you'll need a rear-facing car seat. This should come with a head-hugger, a soft, padded insert to support her head.*

Going home

Leaving the confines of the hospital can be nerve-racking, especially because you may be discharged just eight hours after the birth. Accept all offers of help, especially with chores such as shopping and cooking, and don't expect too much of yourself in these early days.

Travelling from the hospital

You won't be able to travel home by car or taxi unless you have the correct infant car seat for your baby. Some shops will check the fit when you buy a seat as not all car seats fit securely in every car. Safety is essential so only use a second-hand seat if you have the fitting instructions and know its history – a car seat that has been in an accident may not protect your baby. If your car has airbags fitted, don't put the infant seat in the front as an airbag could seriously injure your baby.

You will need to dress your baby according to the weather. A vest and a sleepsuit, with a coat and hat if it is cold, are fine. You can always take a baby blanket to tuck over her if she needs an extra layer.

Support for you

This can be a confusing and challenging time, with much to learn and a constant stream of visitors offering advice and requiring tea. Make sure that the people who are visiting in the first few days are helping rather than hindering. Don't be afraid to ask those close to you to help with specific tasks, such as preparing a meal. A midwife will visit you at home intermittently over the first 10 days to make regular checks on you and your baby. When she signs you off, the health visitor (see page 61) will get in touch and will usually visit you to introduce herself.

Sleep

New babies generally sleep around 16 hours a day, although they may not do so for hours at a stretch and they certainly won't sleep according to your conventions. After years of working all night in a hospital, I thought

I was an expert at sleep deprivation, but not so. The realization that with a new baby we would be on call all night, every night, was daunting. Try to catch up on sleep during the day when your baby sleeps. In the first few weeks she shouldn't go for more than six hours between feeds, so wake her up if she has slept for this long. After this, it is fine if she sleeps for longer periods. Your newborn may make sudden jerky, twitchy movements in her sleep. Don't worry – this is normal.

A Moses basket or carrycot is ideal for your newborn and you will need pram-size sheets and light cellular baby blankets. These can double as a shawl if you want to wrap her up and sheets are useful for swaddling a restless baby (see pages 64–65). It is recommended that your baby sleeps in the same room as you for the first six months.

Safe-sleeping guidelines

As a doctor, it is devastating to deal with the sudden unexpected and unexplained death of a baby. Sudden infant death syndrome (SIDS) or "cot death", while rare, is a source of anxiety for all new parents but there is a lot you can do to reduce the risk.

Don't:
▶ Smoke (dads too), or allow anyone else to smoke in the same room as your baby.
▶ Let your baby get too hot – avoid duvets, quilts, and pillows. Remove your baby's hat and extra clothing when you come indoors.
▶ Share a bed with your baby for the first three months, or at all if your baby was premature or small for dates. (Breastfeed then put her in a cot next to you.) Do not sleep with her on a sofa or armchair, either. If you decide to co-sleep after three months, never share your bed with your baby if you or your partner have been drinking alcohol or taken medication that causes drowsiness, are exhausted, or have been smoking.

Do:
▶ Place your baby in the correct position in her cot (see right).
▶ Breastfeed your baby.
▶ Keep your baby in your bedroom at night for the first six months.
▶ Seek medical advice straight away if your baby is unwell.

For support and advice, contact The Foundation for the Study of Infant Deaths (see page 312).

PUTTING YOUR BABY IN HER COT
Always place your baby on her back to sleep. Make sure her feet are at the foot of the cot so she can't wriggle down under the covers.

Everyday care

You may not feel confident about handling and caring for your newborn initially, but the midwives should be on hand at first to give you help and advice, and you will soon find that looking after your baby becomes second nature. Always take your time and make sure you have what you need to hand before you start.

Lifting and holding your baby

While you need to be gentle when handling your newborn, do remember that babies are quite resilient. Be confident in your actions, and trust that you won't harm her in any way.

The most important thing to remember is that your baby's head is heavy. She has no control over her neck muscles and will only

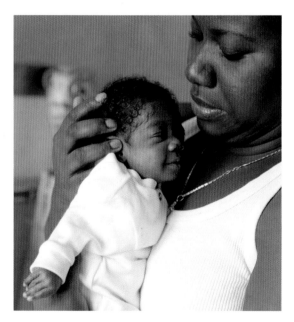

FIRST CUDDLES *Hold your newborn baby close to you in whichever way feels comfortable for you, but always make sure his head and neck are supported.*

begin to gain some when she is around four weeks old, so always support her head when you handle her. Here's how –

■ **Picking her up:** either lift her under the arms with your fingers behind her head, or put one hand under her bottom and the other under her shoulders and head.

■ **Holding her:** move her up to hold her against your shoulder, supporting her bottom with one hand and her head with the other, or cradle her in the crook of your arm. Although she will like to see your face when you are holding her, you may find that she also likes to be held face-down in your arms, with her chin and cheek against the crook of your arm.

■ **Putting her down:** when you put your baby down, you still need to support her head. Hold her with one hand under her bottom and the other under her head and neck, then lower her gently.

■ **The startle reflex:** if you pick your baby up or put her down suddenly and unexpectedly, she may startle, flinging her limbs out, and start to cry. This is a natural reflex (see page 27). If she is a bit jumpy, try talking to her as you are about to lift her, then she will know you are there and be calmed by your voice.

Changing nappies

You don't need to change your baby's nappy unless it is heavy with wee, is soiled, or has leaked. In general, you will need fewer disposable nappies (around 4–6 a day) than fabric nappies, but don't let that deter you from choosing the more environmentally friendly option (see page 67). Get everything you need to hand, including wipes to clean your hands if you have used a nappy cream. If you change your baby on a raised surface, stay with her as it won't be long before she can wriggle enough to move and fall. To change her nappy –

■ **Undo her old nappy:** use it to wipe off as much poo as you can. If you have a baby boy, you will notice that he tends to wee as soon as you take his nappy off, so have some tissues handy or hold the nappy over his penis while he wees before removing it altogether.

■ **Clean your baby's bottom thoroughly:** use water and cotton wool or wipes. When changing your baby girl's nappy, wipe from front to back to avoid spreading germs from her anus to her vagina or urethra. You don't need to clean inside your baby girl's labia or under your baby boy's foreskin. Just clean the areas you can easily get at and if she's done a really horrendous poo, wash her whole nappy area in a bowl of warm water.

■ **Using cream:** if you are using a fabric nappy, put on a barrier cream, such as zinc and castor oil. If you are using a disposable nappy, avoid cream unless your baby's bottom is sore as it reduces the absorbency of the nappy.

■ **Dry your baby's bottom:** once your baby's bottom is clean and dry, put on a fresh nappy.

Dressing

When your baby is tiny, the main clothes she will need day and night are vests and stretchsuits –

■ **Vests:** hold the neck wide open and gather up the rest of the fabric. Lift her head gently and put the back of the neck behind her head, then lift the front of the vest up and over her face. Take each sleeve, open it wide and reach through it to hold your baby's hand. Bring the sleeve over the hand and arm, pulling at the vest, rather than the baby. Pull the body part of the vest down and fasten the poppers.

■ **Stretchsuits:** spread the suit out with all the poppers undone. Lie your baby on top of it. Put your baby's legs into the stretchsuit, then gather up each sleeve and put them over your baby's arms. Do up all the poppers.

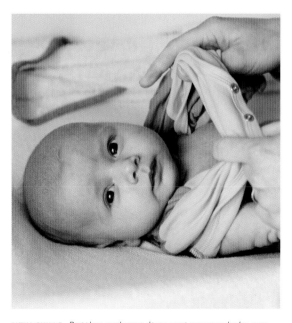

NEW SKILLS *Putting a sleepsuit or vest on your baby can seem tricky at first, but you will soon become highly skilled at dressing and undressing him.*

Keeping your baby clean

During the first week you don't need to put yourself through the stress of bathing your baby. Tiny babies, unlike adults or older children, just don't get dirty very quickly; so fewer washes are fine. Also, most newborns hate being naked, so you might as well minimize the trauma by keeping bathtimes occasional and just washing the bits that need cleaning for the rest of the time. "Topping and tailing" – washing her face, hands, and nappy area – will be adequate. All you need is a bowl of water, cotton wool, a soft flannel or sponge, and a towel. You don't need soap or bath liquid, but if you do want to use them, ensure they are specially formulated baby products as adult toiletries will irritate her skin. Just wash what you can easily get at – the insides of the nose and ears, and the hidden parts of your baby's genitals, are all self-cleaning. Start with her face and wash her bottom last because that way you won't spread germs. Don't be anxious about washing your baby's fontanelles. These soft spots on her skull are tougher than they look and so you can wash her head in the same way you wash the rest of her. Dry your baby thoroughly, especially in the creases and folds of skin, such as her neck and nappy area, to prevent her getting sore.

"Trying to bath my first baby in the hospital, with the midwife looking on, made me flustered as I was nervous about holding him in the water and washing him at the same time. Until he was ready to enjoy the bath, my second baby only got washed when he needed it, and he suffered no ill-effects."

TOPPING AND TAILING *Keeping your baby clean by using cotton wool and water is perfectly adequate until you feel ready to give her a bath. Always use separate cotton wool for the face and genitals.*

Common concerns

▶ **How do I know whether my baby is warm enough?**

In the first week or so, babies are not very good at controlling their temperature, and as your baby is smaller and less active than you, she will get cold more easily. A good rule of thumb is to dress her according to what you would wear while sitting still in the same environment.

The most important thing is not to over-wrap her as this can increase the risk of cot death (see page 39). Be particularly cautious about using too many blankets or covers, and if you're still not sure if she's warm enough, feel the back of her neck – it should feel comfortably warm, not hot and clammy. If her body is warm enough, don't worry if her hands and feet are cool, since newborn circulation is not as efficient as it will be later on.

▶ **My newborn baby is very unsettled. Could this be due to a difficult labour?**

There is no doubt that being born is traumatic. Even with the calmest of deliveries, a baby has to endure many hours of labour followed by the head squeezing through a tight gap. When help is needed, such as in a forceps or ventouse delivery, it's not surprising that some babies are left rather traumatized afterwards.

In most cases the baby recovers quickly, but there are certainly some babies who seem irritable and take a while to settle and establish feeding. These babies may benefit from an assessment by a cranial osteopath, who by almost imperceptible manipulation can detect and help correct problems resulting from the stress of the delivery.

▶ **I don't seem to be able to stop crying, especially in the evenings. Is this normal?**

Yes, it's a rare new mum who doesn't feel a bit low and weepy in the beginning. Your body is adjusting to pregnancy ending and breastfeeding beginning, and it is thought that the sudden drop in pregnancy hormones, and the hormonal changes that go with the beginning of milk production, are responsible for the almost universal weepiness that occurs on the third or fourth day after delivery. Known as the "baby blues", this often happens after the excitement and anticipation of meeting your baby is replaced temporarily by the shock of having to meet her needs day and night, when you're still trying to recover from the birth.

It's perfectly normal to feel resentful of the baby, particularly if your labour was difficult or if you haven't begun to bond yet. For most mums this is a problem that quickly resolves itself. Your midwife, health visitor, and GP can all offer support, advice, and reassurance during this time so do talk to them, as well as to your partner. If the symptoms persist, you may have postnatal depression (see page 101), so seek medical advice.

▶ **It's cold and wet outside. Will my newborn baby catch a cold if I take him out?**

Don't worry – babies can't catch a cold simply by being chilly, but you do need to wrap him up and make sure he wears a hat because a small baby can lose heat quickly. It is best to dress him in layers so that you can easily adapt what he is wearing.

GETTING TO KNOW YOU

1 2 3 4 5 6 7 8 9 10 11 12

MONTH

SLEEPY HEAD YOUR BABY WILL LOVE TO SLEEP BUT, UNFORTUNATELY FOR YOU, IT WILL BE SOME TIME BEFORE HE CAN DISTINGUISH BETWEEN NIGHT AND DAY

EYE COLOUR THE PIGMENT IN YOUR NEWBORN BABY'S EYES IS NOT FULLY DEVELOPED, AND THE COLOUR WILL GRADUALLY CHANGE IN THE COMING WEEKS AND MONTHS

I'M HUNGRY AS YOU GET TO KNOW YOUR BABY, YOU'LL BEGIN TO UNDERSTAND WHAT HE'S COMMUNICATING THROUGH HIS CRIES

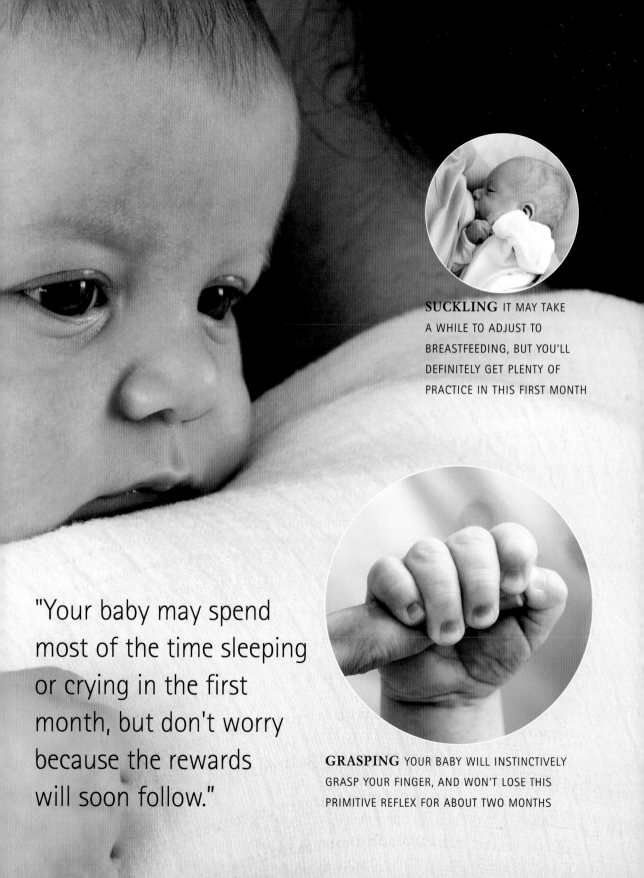

SUCKLING IT MAY TAKE A WHILE TO ADJUST TO BREASTFEEDING, BUT YOU'LL DEFINITELY GET PLENTY OF PRACTICE IN THIS FIRST MONTH

"Your baby may spend most of the time sleeping or crying in the first month, but don't worry because the rewards will soon follow."

GRASPING YOUR BABY WILL INSTINCTIVELY GRASP YOUR FINGER, AND WON'T LOSE THIS PRIMITIVE REFLEX FOR ABOUT TWO MONTHS

Settling into life

It will take a couple of weeks for your baby to settle into his new environment, but he will gradually adapt and begin to become more alert and communicative. You will be adapting too, and will be getting the hang of the basics, such as changing nappies, feeding, and being a universal provider.

Your baby's senses

To help him adjust to the world outside the womb, and to bond with you, your newborn baby is totally reliant on his five senses –

■ **Sight:** all newborns naturally focus at a distance of around 30cm (12in) initially – the perfect distance to gaze at you while you are feeding or holding him. Faces are fascinating to your baby and he will watch yours intently. Towards the end of this month he may follow your face with his eyes if you are moving within his field of vision.

■ **Smell:** the sense of smell is very important to a new baby. Research has shown that even at a few hours old, a baby will turn his head towards the smell of his mother's milk on a breast pad, rather than that of another new mother. So your baby will not only recognize your smell, he will prefer it.

■ **Taste:** your baby's ability to taste develops while he is in the womb. Scientists believe that unborn babies may be able to differentiate between tastes in the amniotic fluid, gulping faster when it is sweeter and more slowly when it tastes bitter. Your newborn baby will be able to detect slight changes in your breast milk that relate to what you have eaten and because of this, researchers believe that breastfed babies may be more likely to accept a greater variety of foods when they are weaned than babies who are fed on formula milk.

■ **Hearing:** your baby could already hear while he was in the womb, so your voice and that of anyone who shares your life were familiar straight after delivery. Now he will love to hear you talk, sing, and read to him. His hearing is well developed, even at this early stage, but he won't take much notice of sounds other than voices. However, sudden, loud bangs and crashes will startle him and may make him cry.

FOCUSING *It will be several weeks before your newborn baby can see beyond 30cm. He may appear to squint as he tries to focus, but this is normal.*

■ **Touch:** your baby's sense of touch helps him to feel safe and secure when you hold him so he will benefit from skin-to-skin contact with you. Studies show that premature babies who are too sick to be cuddled are calmed and comforted by very gentle touch. Some babies enjoy gentle massage (see pages 84–85) and some relax when they are swaddled (see pages 64–65), possibly because this replicates being held securely by the womb.

How your baby may look

Your baby will regain his birth weight by the time he is around 10 days old and will then start to put on weight regularly, so he will be changing rapidly. If he was born with lots of hair, some of it may start to rub off to reveal what could be an entirely different colour underneath. Any bumps and bruises from the delivery will be fading, but he might have an impressive milk rash, or milia (see page 35). My babies were always at their spottiest at this stage. He may be developing cradle cap (see page 97) and his skin may look mottled at this time.

Everyday care

DRY SKIN It's normal for a newborn's skin to peel in the early weeks. This will right itself naturally so don't feel you have to spend time and money moisturizing your baby.

Your baby won't have any idea of the difference between night and day, and his tiny stomach (about the size of a small lemon when full) will need regular refilling, so he will wake for feeds throughout every 24 hours. If your baby is breastfed, he will also be suckling frequently to get your milk supply going – some babies feed every couple of hours for an hour at a time. In the first few weeks you simply have to accept this; just bear in mind that it is a transitory phase. By 6–10 weeks, most babies will sleep for significant chunks of the night. You can also start to encourage the differentiation between night and day by keeping the lights dim, your voice quiet, and generally not overstimulating him during night feeds.

I found the prospect of continuous night shifts at this stage daunting, but the flip side of this was the overwhelming love I felt for my babies, which helped me through the tough times – and I was able to share the burden with Peter. Bear in mind that once your baby has been fed, your partner can be the one to put him to bed, or sit up with him if he is wide awake. Sharing the difficult tasks can make all the difference and is also good practice for later, when you go out and your partner stays home with the baby. It is important for him to have the space to learn these skills.

Remember, you can't accuse your partner of not helping if he has never had the opportunity to. If you are a single parent and doing the night shift alone, try to get help during the day so that you can catch up on some sleep.

Whether your baby is having breast milk or bottles, it is natural to worry about how much and how often to feed him and whether he should have a rigid schedule or be fed on demand. There is a great deal of opinion about what is best but no right answer. What is right for your baby is usually what you are happy with – if you like to have a strict routine, you may not feel comfortable going with the flow and feeding on demand, but if your instinct is to respond to your baby's body clock in the early weeks, you won't want to leave him to cry

and so will probably prefer to demand-feed. Babies are generally accurate barometers of their parents' moods and if you are unhappy, he will be too, whereas if you are relaxed, he is more likely to be calm and content.

RELAXED PARENTING
You don't have to care for your baby in a set way. Stay calm and in tune with him and you'll soon find you know instinctively what he needs.

Comforting your baby

All babies cry, and there is always a reason for it. In the very early days your baby's ways of communicating with you are very limited, so he cries if he is hungry, tired, uncomfortable, bored, or in need of a cuddle. As you get to know him better, you will recognize the difference between his cries and be able to respond quickly and, as a result, he will gradually cry less.

Crying because of pain is usually easy to interpret. For example, if your baby has colic (see page 98) he may scream and pull his legs up. However, this angry, shrill, inconsolable crying is upsetting and you may find it difficult to deal with at first.

There are plenty of ways to comfort your crying baby. Try motion (putting him in the sling, or in the car if you are not too stressed to drive safely); white noise (placing him in front of the washing machine on a spin cycle or next to a de-tuned radio); or try a dummy if he needs to suck. However, there will be times when your baby picks up on your stress and the more you try to settle him down, the more upset he becomes. If your baby has a full tummy, a clean nappy, is not in pain, and doesn't respond to calming measures, try leaving him somewhere quiet to sleep – he may simply be telling you he needs some peace. Another strategy is to hand him over to someone else who is less emotionally involved so you can get a breather.

Advice from others

Now that you have this new little person in your life, you are likely to have doting grandparents, friends, and various random strangers, giving their views on what is best for him. Although well meant and sometimes useful, a lot of this advice will be conflicting and leave you wondering exactly how to proceed. While it is worth being tactful with grandparents even when you don't agree with their views on childcare, it is important to start believing in yourselves as parents and doing things your way. You may make mistakes but as you get to know your baby and how he responds to things, you will find out for yourselves the best way to care for him. You can become better informed by looking to parenting books, magazines, or internet sites for advice on a particular subject. Many websites have chat rooms where you can share problems or concerns with other parents who are in the same situation. Finally, if you really do have doubts about any aspect of your baby's care, speak to your health visitor.

If it all gets too much

Sometimes your baby's crying can seem endless, especially if there is nobody to hand him over to. Every parent has been there. What is important is to recognize when you are becoming so angry you might handle your baby too roughly. Being shaken can seriously injure your baby's brain so if you are at the end of your tether and scared you may hurt him, put him somewhere safe, such as his Moses basket, go out of the room and take 10 minutes to have a cup of tea (or a glass of wine!) and calm down. Don't feel guilty about leaving him for a few minutes – he will be fine. It is normal to have difficult days and feel down at times (see page 43), but if you are really struggling to cope, do tell someone.

Daddy's first steps

It's an excellent idea to take time off after the birth. You are entitled to take 1–2 weeks' paternity leave and as your partner will be exhausted she will be glad to have you around. Once home, there are a host of jobs to be done, from answering the phone, making tea for guests, and ensuring your partner gets some rest, to getting to know your baby (don't forget this one).

Many first-time dads feel nervous of their new charge, but there is no need to be – babies are remarkably robust. Some fathers don't find newborns that interesting and while, admittedly, they don't appear to do much at first, appearances can be deceptive. It's amazing how quickly your baby will start to engage with you, and as this is a time that you will never have again, don't miss it. It can be every bit as exciting as buying him his first train set. If your partner is breastfeeding, you can get involved by generally encouraging her and by winding your baby halfway through and afterwards. Give your partner breaks, too – I used to love taking our daughter out in her sling after a feed.

Try to take a few more days' leave when your baby is a few weeks old. Mums can feel a little abandoned at this stage and it can be a magical time together as a new family.

FATHER'S VIEW

Getting to know your baby

Even if you have little experience of babies, trust your instincts and try to relax when it comes to caring for your newborn. He will feel safe when you hold him, studying your face, and listening intently to your voice. Don't be afraid to communicate with him: most babies like to interact, and chatting to him, with your face not far from his so he can focus on you, may settle him very quickly. Try mimicking his facial expressions, as he will find this fascinating. You will soon come to know your baby better than anyone else, so enjoy him, discover what works best for you in caring for him, and try not to feel guilty or worried if you don't get things right first time. Interestingly, many parents agree that first babies cause them more anxiety than their younger children, who just have to get on with it because Mum and Dad's time is in shorter supply. These second and third babies are often more relaxed and "easier".

DAD TIME *Remember that you are a parent in your own right and not just Mum's helper.*

Expert breastfeeding

Breastfeeding may feel like hard work at first, but within a few weeks you and your baby will be experts. Start by making sure you are comfortable, with your back and arms supported and your baby in a good position to feed. Try some of the different positions shown here until you find the ones that work best for you.

The letdown reflex

When you put your baby to the breast, his suckling stimulates your body to produce two hormones. One of these, prolactin, sends signals to your breasts to make milk, while the other, oxytocin, causes the milk ducts to contract, releasing milk into the nipple. So if your baby feeds often, as he will in the early days, you will make as much milk as he needs.

You will start to notice a full, tingling, pulling sensation in your breasts when you are preparing to feed. This is caused by the release of oxytocin and is called the "letdown reflex". It happens more easily if you are calm, which is why feeding is sometimes more difficult in the early evening when you are tired.

Once breastfeeding is established, your letdown reflex becomes so sensitive that it can be triggered by hearing your baby cry or even by thinking about feeding him. Using breast pads will help prevent the inevitable wet patches down the front of your clothes.

Breast milk is thinner than the creamy colostrum your breasts produced in the first few days, but it is nutritionally just right for your baby. When your baby first latches on to the breast, he quenches his thirst and satisfies his immediate hunger with foremilk, which is already stored in the breast. As the feed continues, the milk, known as hindmilk, becomes richer and more nourishing. Let him feed from the first breast until he has had enough, to ensure he gets as much hindmilk as he needs: if you swap sides too soon, he may only get foremilk. Breastfeeding may take a long time to begin with, but you will find that your baby soon becomes more efficient at suckling.

Your individual baby

You may need to adjust the way you feed depending on your baby's mood or temperament.

▶ An excitable baby may flail around and find it hard to settle at the breast. Swaddling him in a light blanket (see pages 64–65) may help to calm him and keep him still enough to latch on.

▶ A sleepy baby may need encouragement to feed, which you can do by gently tapping his feet if he stops sucking.

▶ If your baby gets very hungry, he may become too upset to feed properly. Cuddle, rock, or sing to him to calm him, then try latching him on again.

GETTING COMFORTABLE

CRADLING YOUR BABY *Hold your baby in the crook of your arm with his head and body turned towards you. You could also lie him on a pillow to raise him to your breast.*

LYING BESIDE YOU *Lie down on your side with your baby alongside you and turned towards you. This position is particularly good if you've had a Caesarean because your baby isn't resting on your tummy.*

THE RUGBY BALL HOLD *Sit up with your baby tucked under your arm, his feet pointing towards your back, and his head cradled in your hand. This is a good position for feeding a wriggly baby or twins. Again, you can raise your baby to your breast on a pillow if necessary.*

Your breastfeeding diet

Good nutrition is important because you need a great deal of energy to care for your baby and yourself and produce the milk he needs to grow. A poor diet during these months can slow your recovery from the birth and leave you too tired to enjoy your baby to the full. Healthy eating will boost your energy, restore lustre to your hair and skin, and help to protect your bones and teeth in the long term.

However anxious you are to get back to your pre-pregnancy shape, don't try to lose weight while breastfeeding. You need to eat a balanced diet that includes plenty of fresh fruit and vegetables; a good combination of carbohydrates, such as bread, rice, pasta, and potatoes (slow-release carbohydrates such as brown rice and wholemeal bread are best); dairy produce, such as cheese, yoghurt and milk; and protein from meat, fish, and legumes.

You may not always feel like eating big meals. That is fine – eating little and often will keep your energy levels topped up. Have a drink and a snack to hand when you breastfeed.

Foods you may want to avoid

There is very little you can't eat when you are breastfeeding, although there are some foods you may only want in moderation and a few you might decide to avoid altogether. You may find that eating spicy foods, or wind-producing foods, such as beans or cabbage, causes your baby to produce spectacular nappies. These foods in your breast milk cause a similar reaction in your baby's tummy as they do in yours and so may produce lots of wind and

loose poos. If this is the case and you find it a problem, try modifying your diet for a while.

If you suspect that whole food groups, such as dairy products, may be disagreeing with your baby, talk to your GP or health visitor about whether you should try cutting these out. If you do, try to compensate for the missing nutrients. For instance, if you stop drinking milk, ensure you are getting a good intake of calcium from other sources, such as leafy green vegetables and soya products. Some studies have shown that eating nuts while breastfeeding may increase the risk of allergies developing in susceptible babies; others have indicated that this is not the case. If there are atopic (allergic) conditions (see pages 279–280), such as asthma, eczema, or hay fever, in your family, you might want to avoid eating nuts while breastfeeding.

Drinks

It is important to stay hydrated while you are breastfeeding, so make sure you drink plenty of fluids, especially water. Avoid having too many caffeinated drinks as these are dehydrating. Alcohol is fine in moderation, but drinking too much can affect your milk supply. Don't drink more than a glass of wine 2–4 times a week. Small amounts of alcohol pass into your breast milk so if you want a drink it is advisable to have it 2–3 hours before feeding.

Medication

All drugs go into breast milk so seek medical advice before taking any. It is, however, safe to take paracetamol, ibuprofen, and many antibiotics. Avoid all recreational drugs.

Breastfeeding concerns

▶ **How do I know if my breastfed baby is getting enough milk?**

You won't know exactly how much milk he's having, but what is important is that he is healthy and growing well. Regular weighing – every two weeks at first – at your local baby clinic will help reassure you that your baby is putting on sufficient weight. Breastfeeding is a lovely, reassuring experience for your baby so he may want to feed long after his tummy is full. As a general rule, once breastfeeding is well established, your baby will get most of his feed in the first 10–15 minutes on each breast, so you don't have to spend hours feeding.

▶ **Can I give my baby an occasional bottle?**

Yes, she can have expressed breast milk or formula in a bottle but it's best to wait until breastfeeding is fully established. This is because while you and she are still learning to breastfeed, she may reject the breast in favour of a teat which is an easier option.

Also, be aware that the work of getting milk from your breasts has been found to help a baby's jaw develop properly and may lead to straighter teeth and stronger facial muscles. Once breastfeeding is fully established, you can express milk either by hand or with a breast pump (see page 89).

▶ **There's a sore, red patch on one of my breasts. What is it?**

Known as mastitis, this is inflammation of the breast tissue, and happens when one of the milk ducts in your breast becomes blocked. An infection then starts in the milk spreading into the breast tissue, causing pain and redness, and your breast becomes hot and engorged. You may also feel unwell. See your GP straight away, as you may need antibiotics to clear the infection. You will still be able to feed your baby during treatment, and in fact this will help to clear the infection. Rest assured that neither the infection, nor the antibiotics, will harm your baby. Putting cool flannels or chilled cabbage leaves on your breasts can help soothe the discomfort and you can also take paracetamol or ibuprofen. Avoid taking aspirin as it is dangerous for babies (see page 262).

▶ **Is it safe to breastfeed if I'm ill?**

Yes. Most illnesses can't be passed to your baby through your breast milk and he will have immunity from you to most common bugs. There are a few exceptions to this, such as the HIV virus, which can be passed through breast milk, but these are rare. If you are HIV positive, you will have been advised during your pregnancy about whether it is safe to breastfeed.

▶ **My milk spurts out very fast and makes my baby choke. What can I do?**

While your breasts are getting used to making milk they can go into over-production and you end up with very full breasts and milk that comes out very fast. This will resolve itself, but for now try expressing a little milk before you breastfeed.

▶ **Does it matter if my baby falls asleep while I'm feeding him?**

If your baby seems well, don't worry. Babies usually get as much milk as they need in 10–15 minutes on each breast. If he's fallen asleep after having milk from one breast, start him on the other next time.

Giving your baby formula

Bottle-feeding can feel just as rewarding as breastfeeding and it gives both of you a great opportunity for cuddles and one-to-one time. Never be tempted to prop your baby up with a bottle as he could choke, and always follow the correct instructions for making up a bottle (see page 33) and keeping equipment clean.

Choosing formula

There is not much difference between brands of cow's milk formula from a nutritional point of view. You may notice other kinds of formula milk on sale, such as soya milk or goat's milk, but for most bottle-fed babies cow's milk formula is the best. If you suspect your baby is allergic to cow's milk (see box, below), get a proper diagnosis and seek advice on formula from your GP or health visitor.

Formula milk for young babies contains whey-based protein, which is the most easily digestible for your baby. You will also see infant formula aimed at "hungry babies", which contains casein-based protein that forms curds in your baby's stomach and so keeps him feeling full for longer. However, this milk can make babies of this age prone to constipation, so unless your GP or health visitor advises otherwise, it is better to give your baby the standard whey-based formula and feed him more often if he is hungry.

Special milks

Soya milk may be recommended by your GP if a cow's milk allergy is suspected. However, some babies will also be allergic to the proteins in soya milk, in which case a hypoallergenic milk will be prescribed. This may be preferred because there has been concern that the compounds in soya milk that mimic female hormones may affect the future fertility of baby boys. If your baby has soya milk, you will need to be extra vigilant about brushing his teeth when they appear.

The Department of Health advises against giving goat's milk to babies, and as the types of protein and lactose levels in goat's milk are similar to those in cow's milk, it is unlikely to be tolerated anyway. Special formula milks for babies who have reflux are also available.

Cow's milk allergy

Possible signs of cow's milk allergy:

▸ Diarrhoea – particularly if there is blood in your baby's poo.

▸ Failure to gain weight and vomiting – although most babies who vomit do not have a cow's milk allergy.

▸ Severe eczema – although most babies with eczema do not have a cow's milk allergy.

▸ More rarely, rapid symptoms of wheezing, hives and swelling (see page 280).

Winding

All babies get wind (air in their tummies) from time to time and some are windier than others. However, it is less likely to be a problem for breastfed babies, who are well latched on, than for bottle-fed babies, who may gulp air if the teat is not fully filled with milk.

Try to wind your baby halfway through a feed and then again when he has finished. Don't worry if your baby doesn't bring up any wind – he might not have any. If he is windy but doesn't bring it up now, he may later, along with some milk. This possetting (see page 32) is normal in young babies and will happen less as your baby's digestive system matures and the valve at the top of his stomach stays reliably shut. The idea of winding is to keep your baby upright so that the air bubbles rise to the top and he can burp them out without getting rid of most of his feed at the same time.

If your baby is sleepy, still try to wind him. It may not even rouse him and it is better than him waking later because he is uncomfortable.

As with all aspects of babycare, you will soon find the most effective method of winding your baby. The two most common positions are shown below, but you can also lie him on his tummy across your lap or forearm.

HOW TO WIND YOUR BABY

HOLD HIM AGAINST YOUR SHOULDER *Gently rub or pat your baby's back to encourage the air to come up – it should come up quite easily if he's upright. You may want to use a muslin square to protect your clothes.*

SIT HIM ON YOUR KNEE *Lean him slightly forwards and gently rub and pat his back until he burps. Because your baby's head is still floppy, it's important to support it by resting it on your hand.*

Sterilization

While cleanliness is essential when bottle-feeding, I don't believe that it's necessary to sterilize feeding equipment if you are careful and follow some simple rules. I never sterilized anything for my babies and I'd encourage those of you who want to be relaxed parents to consider this option.

Many scientists believe that a less-than-sterile environment may actually be beneficial to babies, and that exposure to germs may help prevent allergic reactions. Our bodies contain T-cells, which play a key role in our immune system. These cells fight infections but, as we create increasingly sterile environments for ourselves, there are not many germs to activate them so they don't have anything to fight. Because of this, the T-cells in a baby's developing immune system may sometimes respond to harmless substances, such as food, which results in an allergic reaction. Consequently, the removal of all germs from a baby's digestive system may be linked to an increase in atopic (allergic) conditions, such as asthma and eczema. Research has shown that children who are routinely exposed to bacteria, such as subsequent children in the family or those living on farms, are less likely to develop allergies.

If you are not going to sterilize, follow these simple rules –

■ **Clean thoroughly:** use a dishwasher if you have one. If there is old milk stuck to the bottles or teats, use a bottle brush to get into the corners.

■ **Store correctly:** never leave bottles of formula standing around at room temperature. If you are going out, take the correct amount of powdered formula with you in a bottle, then add the required amount of warm, previously boiled, water when you are ready to feed your baby. Always discard any leftover milk. If you are using ready-made formula, the sealed cartons can be stored at room temperature.

If you decide to sterilize

The Department of Health recommends sterilizing for the first six months to prevent babies getting infections from bacteria in bottles. If you feel you may not be scrupulous in following the cleaning rules outlined above, it is best to play safe and sterilize your baby's feeding equipment, to avoid tummy upsets. There are several methods you can use, including –

■ **Electric steam sterilizer:** this is a plug-in device that creates steam and sterilizes feeding equipment in around 10 minutes.

HOLDING HER CLOSE

You can still get close to your baby if you bottle-feed. And there's the added benefit that Dad can enjoy feeding him too.

Bottle-feeding concerns

▶ **How much formula milk should I give my baby?**
General guidelines recommend babies are given 150ml (5fl oz) per kilo of bodyweight but if your baby is alert, healthy, and producing plenty of wet nappies, you can be reasonably sure she is getting the right amount. If you are at all concerned, seek advice from your midwife or health visitor.

▶ **Is it better to stick to the same brand of infant formula?**
While it's important that you give your bottle-fed baby standard cow's milk infant formula, unless your doctor or health visitor advises otherwise, there's nothing to choose between brands nutritionally and a change will do your baby no harm at all. Just as breastfed babies get used to milk that changes its taste according to what Mum has eaten, a bottle-fed baby can cope with a slightly different formula.

▶ **Is it okay to use a ready-mixed formula milk?**
Yes. Ready-mixed milk comes in cartons and is very convenient when you're out and about with your baby. Be aware, however, that it is more expensive.

■ **Microwave sterilizer:** this takes water in its base and has a rack for bottles and a lid. When heated, it creates steam that sterilizes the contents. You can also buy microwaveable sterilizing bags, which are quick and easy to use if you are going away.

■ **Cold-water chemical solution:** this involves using a sterilizing solution made by mixing liquid or tablets with water. You will need a large, lidded container and something heavy, such as a plate, to hold the items fully under the solution. Although non-toxic, cold-water solution has a strong chemical smell that lingers even after bottles have been rinsed.

■ **Boiling:** put everything in a pan of water and boil for at least 10 minutes. Teats that are boiled frequently are likely to become tacky so will need replacing more often with this method.

Bottles and teats

You can buy teats with different-sized holes or a varying number of holes to allow the milk to flow faster or slower, and some teats help prevent your baby swallowing too much air. Bottles come in different shapes and sizes and you will find it easier to put milk powder into wide-necked bottles. Special bottles are available for babies who suffer from colic (see page 98). They reduce the amount of air taken in during feeds and, although they don't always work, they are worth a try if your baby suffers from wind.

Monitoring health and growth

Your baby's weight and length will be plotted on the growth charts in his health record book to give an overall picture of his growth over time. If he is healthy and feeding well, he is likely to be growing well, so don't read too much into weekly fluctuations.

HOW YOUR BABY IS MEASURED

Growth charts use "centiles" to track changes in your baby's weight, length (or height), and head circumference. This system of averages helps your GP or health visitor keep an eye on whether he is growing as expected. Centiles range from the 2nd to the 98th, although charts differ slightly. If your baby is on the 50th centile, he is right in the middle of the range of measurements for his age. Babies come in different shapes and sizes and some will be on a different centile for weight than for length. For example, a baby who is on the 50th centile for weight and the 70th centile for length, is taller and slimmer than average, while a baby who is on the 15th centile for both weight and length is petite. Both may be equally healthy. Similarly, don't worry if your baby is at the lighter or heavier end of the scale.

Mostly babies grow along the same centile line from birth, although there may be a degree of variation. If a baby moves down or up two centile lines, the health visitor will monitor his growth carefully. If the change is more than two centile lines, the doctor may check him over, but in most cases this is nothing to worry about. Centile charts are a useful, but not infallible, guide to a baby's growth.

Height is largely inherited but may be affected in childhood by factors such as nutrition and emotional health. Boys and girls have different charts because they grow at different rates. Babies born with a particular syndrome, such as Down's (see page 307), will need a specific chart.

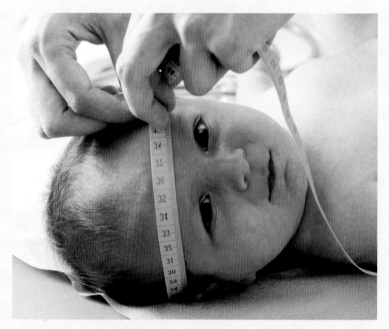

"My partner and I are short so when I saw that my baby was on the 15th centile for height I didn't worry."

HEAD SIZE *Head circumference is also used to monitor a baby's health. Problems are rare, but a slow growth rate can indicate problems with brain development, while a fast rate can be a sign of excess fluid on the brain.*

YOUR HEALTH VISITOR

Health visitors are fully qualified nurses who have had extensive additional training to become experts in child health and development.

Your health visitor will contact you after you have been discharged by your midwife. This is usually about 10 days after your baby is born. She will probably visit you at home to begin with, but after that you can see her at the baby clinic for regular checks or telephone her if you need advice or have any urgent concerns.

Your health visitor is a great resource and for most everyday worries she is the best port of call. She can offer you information and advice, one-to-one support, and access to a network of other parents through postnatal groups and the baby clinic. She will discuss the basics of babycare with you, and if you have a problem with any aspect of looking after your baby, from winding him to coping with sleep problems, she will suggest ways that you can deal with it.

She will also monitor your baby's progress by checking he is feeding well, monitoring his weight and growth, and carrying out any developmental checks that may be needed in the first years of life. Health visitors also support families in other ways, for example those with mental health problems.

If your health visitor is concerned about your baby's health or thinks your baby is ill, she will arrange for you to see your GP. Some health visitors also prescribe certain medications.

WATCHING HIM GROW *A health visitor will weigh your baby regularly and give you advice if she has any concerns about his weight gain.*

Medical care

It is unlikely that you will need to call on your GP during this first month as the community midwife and your health visitor will normally be able to deal with any problems and queries. However, while newborn babies don't fall ill very often, if they do they can become ill very quickly. Your GP will be aware of this and if you do have any concerns about your baby's health, he will be happy to see you. If you need to book an appointment, he will try to fit you in as quickly as possible. You will probably get to know your GP very well over the next few years as young children are among the most frequent visitors to the doctor's surgery.

Your baby will need to see a doctor if he:
▶ Has a temperature.
▶ Has difficulty breathing.
▶ Sweats excessively when feeding.
▶ Feeds very poorly or is unduly irritable.

Dial 999 if your baby has severe difficulty breathing, has blue lips or any other part of his body is blue, is floppy, very irritable (with a temperature), cold and clammy or has a bruise-like rash (see page 270). Always follow your instincts and if you are worried, call an ambulance. You can also seek advice from NHS Direct (see page 312).

BREASTFED BABIES

For many years, baby growth charts have been based on the average weight gain for bottle-fed babies, but there is growing evidence to show that healthy breastfed babies don't necessarily put on weight at the same rate as healthy babies on formula milk.

The World Health Organization has published growth charts, similar to those shown here, which are based on the expected weight gain for breastfed babies.

BOYS' AND GIRLS' WEIGHT

The only difference between the two charts is that boys are slightly heavier at a given age than girls. If you are breastfeeding your baby, you may wish to compare your baby's growth on these charts to those in your child's health record book (see page 80), which are based on all babies.

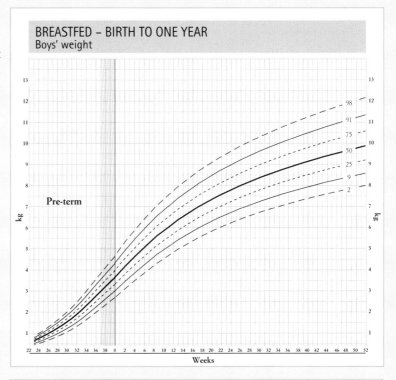

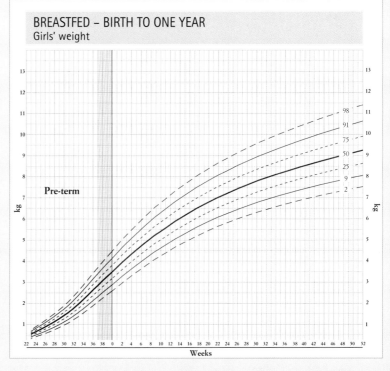

THE FIRST YEAR

The standard growth charts for the first year also have separate measurements for boys and girls. Your health visitor will plot your baby's measurements for head circumference, weight, and length at each health and development check. The 50th percentile is the average and, depending mainly on inherited factors, your baby's measurements will probably fall above or below this. It doesn't matter which centile he is on, as long as the curve of the chart indicates a steady and healthy growth rate.

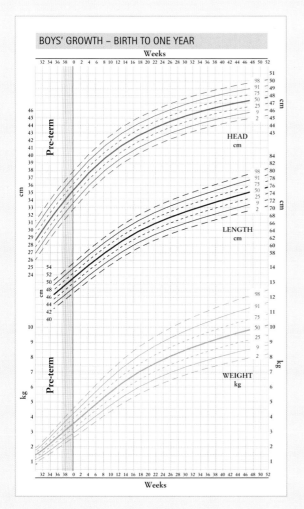

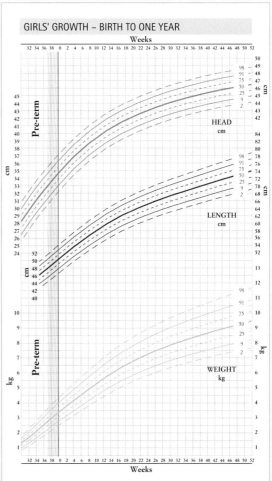

CENTILES *96 per cent of children who are developing normally will fall between the 2nd and 98th centiles for height (length), weight, and head circumference. For example, it is normal for a baby who has tall parents to be on a high centile for length, and a baby who has slender parents to be on a low centile for weight.*

GROWTH CURVES *All babies have growth spurts and periods of slow growth so it is important to look at the measurements over time. For example, a baby whose weight falls by two centiles, and then grows along that centile, is less worrying than a baby whose weight continues to fall off the centiles.*

Everyday care

Handling your newborn baby may be a little less daunting by now. You will still need to support his heavy head, and he may cry when you undress him, but if you handle him with confidence you will find that babycare tasks are wonderful opportunities for spending enjoyable time together.

Beginning a routine

Your baby will sleep as much as he needs to, whenever he needs to. While he won't be ready to sleep through the night without a feed for several weeks, you can begin to establish a bedtime routine – a bath or wash followed by a feed. A story or lullaby may be helpful, too. One thing you can begin to do now, which will help to settle your baby in the long term, is help him learn to fall asleep by himself. If he has had a feed and is sleepy, try putting him to bed awake and he will gradually learn that he can go

HOW TO SWADDLE

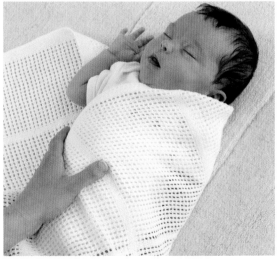

1. PUT THE BLANKET ON A FLAT SURFACE AND FOLD ONE CORNER DOWN *Use a lightweight fabric, such as a cellular blanket or a pram sheet. Lay your baby down with his head just above the folded-down edge. Remember that he is naturally curled up at this age from being in the womb so don't try to straighten him out.*

2. FOLD OVER THE RIGHT-HAND CORNER *Bring the right-hand corner of the blanket over and tuck it snugly under your baby's body so that his left arm is secured under the blanket. You will probably find that his right arm flails about, but he should already be feeling more snug.*

to sleep without being in your arms. If he surfaces from time to time during the night, he is more likely to go to sleep by himself if he doesn't need milk. Swaddling (see below) can help your baby to feel secure and help to settle him, but not all babies like it. Unwrap him once he is asleep so that he doesn't overheat.

Where should he sleep?

Your baby can sleep in a carrycot or Moses basket, or in a cot. If you buy a second-hand cot, buy a new mattress because there is a possible link between toxic bacteria in second-hand mattresses and cot death. The mattress should fit without any gaps around the edges.

Safe sleeping

The Foundation for the Study of Infant Deaths (FSID) (see page 312) recommends that your baby sleeps in your bedroom for the first six months, as research shows that this reduces the risk of cot death. To avoid your baby getting too hot or too cold, the temperature of the room where he sleeps should be 16–20°C (60–68°F) – in the UK that means you normally won't need the heating on at night.

Sharing a bed with your baby is not recommended in the early months. It is safer to breastfeed him in your bed, then put him into his cot next to you. See page 39 for more information on safe sleeping.

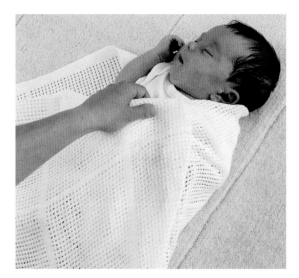

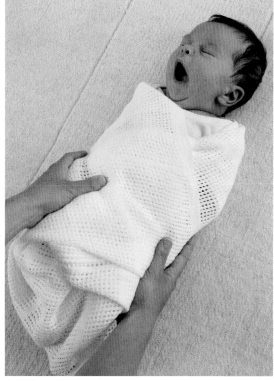

3. FOLD UP THE BOTTOM CORNER *Take the corner below your baby's feet, then bring it towards his chest, and tuck it underneath the fold.*

4. PULL THE LEFT-HAND SIDE ACROSS *Bring the left-hand corner over and tuck it underneath him. Chances are, the first yawns will soon follow. Unwrap him once he is asleep.*

First bedclothes

You will need pram-size sheets and lightweight baby blankets. Alternatively, lightweight sleeping bags without hoods are safe for newborns from 7lb (3kg) – they are designed to be used on their own, with your baby wearing a vest and sleepsuit. He won't need a blanket as well. These are great as they never get kicked off when your baby moves in his sleep and they allow you to spirit up a bed almost anywhere. However, never put your baby in a sleeping bag that is too big for him as he could slide down inside it and overheat.

First clothes

All you need are a few vests and a pack of four plain sleepsuits with front-fastening poppers – these are far easier than pulling clothes over your baby's head. Everything else will probably come as presents. I'm sure you will be tempted to buy lots of lovely baby clothes, but a word of caution – babies grow very quickly and you will probably end up dressing your baby in one or two favourites that seem to get worn most of the time. My babies only wore half the clothes bought for them. Beware of fancy clothes that are often given as gifts – they tend to shrink in the wash and need ironing!

If it is cold, I recommend little booties with elasticated ankles rather than socks – my babies never kept their socks on. Whatever your baby has on his feet, whether it is sleepsuits, socks, or booties, make sure they are loose-fitting, as his feet are very soft and easily squashed.

Buying for your baby

Your baby needs very little to keep him comfortable and safe. As newborn gear gets very little use, becoming a new parent is an ideal opportunity for recycling. There is plenty of second-hand clothing and equipment on sale in small ads, in local papers, and on eBay, and you'll be able to hand much of it on again when you have no further use for it.

Check that second-hand car seats have not been involved in an accident and make sure you have instructions for any equipment.

DESIRABLE BUT NOT ESSENTIAL

A bouncing cradle chair is useful for propping your baby up after the first couple of weeks and rewards him for making movements by gently rocking him. If you feel like splashing out, or the grandparents want to splurge, baby swing seats have a rocking mechanism and lots of babies find them soothing: some play a tune at the same time. I was given one for my second baby and she loved it. A changing bag is useful, although reasonably capacious pockets (particularly if you are breastfeeding and don't need bottles) will suffice for a newborn nappy, a spare sleepsuit, and a few wipes in a plastic bag. Alternatively, use a rucksack.

NOT NECESSARY

Toys for babies are superfluous in the first few weeks. The only newborn toy that will have any mileage is a mobile hung where he can easily see it (at a distance of about 30cm/12in). Babies respond to contrast, so black and white patterns are a good choice.

The way you decide to dress your baby often comes down to a question of style versus the reality of coping. As one mum told me: "My triplets never lost any socks and always wore immaculate white clothes – maybe that's why I was so depressed during the first year!"

Nappies

You have two options: disposable nappies or reusable fabric nappies (see page 95). Disposables are great for the early weeks, but if you want to use reusables from the start, consider a nappy-laundering service.

Reusable nappies cost more initially, as you have to buy around 18 to 24, but even taking into account laundering costs, they work out considerably cheaper over your baby's nappy-wearing years. You will save at least £500 in total. If you have a second baby, you will be able to use them again, so bringing down the cost even more. Reusables are also more environmentally friendly. While disposables are quicker and easier, especially when you are out, they are becoming a global waste problem. Currently in the UK, eight million disposable nappies are thrown into landfills every day. Whatever you use, the three important factors are comfort, fit, and absorbency. Babies and nappies come in different shapes and sizes, so you might need to experiment to find the best brand for your baby.

A changing mat is useful, but not essential – a towel will do – and you will need either mild baby wipes or cotton wool and water. Nappy sacks are useful, but recycled carrier bags will do the job, too.

Bathing

You may still prefer to "top and tail" your baby at this stage (see page 42), but when you do bath him, have everything to hand as you will need to hold on to him and support his head at all times. Check the water temperature with your elbow – it should feel comfortably warm but not hot. You don't need much water and although it is fine to use baby bath products if you have been given them, they are not essential. You also don't need separate water and cotton wool for his eyes.

Make sure you dry your baby thoroughly after washing, as the creases in his skin can become sore if you don't. Avoid talcum powder as it can clog his pores and may get into his airways, which can cause respiratory problems.

IN THE TUB *You don't need a baby bath – a washing-up bowl is ideal. Or use your bathroom basin with a hand towel wrapped around the taps for safety.*

Common concerns

▸ **How should I wash my newborn baby's hair?**

Your baby's hair doesn't need much attention at this age, but when you do wash it, both of you may feel more secure if you wrap her firmly in a soft towel so she can't flail around. If you're going to bath her as well, you can wash her hair in the bath water first; if not, you'll need a bowl or basin of warm water with a squirt of baby bath liquid if you like. Remember that her head should be supported at all times, so hold her in the crook of your arm with her head pointing towards the water and scoop it over her head from behind to avoid it splashing in her face. Gently dry her head as soon as you've finished.

▸ **How should I cut my baby's nails?**

It is best to cut them with baby nail clippers, or baby scissors which have rounded ends so you won't prick his skin. If you are worried about him wriggling around, try cutting them when he is asleep. His toenails may be long, oddly-shaped, and rather curly at the ends. They can be brittle, too, but this is normal and all you need to do is cut them straight across with baby nail scissors or clippers.

▸ **My baby was born with a tooth. Is this normal?**

By the time your baby is born her milk teeth are already formed in her gums but a few babies are born with a tooth already through. If the tooth is loose or interferes with early feeding, your doctor may suggest removing it. Otherwise, it's nothing to worry about.

▸ **Should I give my baby a dummy?**

Babies are born with a need to suck. Your baby will find comfort from sucking and if you are breastfeeding he may happily stay on the breast after he has satisfied his appetite. Some babies find their thumbs at this age (many suck their thumbs in the womb) – but if yours isn't a thumb-sucker, you may want to give him a dummy. Although you may not like dummies, if they soothe your baby there's no reason not to give him one. You don't need to sterilize dummies, but some level of cleanliness is required and if your baby's dummy falls on the floor, wash it before giving it back to him. Don't clean the dummy by putting it in your mouth. As babies get older, the constant use of a dummy can be associated with language delay (it's hard to speak with a dummy in your mouth), so save it for when nothing else soothes him.

▸ **I think my baby may be constipated. What should I do?**

If your baby is breastfed, she is less likely to get constipated because breast milk is easily digestible. Bottle-fed babies tend to poo less frequently, sometimes only a couple of times a week, but this doesn't necessarily mean she's constipated. Don't be surprised if your baby appears to make considerable effort when opening her bowels, although this shouldn't cause her distress. If it does, or if her poos are small and hard, she may be constipated (see page 276). If your baby is having trouble opening her bowels, try giving her extra drinks of cooled, boiled water. If she's bottle-fed, make sure you're not putting heaped scoops of powder into her bottles as concentrated formula can cause constipation.

Your life as new parents

One month down the line as new parents you may find it hard to remember a time when your baby wasn't there. While he is still your main focus, make sure you take time to look after yourselves and talk to each other. Getting out of the house regularly is a good start.

Going out and about

Take time alone and as a couple to do the activities you enjoy or visit friends with your baby on board. My babies have been on long country walks, the London Eye, buses and tubes, and to parties, restaurants, and art galleries. If you can, enjoy your baby's portability while he's tiny.

HANDS-FREE *A sling or carrier is handy. Make sure it supports your baby's head, neck, and back.*

You can travel light in the early weeks, especially if you are breastfeeding, as your baby will be quite happy in his car seat or sling. Experiencing new sights, sounds, and places will help him learn to be comfortable in a variety of settings, which is good for him as well as for you.

Many new parents worry about exposing a tiny baby to the outside world, but there is no need to be concerned. I would, however, suggest the following –

■ **Avoid smoky areas:** also, don't allow anyone to smoke near your baby.

■ **Dress your baby appropriately:** if it is cold outside but you are going to be in and out of shops or cafés, dress him in layers that can be removed or added as necessary. Take spare clothes with you, too.

■ **Avoid strong sunlight:** your baby's skin is delicate and can easily burn.

■ **Be equipped:** take a spare nappy and wipes, plus, if you are bottle-feeding, bring bottles with milk powder to mix with cooled, boiled water.

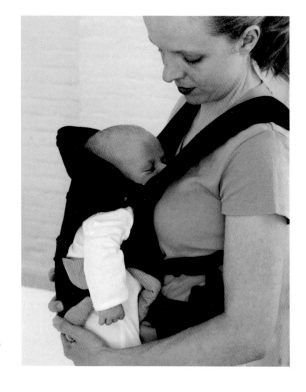

Slings

Your baby will love being carried close to you in a sling and it will be a real pleasure for you, too. Choose a soft, comfortable carrier that will support your baby's head and last until he is around 6–8 months old. If it is second-hand, make sure you have the instructions, as some are complicated to put on. I recently rang to arrange to meet a colleague (a child psychiatrist and paediatrician), and she confessed that she hadn't ventured out in the car with her month-old baby as she couldn't work out how to use the sling or how to collapse the pram!

Prams

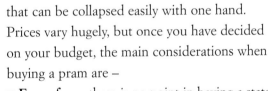

TERRAIN BUGGY *Three-wheeler buggies are good for terrains such as grass or muddy paths, so are great for walks in the country, but can be unwieldy on buses and in shops.*

Don't blow your savings on a designer pram that is tricky to collapse, takes up all the space in your hallway, and won't fit in your car boot. There is a wide variety of pushchairs, prams, lightweight buggies, and travel systems. Some have seats that lie flat; others have a carrycot and/or a car seat (make sure it fits your car) that attaches to the chassis. You can buy them with three or four wheels and most can be bought in twin or triplet versions.

You can use a lightweight buggy at this stage if it lies flat, or has a car seat or carrycot attachment for newborns. The most practical are those

that can be collapsed easily with one hand. Prices vary hugely, but once you have decided on your budget, the main considerations when buying a pram are –

■ **Ease of use:** there is no point in having a state-of-the-art pram if it is difficult to fold and unfold, so check this before you buy.

■ **Manoeuvrability:** before buying, check to see what it feels like to push and whether you can get it up and down kerbs easily.

■ **Handle height:** you can end up with long-term backache if you are stooping to push a pram. If you and your partner are different heights, look for a model that has easily adjustable handles.

■ **Size:** check your pram or pushchair will fit in your hallway and in your car boot.

Adapting to parenthood

▶ **I'm breastfeeding on demand but my partner thinks it is too time-consuming and would like us to work to more of a schedule. How can we find a compromise?**
Try to get to the root of the problem. Is it because your partner generally likes to be more organized or because he doesn't like "sharing you" with the baby? Get him to read about the importance of breastfeeding and why demand-feeding can be a good thing. It is important to address the issue and find an agreed way forward that you both feel comfortable with.

▶ **Every time visitors come to the house they make a fuss of the baby and me, but just expect my partner to make the tea! I can see he's feeling marginalized, but how should I handle it?**
Talk to your partner about how this makes him feel. He's probably overwhelmed, euphoric, exhausted, and quite possibly scared – just as you are – but you're getting most of the fuss, praise, and presents as you're the one who has been through pregnancy and delivery. As long as your partner knows that

you understand his feelings and appreciate that this is a life-change you're both experiencing, you will be able to laugh off other people's insensitivities together.

The important thing is not to let resentment build up on either side. You're both tired and have been through a huge emotional upheaval and you need each other's support.

▶ **I was desperate to have a girl and now my baby boy has been born I can't shake off my feelings of disappointment. I'm too ashamed to admit this to anyone. Will I be able to bond with him?**
Every pregnant woman has an image of what her unborn baby will be like, whether this is in terms of character, size, looks, or sex. This is normal and it's equally normal to have difficulties adjusting to the reality of the baby you've given birth to, as opposed to the baby you've been imagining all this time. Please don't be ashamed – this is far more common than you think and many women (and men) secretly hope for a baby of a particular sex. Rest assured, though, that as you get to know and care

for your son, the love will grow and whether it takes weeks or months, you will bond with him and won't be able to imagine life without him.

▶ **I'm a single parent and am finding the practical side of being a new mum harder than I thought it would be. My mum is happy to help, but I don't want to rely on her too much. What can I do?**
In these early weeks it is important that you get some rest and accept help when you need it. This doesn't necessarily mean handing over your baby all the time, but as your mum is happy to help do take the opportunity to arrange regular baby-free time so you can meet friends for an hour or so, see a movie, or just catch up on some sleep.

It might help to meet other new mums in your situation and your health visitor will be able to tell you about any postnatal or baby groups that meet locally. These can offer companionship and support, and the opportunity to swap notes. You might also benefit from communicating with other single parents through online chat rooms, if you have access to a computer.

Caring for twins

If you are new parents of twins, you probably knew you were expecting more than one baby from the time of your first scan, but having to cope with two newborn babies at once may still come as something of a shock.

You will have many of the same anxieties as parents of single babies, but many more they don't share, such as "Will they overheat if I put them in the same cot?" or "How can I possibly breastfeed?" The biggest question, though, is likely to be "How will we cope?" If they are identical, you may wonder if you will be able to tell them apart. Don't worry – you will be able to very quickly, but you could leave their hospital tags on until you're sure.

COPING IN THE EARLY DAYS

You will need lots of practical help as you get used to feeding two babies, changing two lots of nappies and getting to know two very different small people. When you have twins, Dad is much more likely to get involved with all aspects of care because he will have to. If your twins have been in special care, it may take a while to adjust to being home with them and coping on your own.

Lack of sleep can be a problem if your babies don't sleep at the same time, as can the sheer amount of practical tasks, such as washing, changing, and feeding. Ask for help if you need it and don't turn down any offers! It's worth joining a support organization, such as TAMBA, the Twins and Multiple Births Association (see page 312), who will be able to offer advice and practical tips, as well as put you in contact with other new parents of twins or more.

BONDING

Even if your babies are identical, they will have their own personalities and you will quickly get to know each baby as an individual. You may find that it helps to have some one-to-one time with each baby when possible – and it will definitely help you to have an occasional break from both babies,

SPECIAL CARE

Twins may need time in special care as they are often born prematurely and have complicated deliveries. Identical twins may be affected in the womb by twin-to-twin transfusion where more blood goes to one twin, putting the other's life at risk. Twins will usually be in separate incubators, but brought together whenever it is possible.

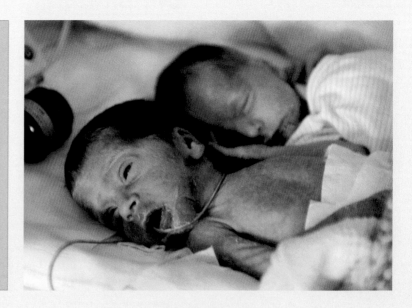

even if it is only going for a 10-minute walk in the fresh air while someone else holds the fort.

SLEEPING

Your twin babies can sleep in the same cot or separately, depending on your preference. Research has indicated that there is no added risk of cot death if your twins co-sleep in the early months, although it is important to adhere to the other advice for reducing the risk of SIDS, including positioning your babies correctly, with their feet at the foot of the cot, keeping their cot in your room for the first six months, and ensuring they don't overheat. See page 39 for more information on reducing the risk of cot death.

FEEDING TWINS

It is possible to breastfeed your twins, although it will require a bit more patience than breastfeeding a single baby. You can feed them one at a time or together. The rugby ball hold (see page 53) is a good position for feeding twins simultaneously, and there are also special cushions available to raise them up to your breast and help you stay comfortable.

Your only logistical difficulty will be getting two hungry babies into position and helping each of them latch on. Your community midwife or health visitor will spend time helping you manage this, but when they are

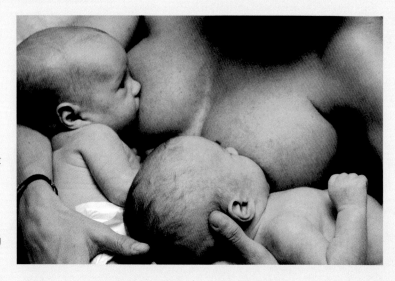

not there, your partner, mum, or friends come in to their own. You can get one baby latched on while someone holds the other, then passes him over to you. That said, don't feel a failure if you end up bottle-feeding your babies – most mums of twins end up giving at least some bottles because it allows other people to help out with the feeding.

If you combine breastfeeding and bottle-feeding, it is important to ensure that both babies have the same amount of each. The easiest way to do this is to give one the breast and the other a bottle, then swap them over at the next feed. This is one situation where I would recommend you get your babies into a routine as soon as you can, because if you feed your twins on demand you can easily end up in a continual cycle of feeding without breaks or sleep.

ENOUGH FOR TWO *You may worry about having enough breast milk to feed both of your babies, but the law of supply and demand means the more you breastfeed, the more milk you will produce.*

BE KIND TO YOURSELF

Adapting to being a new parent is difficult at the best of times, but when you have two newborn babies to look after it can be much more of a strain and it is important not to be too hard on yourself. Keep housework to a minimum – better still, get someone to do it for you if you have any willing helpers or if you can afford to pay someone. Plan to take as much maternity leave as you can – for the first few months you will simply "exist" and will need longer to adjust to the joys and challenges of looking after two babies.

YOUR YOUNG BABY

LOOK AT THAT A WHOLE NEW WORLD WILL OPEN UP TO YOUR BABY AS HE BEGINS TO BE ABLE TO SEE FURTHER – IT WON'T BE LONG BEFORE HE TRIES TO REACH FOR THINGS, TOO

LITTLE WRIGGLER YOUR BABY WILL BECOME MORE PHYSICALLY ABLE BY THE DAY AND WILL WRIGGLE WITH EXCITEMENT WHEN SHE SEES YOU

I'VE GOT HANDS AS SOON AS YOUR BABY DISCOVERS HIS HANDS, THEY WILL NEVER BE VERY FAR AWAY FROM HIS MOUTH

A SPECIAL BOND YOU ARE YOUR BABY'S WORLD – HE'LL LOVE TO LOOK AT YOU AND LISTEN TO YOU

THAT'S MINE HOLDING A TOY BRIEFLY IS A SKILL THAT WILL DEVELOP OVER THE NEXT COUPLE OF MONTHS

"Prepare to be amazed as your baby begins to embrace her world."

Your baby's development

Between 4 and 12 weeks you will see rapid changes in your baby as his body and personality unfold and he evolves from a helpless bundle into a small but complete individual. From his first tentative smiles to beams of delight at seeing you, his responses will become more and more rewarding.

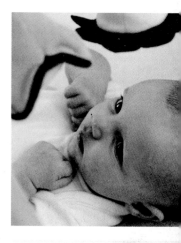

Using his body

Your baby's movements will start to become less random and he may even begin to roll from his back to his side in the third month, so it is important not to leave him unattended on any surface he could fall off. He is becoming stronger, and you will see him start to kick his legs and wave his arms when he is excited.

At some point during his second month, your baby will discover his hands and feet and by 12 weeks he will be able to hold his hands together. However, he doesn't yet understand that his hands and feet belong to him, so when they accidentally come into view he will be fascinated. You can make the most of this phase by buying bootees and mittens with rattles attached; if you put these on (one at a time to start with), he will be drawn to the sound he makes as he waves his arm or kicks his leg – the very beginning of learning about cause and effect.

Your baby will lose his instinctive grasp reflex in the second month and this will eventually be replaced with a deliberate grip that he will use to hold objects. His hands are beginning to relax and open out and if you put a light rattle against his palm he may hold it briefly. He will also begin to reach out towards objects, such as a mobile that is hanging above his cot, and may attempt to swipe at objects within reach, too – this skill will be very hit and miss and it will take time before he is able to grab things accurately.

If your baby was premature, keep in mind that he is likely to reach milestones according to his original due date. So, if he arrived a month early, for example, he may not smile until his third month. You can talk through any concerns at the development checks with your health visitor.

EARLY PLAY Encourage your baby's interest in brightly coloured toys by lying her under a baby gym. If you move a toy in her line of sight, her eyes will follow.

Head control

Your baby will have increasing control over his head as his neck muscles become stronger, and he will progress from being able to hold his head up briefly without support to reliably holding it steady by around 12 weeks. He will enjoy being in his bouncy chair and if you have a carrycot, put a folded pillow underneath the top half of the mattress to raise him up and give him a better view of his surroundings.

As soon as your baby starts to have a little head control, do ensure he has regular time lying on his tummy when he is awake. I see so many babies whose heads have become misshapen because they always lie on their backs. Over time, this can flatten the back or side of a baby's head. While it is important that your young baby sleeps on his back, this "tummy time" when he is awake and you are around to keep a close eye on him, is vital for his healthy development. Babies who spend a lot of time on their backs may be slower to roll over and crawl, and some who are not placed on their tummies at all in the first few weeks become very distressed when they are. Being on his tummy is also a more comfortable position if your baby has reflux (see page 98).

While he is on his tummy, your baby will soon be able to raise his head up a little before collapsing back down again. Try putting a rattle or soft toy in front of him to encourage him to lift his head up. From around seven weeks, rather than having his legs tucked under his body when you put him on his front, he will begin to stretch them out behind him. By 12 weeks he may be able to lift his head higher and possibly raise his chest by pushing up with his arms.

Improved vision

Your baby's eyesight will be improving and he will be able to see further so he will enjoy lying under a mobile or baby gym. He will also gradually be able to follow your movements with his eyes – this skill is known as "tracking". You can encourage him by getting his attention, then moving slowly within his field of vision to see if his eyes follow you.

Being in a variety of different environments will stimulate your baby's vision and other senses, and will get him used to being in new places and around unfamiliar people, so don't feel you need to keep him away from crowds or inclement weather.

TUMMY TIME *Help your baby develop head control by lying him on his tummy. Some babies don't like this, so follow his lead and put him on his back if he becomes unhappy.*

You and your baby

As you get to know your baby you will find the best ways to handle him and play with him. You will also get to know when he has had enough and wants to rest. If your baby is fearful and startles easily, handle him gently and talk to him softly. If he is very active and alert, give him as much opportunity as possible to see what is going on around him. You will soon see what makes him happy and what upsets him so follow his lead and respond accordingly.

Your baby will be happiest when he is close to you. Even if he is not in your arms, you can chat and sing to him. If he cries and you can't pick him up straight away, your voice may soothe him and will let him know that you are nearby. However busy you are, try to have a bit of quiet time with him to enjoy those new smiles, which will appear more and more often during the coming weeks.

During these two months your baby will begin to turn towards sounds that are close to him and will make noises other than crying, for instance the soft vowel sounds that are known as cooing. By the time he is 12 weeks old, he may begin to chuckle and laugh.

Giving her down time

You can't hold your baby all the time and sometimes it's good for her to lie on a playmat or rug with you close by. Although sheepskin and lambskin rugs are soft, your baby may get too hot if she's lying on her tummy so don't lie her down to sleep on one.

As well as spending time on her tummy, she will enjoy lying on her back so that she can move her arms and kick. She will enjoy this all the more if you take off her nappy and lie her on a towel to kick freely. This will help if she has nappy rash, too. If you put your baby down, make sure that she has something to occupy her – either toys to look at on a baby gym or attached to her bouncy chair. She will also enjoy watching you around the house so chat to her as you go about your chores. For safety, don't put her bouncy chair on a raised surface, such as a table or bed, as her movements could easily cause it to slip and topple over.

The six-week check

You and your baby will both be due for a check-up six weeks after the birth, or at eight weeks depending on where you live. Your GP will want to make sure that your baby is in good health and that you have recovered from the birth, both physically and emotionally.

Examining your baby

The physical examination at this check-up is similar to the one your baby had at birth. Your GP will pay particular attention to your baby's eyes, heart, hips, the pulses at the top of her legs, and the shape of her spine. If you have a boy, your doctor will check to see whether his testicles are present in the scrotum (see page 305). The following aspects of your baby's development will also be checked –

■ **Vision:** a baby's eyes should be able to fix on and follow a face by this age, although he can't yet see clearly at any distance.

■ **Hearing:** he should still become startled by loud noises and calm down when he hears your voice.

■ **Smiling:** most babies have begun to smile by 6–8 weeks.

■ **Physical control:** your baby will be examined to check whether his arms and legs are moving equally and whether he can support his own head for short periods of time.

■ **Feeding:** his overall growth will be checked and you will be asked if he is feeding well.

A health record

The information from this check, and your baby's subsequent development checks and vaccination records, will be entered in his personal child health record, or "red book". This record will help you and health professionals keep track of his progress.

YOUR BABY'S HEALTH
A thorough physical examination will be carried out on your baby. Don't be afraid to raise any concerns you have about his health, however small.

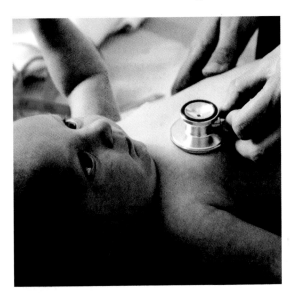

Registering the birth

If your baby was born in England, Northern Ireland, or Wales, you will need to register his birth by the time he is six weeks (42 days) old. If he was born in Scotland, you need to register by 21 days.

Staff at the hospital where your baby was born, or your home-birth midwife, will have given you full details of where to register your newborn baby, along with the relevant paperwork to take with you. If you are married, either of you can register the birth, but if you are not and you want the father's details on the birth certificate, you will both need to attend.

You can, of course, call your baby whatever you like, and have unlimited names, but it is worth giving some thought to how a name might be perceived as your baby grows up. A celebrity name that is popular now may sound very dated later on; a very old-fashioned or unusual name may lead to teasing; and twins are unlikely to thank you for combinations such as Bill and Ben or Tom and Jerry. Names that are difficult to spell or pronounce may cause problems throughout your child's life. Also be aware of what your baby's name may be shortened to.

It is definitely worth checking what your baby's initials will spell, so that you don't saddle him with a ready-made nickname for when he goes to school.

Examining you

Your GP will probably check your blood pressure and if you are having problems passing urine, he or she may ask for a sample to test for infection. Many new mums experience some degree of incontinence – don't be embarrassed to mention this as it can be treated, initially by doing the pelvic floor exercises you learned in pregnancy. You will be asked whether you are still having any discharge (lochia) or fresh bleeding. Any stitches should have dissolved by now, but if you are still experiencing discomfort then it is a good time to get this checked to ensure you are healing well. If you are struggling with exhaustion and/or depression, it is vital to raise this. Postnatal depression (see page 101) is treatable, but needs to be addressed as early as possible, so do ask for help.

You may have resumed your sex life despite the exhaustion, or you may be horrified at the notion of ever having sex again. If penetrative sex is causing you discomfort, mention it to your GP. You will be reminded about contraception – however low a priority sex may be, it is possible to get pregnant before your first period so be prepared, unless you want a 10-month gap between babies.

Communicating with your baby

Although your baby is still several months away from uttering his first word, his relationship with you is all about communication – from energizing you into action through his cries to delighting you with his first smiles and interacting with you through sounds, play, and body language.

Talking

THAT'S FUNNY *At 8–12 weeks your baby may begin to chuckle, and you will soon discover many ways of making him laugh.*

For most parents, starting a conversation with their baby comes naturally, but if it doesn't it is well worth making the effort. As you chat, pause regularly to give him time to make sounds in reply. Then respond to these by talking back to him – "Did you?", "Yes, it's time for your bath!", "Look, here's your nappy!" He won't understand the words, but he will understand the tone and your intention to communicate. Parents naturally pitch their voices higher and exaggerate their facial expressions when they talk to their babies, and while it is not necessary to use baby language (although it doesn't matter if you do), research shows that babies are especially tuned to respond to this way of speaking, which has become known as "parentese" or "motherese".

Body language

As your baby's body uncurls he will have more control over his limbs and head, and will be increasingly able to give you cues to how he is feeling. He will gradually lose the "moro", or startle, reflex – a very eloquent way to communicate fear – and will be able to show he is happy by wriggling with excitement and smiling; contented by relaxing into your arms;

Your baby's personality

By now you may have some strong clues to your baby's personality, but try not to label him as "difficult" or "placid". Babies do change.

Some are calm from the start, while others may be restless or fretful. Bear in mind that many "difficult" babies become easy toddlers, so don't panic if yours is a crier. A baby who is only happy when you are giving him attention may just be very sociable, and really come into his own in his second year.

A baby who is very active may be miserable early on because he is frustrated or may be restless and not a good sleeper – he will probably be happier and more settled once he has more control over his body.

Try to remember, too, that, like adults, babies sometimes simply have a bad day.

and distressed or angry by stiffening his limbs and crying. He will also begin to let you know when he has had enough of playing or feeding by turning his head away.

The importance of play

Having you as a playmate will make your baby feel secure as well as help to develop a powerful bond between you. He explores his world through play and it is key to his development. By playing he learns motor skills, co-ordination, and how to interact with others.

He will love gentle rocking, chatting, and listening to you sing nursery rhymes. By the time he is around 12 weeks old, he may take a toy that you offer him, although it will be months before he is able to deliberately let it go. He will begin to be aware of cause and effect, as he holds a rattle and hears the noise it makes when his arm moves. Out of sight is out of mind, though, so the moment he is distracted the toy will drop out of his hand and will no longer exist for him.

"I hold my baby facing me and when he makes a sound I reply and watch his face light up. These moments are pure magic."

Massaging your baby

Massage has been used for thousands of years and is, quite simply, touch that feels good. As well as being a relaxing activity, it is a wonderful way to communicate with your baby and can benefit him by soothing his crying, and relieving colic or wind pain. Research also shows that babies who are massaged may sleep better.

Learning baby massage

There may be a class in your area where you can learn baby massage techniques. Your health visitor may be able to recommend one. However, remember that you will naturally massage your baby all the time – when you rub his back to soothe him, stroke his hair, or play with his hands and feet, so don't worry too much about the finer details of the techniques – just make sure you and your baby have fun together and all your movements are gentle.

What you will need

Using a massage oil is not essential, but it will enable your hands to glide easily over your baby's body without uncomfortable friction.

HOW TO MASSAGE

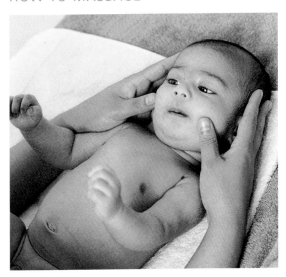

1. HEAD MASSAGE *Lay your baby on his back on a soft towel. Lightly massage the crown of his head using circular strokes (avoid his fontanelles), then work down the side of his cheeks. Give him plenty of eye contact.*

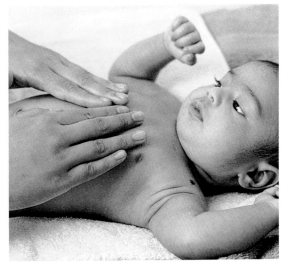

2. CHEST AND TUMMY *Gently stroke your baby's chest using a downward motion. Rub his tummy using a circular motion, working clockwise and outward from his belly button with your fingertips.*

Olive oil is suitable but avoid aromatherapy and nut oils; there is a possible link between nut oils and the development of nut allergy. Lay your baby on a soft surface and either put a nappy or towel underneath him in case he wees or poos, or leave his nappy on. If he is not comfortable being naked, don't bother with the oil and leave his clothes on.

It is important to ensure that your baby is warm while you massage him so ensure that the room is a comfortable temperature. If you choose the right time, he is more likely to be relaxed and enjoy the experience, so don't massage him just after he has had a feed or when he is hungry. Try to choose a time when you are relaxed, too, as babies have a way of picking up on our moods.

Getting started

Don't expect a massage to last more than a few minutes to begin with while your baby is getting used to the experience. To start with you can simply try stroking his arms and legs firmly, then massaging his abdomen lightly in a clockwise direction.

Talk to your baby as your massage him and watch his response. You might want to play some calming music to create a truly relaxing atmosphere. If he doesn't seem happy at any time, stop the massage. Your baby will give you cues to tell you whether he is enjoying it, such as making eye contact, staying relaxed, and smiling or cooing. If he wants you to stop he may turn his head away, shut his eyes tightly, whimper, or cry.

3. LEGS, FEET, AND TOES *Work from your baby's thighs to his knees, stroking in a downward motion. Lift each leg and gently squeeze his shins. Rub his ankles and the soles of his feet, then gently massage each toe in turn.*

4. INTERACTION *Keep your baby interested by giving him lots of smiles and talking or singing to him. When you have massaged his front, turn him over and massage his back, working from the head down.*

Routines and feeding

There is a lot of rather pedantic advice about sticking to rules and routines in babycare, but I believe they are unnecessary unless this happens to be the way you prefer to do things. If you tune into your baby's needs, you can be a more relaxed parent and find your own style.

Sleep routines

NIGHT-TIME SLEEP

A sleep routine isn't essential, but it will help your baby learn the difference between night and day – the sooner that happens, the sooner you'll get a good night's sleep.

By your baby's third month you may be longing for the day that your baby sleeps through the night and be deeply envious of parents who appear to have cracked it. The earliest your baby will be physically able to go through the night without a feed is around six weeks, but babies vary considerably and yours may need sustenance during the night for longer than this. However, some six-week-old babies can manage 5–6 hours sleep at night if they have been given a late feed. It is therefore worth trying to give your baby a breast- or bottle-feed at around the time you go to bed. There is a chance that this longer stretch will then give you some semblance of a "full" night's sleep.

It's funny how new parents often describe a six-hour sleep as "sleeping through the night". It's certainly a milestone to be celebrated. The trick is to coax your baby into co-operating with a sleep routine. If your baby doesn't yet recognize the difference between night and day (many don't at this age), a bedtime routine that involves changing into night-time clothes, having a bath or wash, a story, cuddle, and a last breast- or bottle-feed will give him sleep "cues" that he will begin to understand as soon as he is developmentally ready.

"I couldn't bear making my baby wait for feeds and breastfed him throughout the night for months. Being flexible suited our family and if I could go back I wouldn't do it any differently."

Feeding routines

Some parents prefer to feed their babies every three or four hours, while others demand-feed almost constantly throughout the day and night. All families and babies are different and most will find a happy medium somewhere between these two extremes. The choice really depends on what sort of person you are and your lifestyle. As with all aspects of parenting, do what feels right for you.

Bottle-fed babies take longer to digest their milk than breastfed babies, so it may be possible to get them into some sort of feeding routine after the first few weeks. A breastfed baby, however, will need to feed frequently early on as he is growing fast and this is how he ensures that your milk supply increases to meet his needs.

As your baby matures, you will find that his feeds gradually become more spaced out. This is because his stomach is bigger and can hold a greater quantity of milk, which takes longer to digest. Having had a longer gap since his last feed, he will be hungrier and therefore drink more milk, which will fill him up for longer. So he will naturally be inclined to take more time between feeds as he gets older. The exception to this is the breastfed baby who feeds more often and longer simply for comfort. If your baby does this, he will want the breast frequently, day and night, and you can choose whether you allow this or whether you offer him some other form of comfort. You could give him a dummy or encourage him to suck his thumb (some will, but some won't), or give him lots of attention and cuddles, but not the breast unless he is hungry.

If you prefer a strict feeding routine, your baby will get used to this, and having regular feeds may also make him easier to settle and make his sleep patterns more predictable. On the other hand, if you prefer to be flexible, that is fine, too. Just go with the flow and he will soon establish a feeding pattern of his own.

BOTTLE-FED BABIES
It may be easier to establish a feeding routine with a bottle-fed baby because formula takes longer to digest, keeping a baby fuller for longer.

"I fed my baby on demand during the day, but gave him the bare minimum at night and got him into a sleep routine as soon as I could. I found that this way I could cope rather than constantly being exhausted."

Feeding your growing baby

You will probably be over the worst of any breastfeeding problems by now. However, you may still feel concerned that your baby is not getting enough milk and sometimes wonder whether he is still hungry or just needs a cuddle. Some mums just feel too tied to their baby's demands. During these difficult times, you may be tempted to offer your baby a bottle of formula milk. Don't – because all the problems are about to settle down and as you have come this far it is really worth persevering with breastfeeding. If you haven't given your baby formula milk yet and he is growing well, you can call yourself an expert breastfeeder and it should be plain sailing from now on.

If you offer your baby the breast when he is hungry, and stop when he is full, he will have as much milk as he needs. You don't need to coax him to feed unless your GP or health visitor has expressed concern that he is not having enough milk. This is uncommon, as babies usually grow at the rate that is correct for them. If you are bottle-feeding, don't be tempted to put extra formula in his bottle to encourage him to sleep at night. Sneaking in extra calories may cause your baby to gain too much weight and become constipated. Trust your baby's instincts – he knows when he is hungry and if you listen to what his appetite is telling him now, he will be able to do this for himself as he grows.

"My two-month-old baby seems to be much more efficient at feeding now, and she is gradually spending much less time at the breast."

Supplementary bottles

Healthy babies come in all shapes and sizes: some are naturally chubby, while others are designed to be slim. I do see some babies, however, who are very underweight and may also be listless and extremely miserable. This is called "failure to thrive". If there is no medical problem, their condition is usually due to inadequate calorie intake and the doctor or health visitor may suggest a few supplementary bottle-feeds to get breastfeeding back on track. By having these additional feeds, a baby will have the energy to suckle more, which will, in turn, boost milk supply.

If this is recommended for your baby, it does not mean that you have done anything wrong. Despite the word, "failure", some babies simply need an extra boost to get them growing well.

Expressing and storing milk

Once breastfeeding is fully established, you can express milk for your baby to take from a bottle, giving you flexibility and giving your partner a chance to have a turn at feeding. Being able to leave expressed milk in a bottle also means that you can go out alone for an evening and not worry about your baby waking and wanting a feed.

To express by hand, place your hand around your breast a couple of centimetres away from your areola (the dark skin around your nipple), starting with your thumb at the top and your fingers at the bottom. Then press downwards and forwards towards your nipple, exerting gentle pressure to mimic your baby's action of "stripping" the milk from the breast. Move your hand round as you express and catch the milk in a clean, wide-mouthed container.

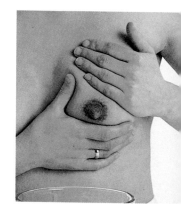

EXPRESSING MILK By expressing, you will get a break from feeding but still be giving your baby the benefits of breast milk. You can express by hand or use a manual or electric pump.

To express with a breast pump, place the device over your breast as instructed then either turn the pump on if it runs on electricity or depress the lever to operate it manually. These pumps work on a suction basis, pulling the nipple and areola, along with the surrounding area of the breast, into the cup to imitate the action of a breastfeeding baby. They have a container attached to catch the milk and some come with a bottle attachment so all you have to do is add a teat when you are ready to give the milk to your baby. If the pump doesn't feel right, or is uncomfortable, check the instructions to ensure it is positioned correctly. If you are finding expressing difficult or painful (it shouldn't be), ask your health visitor for help or to put you in touch with a breastfeeding counsellor.

Breast milk should be stored in the fridge or the freezer. Milk will keep in the fridge (below 5°C) for 3–5 days, or in the freezer (below -18°C) for three months (write the date you expressed it on the bottle to keep track). Defrost frozen milk overnight in the fridge or put it in a bowl of warm water. Once defrosted, you can keep the milk in the fridge for 24 hours. Ideally, as with bottled milk, don't use a microwave to defrost or heat milk as it can create "hot spots" that might burn your baby; microwave heating can also damage the antibodies in breast milk.

Combining breast and bottle

If you are not going to be with your baby for every feed, or you want to share feeding with your partner, you may want to give your baby a combination of breastfeeds and formula milk. Once breastfeeding is well established, this will be fine as long as you continue to breastfeed regularly to maintain your milk supply. If you replace some breastfeeds with bottles, you may find that your breasts become engorged for a few days while your body learns to make less milk, but this will quickly settle down.

If your baby has been fully breastfed until now, he may need coaxing to take a bottle. You can buy teats that have been specially designed for babies who are accustomed to the breast and are shaped to encourage him to "latch on" and suckle the milk in a similar action to breastfeeding. If he refuses formula at first, try getting him used to bottles of expressed breast milk to start with, then switch over once he has got the hang of it.

If your baby is reluctant to take a bottle from you, this is probably because he associates you with breastfeeding, which he prefers. Your partner, a friend, or family member may therefore have more success, but you may find you have to stay out of the way so that your baby can't see you, hear you, or smell your milk. Once you have a second baby, this can be a good ruse to get a jealous older sibling involved – your baby is more likely to take a bottle from his older brother or sister, with dad's help, than he is from you. And it can be a great way to encourage them to bond.

Breastfeeding in public

It is possible to discreetly breastfeed anywhere, so don't feel you should slink off to the loos if your baby needs feeding in a public place. A loose T-shirt will allow easy access without revealing much flesh, or you can drape a sarong or shawl around you and your baby. The more women breastfeed in public, the more people will get used to it and this will encourage other mums to follow suit. It is normal to feel self-conscious at first, but you will soon overcome that. To begin with, it can help to feed your baby in a public place where there are other mums and babies, such as baby-friendly cafés or drop-in baby groups.

The vaccination debate

Vaccines work by stimulating your baby's body to make antibodies to particular diseases so that he becomes immune to them. There have been controversies about particular vaccines, but by and large, they are a safe and effective way of protecting children from potentially dangerous illnesses.

Weighing up the risks

Peter's parents remember that, during their childhood, after the summer holidays one or two classmates would not return to school because they had been struck down by polio. We don't see this illness in the UK these days, due to effective vaccination, but not long ago it commonly caused paralysis, disability, and sometimes death. The decision to have your baby vaccinated can be a difficult one as there are sometimes concerns voiced about the safety of vaccines. However, the risk of a serious reaction to a vaccine is incredibly small, especially if you compare it to the risk to your child of contracting the illness itself. All our children have been immunized.

In the 1970s there were concerns that the whooping cough (pertussis) vaccine might be a cause of fits in some children, and many parents decided not to have their babies immunized. The result was an epidemic of whooping cough among unimmunized children, with some of them suffering brain injury or even death as a result of the disease. We now know that the whooping cough vaccine does not cause fits and so the suffering and deaths of these children were unnecessary.

Some babies who are prone to having febrile convulsions (see page 259) may have one following the MMR vaccination, but the risk is small – around 1 in 1,000. An unimmunized baby who catches measles has a 1 in 200 risk of having convulsions, as well as a significant risk of other serious complications or even death. Unfortunately, suggestions that there is a link between the MMR vaccine and autism and bowel problems, have caused a drop in the take-up of this vaccination, even though subsequent research has found no connection whatsoever. This has led to an inevitable rise in cases of the diseases, along with the attendant dangers.

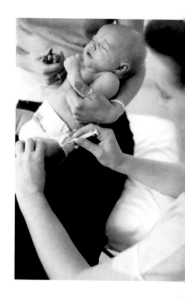

FIRST APPOINTMENT
Immunizations are usually given by the practice nurse at your clinic or GP surgery. You will be asked to hold your baby while the injection is given.

"It was quite difficult watching my baby have her vaccinations, but I knew it was the right thing to do."

Think of it this way. Travelling on a motorway always carries some risk, but if you had the choice of being in a top-of-the-range car with seat belts, crumple zones, and anti-lock brakes (being immunized) or a rusty old three-wheeler (risking the disease), the decision would be easy.

What do the diseases do?

The UK immunization programme protects against the following diseases, some of which can kill if they are not spotted and treated early –

■ **Diphtheria** is an infectious bacterial disease that causes breathing difficulties and can damage the heart, nerves, and glands.

■ **Tetanus** is a bacteria present in the soil that enters the body via cuts and grazes. It causes paralysis, painful muscular contractions, and can be fatal.

■ **Whooping cough or pertussis** (see page 274) is a very infectious disease that causes long coughing spasms, with a characteristic "whooping" sound as the baby takes in air. It can cause pneumonia, brain damage, and death, particularly in babies under six months.

■ **Polio** is an extremely infectious virus that affects the central nervous system and can cause paralysis.

■ **Hib (haemophilus influenzae type b)** is a bacterium that can cause illnesses such as meningitis, septicaemia (blood poisoning), and pneumonia.

■ **Pneumococcus** is a bacterium that causes serious illnesses, including pneumococcal meningitis, pneumonia, and septicaemia.

■ **Meningococcus C** is a bacterium that can cause meningitis and septicaemia.

■ **Measles** (see page 271) is a highly infectious bacterial disease that can cause ear inflammation, problems with the nervous system, brain damage, and pneumonia.

■ **Mumps** (see page 272) is a viral infection that can cause severe complications such as meningitis, deafness, and infertility in males.

■ **Rubella** (see page 273), also known as German measles, is a mild, infectious disease caused by a virus. If caught in pregnancy, it can cause severe problems in the unborn baby.

Having vaccinations

Your baby may become distressed when he is given the injections. Giving him a reassuring cuddle should help to calm him down, or you can offer him the breast or a bottle. Many babies won't have any obvious reaction to being vaccinated, but some will develop a fever over the following 24 hours and may become irritable. This can be treated with 2.5ml of infant paracetamol suspension, which can be repeated after six hours if necessary. I always gave my babies paracetamol before the immunizations, too. Occasionally the injection site will be red for a day or so, which is nothing to worry about, but if the reaction doesn't calm down, or is bigger than a 10p coin, show your health visitor or GP.

Very occasionally, the injection site can become infected, which will require antibiotics. Rarely, a baby can have a strong reaction to an immunization. If this happens, you will be given advice about whether or when your baby should have the subsequent injections.

Your baby's vaccinations

Your baby's immunizations will be given at specific ages. You will be sent a reminder by your GP surgery when they are due.

WHAT IS GIVEN	WHEN
▶ Tuberculosis (BCG) for babies who are at a high risk of contracting the disease (1 injection)	At birth, if necessary
▶ Diphtheria, tetanus, whooping cough (pertussis), polio, and Hib (1 injection) ▶ Pneumococcal infection (1 injection)	Two months
▶ Diphtheria, tetanus, whooping cough (pertussis), polio, and Hib (1 injection) ▶ Meningitis C (1 injection)	Three months
▶ Diphtheria, tetanus, whooping cough (pertussis), polio, and Hib (1 injection) ▶ Meningitis C (1 injection) ▶ Pneumococcal infection (1 injection)	Four months
▶ Hib and meningitis C (1 injection)	12 months
▶ Measles, mumps, and rubella (MMR) (1 injection) ▶ Pneumococcal infection (1 injection)	13 months

Everyday care

The basics of caring for your baby are becoming easier now that he has more control of his body, and he may now be more interactive with you during activities like nappy changing. You may also have begun to establish some sort of routine to your day and learnt to anticipate his needs.

Time together

You can often incorporate time with your baby into the jobs you have to do around the house – if you are hoovering or sorting the laundry, he can sit in his bouncy chair and watch you. Having said that, there will be times when you have to leave your baby while you're doing something. Don't be too concerned if he cries and you can't get there immediately – he won't come to any harm if he has to wait a few minutes for your attention, so don't feel you have to drop everything and rush to him the moment he whimpers.

Carrying your baby

Once your baby can reliably hold his head up, possibly by the end of the third month, you can turn him to face outwards in his baby sling or carrier, if the design allows for this. Lots of babies are delighted with this fresh perspective on the world and have the dual pleasure of being held close to you and having lots of new and interesting things to look at.

Consider also using the sling when you are working around the house. This enables you to have both hands free to get on with things but keep your baby with you and stimulated.

Nappy rash

Soreness and inflammation in the nappy area is common and is a consequence of your baby having urine and faeces next to his skin. The delicate skin on your baby's bottom and genitals may also be spotty and moist-looking. There are, however, to prevent it getting worse. The best way to help it heal is to keep your baby's nappy area clean and dry, and leave his nappy off so air can get to his skin whenever it is practical. Lie him on a towel or nappy to minimize any mess.

Even the most absorbent nappies can leave some dampness so if your baby is sore change his nappy regularly, and straight away if he does a poo, to avoid making the rash worse. Make sure he is thoroughly dry before you put a clean nappy on. If your baby wears fabric nappies, use a nappy cream, which will form a barrier on his skin to protect it from the effects of moisture. Make sure your baby's nappy isn't too tight – there should be room for air to circulate.

If your baby's nappy rash is very severe or persistent, he may have a fungal or bacterial infection (see page 283). See your GP or health visitor, who will be able to prescribe treatment with more active creams.

Reusable nappies

Disposables were probably indispensable in the first few weeks, but you may now feel ready to try reusable nappies. You can choose between traditional terry or shaped fabric nappies –

■ **Traditional terry squares:** these nappies can be folded into different shapes, depending on your baby's size and gender (boys and girls will wet in different areas of the nappy), and are secured with a pin or clip.

■ **Shaped nappies:** these are neater and slimmer nappies than terry squares and are fastened with poppers or Velcro. Some makes have a separate folded muslin nappy and an outer wrap, while others are all-in-one.

Whichever type you use, a disposable liner inside will help to protect your baby's bottom, and you can use booster pads to provide extra absorbency at night. You will also need a bucket with a lid to store the dirty nappies.

PUTTING ON A REUSABLE NAPPY

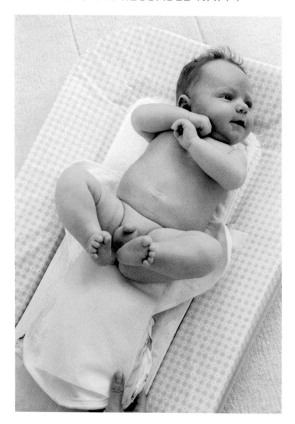

INNER LINING *A disposable inner lining can be used with all fabric nappies. Simply lay the nappy on the changing mat and place the lining on top. Dispose of the lining once it is soiled or wet.*

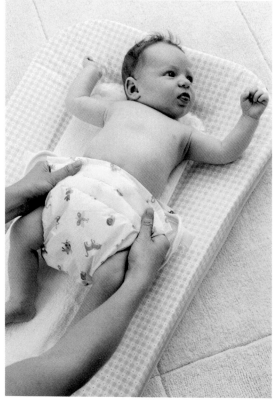

ALL-IN-ONE NAPPIES *Usually, these have a combined inner nappy and outer wrap, but sometimes they are separate. Fold the outer pants over and fasten the Velcro tabs or poppers securely at the sides.*

Bathtime

Although some babies are still wary of the bath at this age, many love it and find bathtime a real pleasure. If your baby happily splashes and plays in the water, bathtime can become an enjoyable start to his regular bedtime routine that will help him to wind down. If your baby is not keen, don't worry. Just carry on washing the bits that need it for now and try again when he feels a bit more confident.

There is a range of bath seats available that support your baby in the water, leaving your hands free. You must, however, still stay with him at all times. You could try a cradle bath seat or support, which is made of plastic, foam, or fabric. These support your baby above the water and they may be a good option if you don't feel confident, or tire easily, when you are holding your baby in the bath. A new addition to the market is a bucket-shaped bath. Designed for babies aged up to six months, this deep bath supports the baby in a foetal or seated position. Another option is bathing with your baby. Place him on your lap facing you and make sure you have someone to hand him to before you get out of the bath.

SUPPORTING YOUR BABY IN THE BATH

HOLDING HIM STEADY *When bathing your baby, support his head and neck at all times with one hand, and use your other hand to gently wash him.*

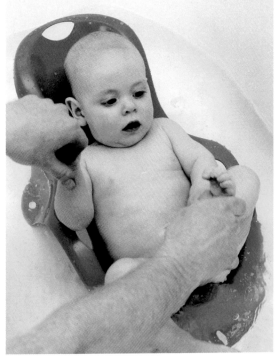

USING A SEAT *A bath seat will support your baby in the water, enabling you to wash him more easily because both of your hands are free.*

Common concerns

▶ **Should I be concerned that my baby is still being sick after feeds?**
If your baby is simply possetting, don't worry as this is the normal bringing up of milk in a very young baby and he will grow out of it in a few months. However, if your baby suddenly starts vomiting having not done this before, or seems ill when he vomits, or if his vomiting is becoming more severe, seek medical advice (see page 258). Similarly, see your GP if your baby is not gaining weight, or seems distressed by feeding or possetting.

▶ **My baby has yellow scales on her scalp. What are they and should I try to remove them?**
These scales are called seborrhoeic dermatitis, or cradle cap, a very common and harmless condition. It doesn't need treatment, but if it looks unsightly and you want to remove the scales, you can soften them with a little olive oil. Leave this on overnight, then wash your baby's hair in mild baby shampoo or baby bath liquid in the morning. You may need to do this a few times to get rid of cradle cap, but

don't be tempted to pick at the scales as this can make her scalp sore and leave her vulnerable to infection. If left alone, cradle cap will generally clear up on its own.

▶ **Sometimes when I'm washing or changing my baby I notice that he has an erection. Is this usual?**
Yes, this is normal and nothing to be concerned about. The penis is a sensitive organ and all baby boys will have erections from time to time, some more than others – baby boys have even been observed to have erections in the womb.

▶ **Why is my baby's skin always so dry and how can I treat it?**
Dry skin in young babies is very common and is normally nothing to worry about. If a baby is overdue, the creamy vernix that protected her skin in the womb may have been absorbed by the time she is born, and this can cause dry, flaky skin in the early weeks of life. For other babies, dry skin is simply part of the natural settling-down process as her body gets accustomed to life outside the womb.

Try rubbing in some olive oil or use an emollient once or twice a day until things improve. If you don't notice an improvement, or yout baby's skin is sore, seek advice from your health visitor or GP.

▶ **I always pick my baby up as soon as he starts crying. Am I spoiling him?**
It's impossible to "spoil" your baby at this age by responding quickly to his needs: rather, you'll show him that he can rely on you to come when he calls you so he will probably cry less often. Your baby is programmed to want to be close to you – this is essential for his survival – and your attention will help him feel secure. If he is particularly miserable and you can't work out the cause, you may find that he settles if you take him for a walk or put him in the sling and carry him around.

That said, it is always worth waiting a few moments when your baby starts to whimper as he may settle quickly without starting to cry, particularly if you talk to him. He may just want reassurance that you are there.

QUESTION&ANSWER

Understanding your baby's cries

While all babies cry, some cry considerably more than others. Crying is normal, but a cry of pain or discomfort, or continuous, excessive crying for which there seems to be no apparent cause, should be investigated.

WHY YOUR BABY MAY CRY

There are several reasons why your baby might cry –

▶ **Hunger:** this is the most common reason and is likely to be the cry you identify most easily.

▶ **Boredom:** your baby may be in need of company. Try putting him in the sling or carrier so that he can be close to you as you do your chores.

▶ **Over-stimulation:** sometimes a bit of quiet, calm time is needed – maybe a breastfeed in another room.

▶ **Tiredness:** like the rest of us, babies can get to the point where they find it hard to fall asleep – try leaving your baby in his Moses basket to drop off.

▶ **Discomfort:** this is not quite a cry of pain, but may build up to it if you can't identify the cause.

▶ **Pain:** your baby's cry will sound urgent and may rise to a scream. It is a cry you can't ignore and you will respond to him instinctively.

EXCESSIVE CRYING

In medical terms, excessive crying is defined as continuous crying lasting more than three hours in 24 hours. It may seem as though your baby is crying non-stop, but you will probably find that the total is less than three hours. On rare occasions, doctors will admit babies to hospital to check that there are no medical problems causing excessive crying. This will also give you a chance to get some sleep.

REFLUX

The most common medical cause of excessive crying is gastro-oesophageal reflux. This is where the immature valve at the top of a baby's stomach allows milk to come back up. The stomach acids in the regurgitated milk can burn a baby's oesophagus (food tube), which is sore and makes him cry.

A refluxing baby will often arch his back with pain and dislike lying flat. He may vomit and his pain will usually be worse after feeds. Although reflux can be miserable for your baby and for you, try not to worry. This condition can be treated (see page 275) and your baby will eventually grow out of it.

COLIC

One cry that lots of parents get to know all too well is the screaming that comes with colic. It frequently occurs in the evening and often seems worse because this is when you are likely to feel particularly tired. We are not exactly sure what causes this tummy pain in young babies, but it is most common in babies aged around 2–3 months and may be due to excess wind or an intolerance of lactose, the natural sugar that is found in milk. If your baby cries for hours and seems to be in pain, screaming, and pulling his legs up to his tummy, he may have colic.

I personally think that colic drops are probably more helpful for parents (who need to feel that they are doing something) than for the baby. However, some parents swear by an expensive colic remedy that breaks down the lactose in milk, so this could be worth a try. Ask your doctor or pharmacist for advice. It is also worth trying the comforting techniques opposite. Every baby is different and you will probably soon hit on the technique that works best for yours.

Trying to stay calm will help. This may be easier said than done, but be aware that your tiny baby may pick up on your stress and this can result in his crying becoming worse. Get your partner, a family member, or friend to take a turn if possible so that you can have a break. Comfort yourself with the knowledge that colic rarely lasts longer than a few months and, although it is uncomfortable for your baby, it won't harm him in any way.

COMFORTING YOUR CRYING BABY

If your baby cries a great deal it can be difficult, but don't despair. My youngest cried so much when he was tiny that we referred to him as "the miserable git"! He is now an adorable and happy child.

There are lots of ways to soothe your baby and he is likely to settle fairly quickly once the crying cycle has been broken, especially if you have been reassured that there is nothing wrong with him. The hope is your baby will respond to one or more of the following techniques –

▶ **Cuddling him:** your baby may be calmed if you hold him close and rock him gently. You will soon find the position that is most effective at soothing him.

▶ **Motion:** put your baby in the sling, wheel him in the pram if you have one, or drive him around in the car. A word of warning, though: try not to get into the habit of driving your baby around to calm him down. This technique should only be a last resort or you will find yourself driving a crying baby around every evening.

▶ **White noise:** try putting your baby in front of the washing machine on a spin cycle. It sounds bizarre, but many parents swear by it. The vacuum cleaner or a detuned radio are also sounds that seem to calm babies, or you could try making gentle shushing noises while you're holding him.

▶ **Comfort sucking:** babies are programmed to suck and yours may be soothed by the breast, even if he is not hungry, or by sucking his thumb, fingers, or a dummy.

▶ **Massage:** try gently massaging his tummy in a clockwise motion (see pages 84–85), which may give him some relief.

▶ **Swaddling:** if he is flailing around, being swaddled (see pages 64–65) may help to calm him down.

▶ **Talking to him:** hold him face to face and engage him in a conversation.

ROCKING *Simply rocking your baby to and fro may be enough to ease her crying. Try singing her a lullaby or talking to her as you rock her.*

"LEOPARD IN A TREE" *Position your baby on your forearm and rest her head on your hand. You can easily rub her back which can help to soothe her.*

SLING *Holding your baby close to you in a sling may make him feel secure and ease his crying. This also has the advantage of keeping your hands free.*

Being a parent

While we all talk about the enormous change having children will make to our lives, most of us don't plan what to do about it. We assume our existing relationships will simply fit around the baby, but in reality you will need to be organized and try to plan some baby-free time in advance.

Taking time out

It is amazing how liberating two hours without a baby can be. Wanting time apart from your baby doesn't make you a bad parent – in fact, taking time out for yourself, nurturing your relationship with your partner and coming back to your baby with renewed delight will benefit everyone. Because spontaneity is difficult, it is a good idea to arrange nights out in advance. When life is so hectic it can be hard to get organized, but if you book a babysitter you are more likely to go out and have a break. Being vague about arrangements usually means you end up staying in.

TIME TOGETHER *Having some baby-free time is a necessity, not a luxury, so don't feel guilty.*

Health concerns

▶ **I can't stop smoking. Will my baby be affected?**
Yes, cigarette smoke is harmful for your baby. It increases the risk of cot death (see page 39), as well as the risk of frequent ear and chest infections and if you haven't been able to give up before now, I urge you to keep trying. There are support clinics that can help you, and your GP or health visitor will be able to give you advice. Smoking in a separate room isn't enough. Even then, some of the particles from your cigarette smoke will find their way to your baby's lungs, as they cling to your clothes and hair.

▶ **Can I take the contraceptive pill while I'm breastfeeding?**
Yes, it is important to use contraception as soon you start having sex again as you can get pregnant soon after giving birth, even if you're fully breastfeeding. The combined contraceptive pill contains the hormones oestrogen and progesterone and this is not recommended during breastfeeding because it can affect the amount of milk you produce. However, the mini-pill contains only progesterone and is safe to use. You may need to use additional contraception, such as condoms, for the first few days until the pill becomes effective.

QUESTION&ANSWER

Baby blues or postnatal depression?

If you are still feeling down, it is time to get help from your health visitor or GP as the "baby blues" (see page 43) should have passed by now. You may be suffering from postnatal depression (PND), a condition that affects up to one in 10 mums and can become severe enough to interfere with the ability to get on with life. Mothers of twins or special needs babies are particularly vulnerable to PND. It frequently starts within a month of the birth, but can occur up to a year later. Symptoms can vary but include feeling low, anxious, negative, and sleepless; plus a loss of appetite, and an inability to cope. These feelings can become completely overwhelming and may be accompanied by guilt and panic attacks.

Mothers feel that they are expected to be happy with their new baby and are often ashamed about feeling low, but PND can happen to anybody and needs to be treated as early as possible. Counselling and/or medication are very effective, so don't subject yourself to unnecessary suffering. Untreated, PND can ruin your joy in your new child, interfere with bonding, and set destructive parenting and relationship patterns that may persist for years, so do seek help as soon as possible. Most women who are not diagnosed for some time regret it was not recognized earlier.

Fathers' blues

Everyone has heard of new mums getting the baby blues, but the daddy blues is less well acknowledged. The trigger for this is the complete life-change that a new baby brings, particularly the change it brings to your relationship. While new mums often feel that their bodies are no longer their own, their partners frequently feel that they are suddenly second in line.

The physical and emotional closeness that sex can bring may still be absent because even if your partner has recovered from the birth she may not feel very sexy anymore. This feeling of being excluded, coupled with exhaustion and the fact that some men find tiny babies relatively uninteresting (so that the compensations for this loss of position in your partner's life may seem small), can make new parenthood a dangerous time in your relationship.

The most important thing is to keep talking. It's essential to communicate so that problems are discussed, shared, and understood and don't fester into misunderstanding and resentment. Cuddle and be physically close – although she may not want to have sex, your partner will notice if you seem reserved and lacking in affection. Get involved in babycare and make sure you spend time alone with your baby.

FATHER'S VIEW

YOUR PERSONABLE BABY

1 2 3 **4 5 6** 7 8 9 10 11 12

MONTHS

"Your baby will greet you with gurgles and smiles, and there'll be fewer tears."

PLAY WITH ME BEING A PARENT BECOMES MORE REWARDING BY THE DAY AS YOUR BABY LEARNS TO PLAY AND "CHAT"

I'VE GOT FEET ONCE YOUR BABY FINDS HER FEET, HOLDING AND SUCKING THEM WILL KEEP HER HAPPILY ENTERTAINED

THIS IS TASTY YOUR BABY LEARNS MORE ABOUT TEXTURE BY EXPLORING AN OBJECT WITH HER MOUTH, RATHER THAN HER HANDS

SLEEPY HEAD AFTER THREE MONTHS, YOUR BABY WILL PROBABLY BE SLEEPING LONGER AT NIGHT AND LESS DURING THE DAY

LITTLE GUZZLER YOUR BABY WILL BEGIN TO DRAIN HIS BOTTLE VERY FAST WHEN HE'S HUNGRY

A little person emerges

From the fourth to the sixth month you will see exciting changes as your baby becomes more sociable and physically capable, and begins to interact more. As she becomes increasingly responsive, she will begin to gurgle and laugh and respond to games such as peek-a-boo with squeals of delight.

Physical development

If you hold your three-month-old in a sitting position, she may be able to keep her head steady but won't be able to keep her back straight yet. By four months, she might be able to keep her head level with her body when you take her hands and pull her to a sitting position. By five months she may be one of the few babies who are just about sitting independently, but she won't be able to maintain this position for long. Place cushions around her for support and so that she won't hurt herself if she does fall.

She may enjoy taking some of her weight when you hold her upright on your lap. As long as you allow her to do this when she is ready, rather than trying to coax her to stand, she will have great fun pushing against your legs with her feet. Don't worry if your baby doesn't want to take weight on her legs at this stage as this is true of many babies at this age. Your baby will enjoy having the opportunity to lie on her back and kick, and she will probably enjoy kicking in the bath, too, so have lots of towels ready. Regular playtime on her tummy continues to be good for her, but it is still important to put her on her back to sleep.

STIMULATING PLAY
You can help your baby's emotional and physical development. Encourage her developing strength, but always take your cues from her.

Growing at her own pace

Your baby learns and grows in her own way, at her own pace, and while babies generally follow the same broad arc of development, there are big variations within this. Your baby may be particularly physical, holding her head up early and rolling over, or she may be very alert and sociable, but less forward in her physical development. Either is normal and all babies are individuals so try not to make comparisons with other babies or to worry unnecessarily about her reaching milestones.

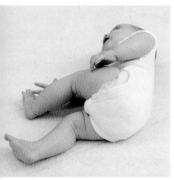

ROLLING OVER *She will gradually learn to roll over on to her tummy or back.*

Your baby's view of the world

As her vision improves, your baby will enjoy having different things to look at. Research shows that babies are still rather short-sighted at this age, but her growing perception of depth means that she will become far more efficient at seeing something and swiping at it. As she gets more skilled at this, she will succeed in grabbing things.

By around five months she may be interested in looking at small objects and try to reach for them. However, she will want to explore everything she holds with her mouth, so supervise her carefully. Don't let her get hold of anything that is small enough to choke her, such as coins or buttons. She will be interested in different textures, too – crumpled paper, bubbles in her bath water, and shiny fabric are all new to her and will be fun for her to explore.

Your baby's senses are becoming linked together, too. For example, researchers found that when three- and four-month-old babies could see both their mum and dad, and were played a recording of one of their voices from a point in between both parents, the babies looked at the parent whose voice they could hear.

Cause and effect

Beginning to understand that things happen as a result of her actions – cause and effect – is a major leap forward in your baby's mental development. As well as grasping that when she waves a rattle it makes a noise, during these next few months she will also come to realize that when she cries for milk, you will pick her up and feed her, or when she "talks" to you, you will reply. In this way, she will gradually develop a sense of having some control over her world. You can encourage this new area of development by responding enthusiastically when she causes something to happen, such as pressing an interactive toy so that it makes a noise.

Your baby's understanding of cause and effect also helps her learn to anticipate. If you have begun a bedtime routine with her, having her bath then a story will teach her to anticipate a calming feed followed by bed. You can harness this new understanding by reading her the same bedtime story every night or singing the same song, so making it a "cue" that it is almost time to sleep. This will help in settling her into a routine that she understands and that helps her to feel secure.

Communicating

Your baby will start to initiate social interaction, waving her arms to be picked up and smiling at you when you come into her field of vision. When you interact with your baby, remember to give her time to respond to you. Her reactions won't be as fast as an older child's so when you chat to her, pause for a few seconds and let her have her turn in the "conversation". She will start to use consonants, such as "ba", and start to repeat these – so she might say "bababababa", a development known as babbling.

When she makes sounds, she will probably enjoy it if you repeat them back to her. She will let you know when she has had enough by turning away, breaking eye contact, or becoming fretful. Act on this, too, as it is her way of communicating that she is tired or fed up. Your baby is learning that communication is a two-way process, and at this age it is impossible to "spoil" her with too much attention, so relax and enjoy her company.

Your baby's thoughts and behaviour

Your baby's thought processes are still developing; understanding how she thinks can help you understand her behaviour, which in turn will help you to be a relaxed parent. Your young baby's instinct is to bond with you and ensure that she gets what she needs from you – food, warmth, and love. Any behaviour that delivers these for her will be reinforced.

Research shows that babies as young as six months old display jealousy when their mum diverts her attention to another baby. They kick and cry furiously until they have her full attention once more. The mothers in the study were shocked by the strength of their babies' emotions and responded by demonstrating their love for their babies, exactly what the babies needed. While babies are capable of demonstrating a whole range of emotions it is important to understand that they have no concept of good or bad behaviour and should never be punished.

BABY POWER *Babies learn that they can have an effect on their world – smile and you smile, shake a rattle and it makes a noise.*

It's playtime

At three months your baby will be able to focus on objects that are a bit further away and will be increasingly accurate in reaching out for them. If you have been itching to buy toys for her, now is a good time, as she will enjoy anything that she can safely attempt to hold and explore with her mouth.

Handling toys

If you hold out a toy for your baby, be patient – at four months, she is still learning to judge the distance of an object. You will see her looking from her hand to a toy and back again before reaching out for it. By the time she is around five months old, she will no longer need to do this and will reach out and hold things with far greater accuracy and ease, adjusting her hand to the size of the object as she reaches for it. A word of warning – your baby can grab at your hot drink just as easily as she can get hold of a toy, so keep anything dangerous well out of her reach.

Your baby will enjoy lots of different sounds – some predictable, some new. A specially designed playmat for when she is lying on her tummy is often a big hit as these have sections that crackle, rattle, and squeak as she touches them or rolls on them. A rainmaker may be popular with your baby – this is a hollow, sealed tube with small beads inside that make a sound when the "rain" is inverted. However, some rice shaken in a jar is just as effective. Try also scrunching up paper, clapping along to songs and nursery rhymes, or playing her music on the stereo. A musical box attached, or near, to her cot can be a good buy and may become an enjoyable part of her bedtime routine.

Baby bouncers

Babies love the kind of bouncer that you suspend from a door frame or a hook in the ceiling. Some come with their own free-standing frame, although these take up a lot of space. Once your baby is able to hold her head up reliably, a bouncer will give her a whole new view of the world. Her toes should just be able to touch the floor so she can bounce and swivel around. Ten minutes or so is probably long enough in a baby bouncer as your baby will get tired, but at least this will give you a bit of time to get one or two tasks done.

Peek-a-boo

This is a game that babies enjoy the world over, and there are versions to be found in most cultures. Your baby doesn't understand that things continue to exist when she can't see them – known as object permanence – and this fun, gentle game will help her get the idea and will probably be a firm favourite for months. Soon, when you cover your face with your hands, she will shriek with excitement as she waits for you to pop out and say, "Boo!" You can extend this game by letting her see you put a blanket over a toy, then lifting it up again. Her excited anticipation of seeing the toy revealed is a sign that she is beginning to understand that things are still there even if she can't see them.

Your clever baby

There is a whole host of products aimed at boosting your baby's mental development, from mobiles and rattles to books, electronic toys, and DVDs. Every year there is generally another "must have" toy or method of stimulation that is guaranteed to ensure that your baby will be the next Einstein. Perhaps the most well known of these are products based on the apparent effect on babies of listening to Mozart. These purport to enhance a baby's "spatial, temporal reasoning". Needless to say, the evidence that underpins this programme has been debunked, although music does have a place in your baby's development later on (see page 219).

The most important thing is to enjoy play with your baby so she is stimulated regularly. Babies who are not stimulated may eventually withdraw and fail to interact with people. Once this ground is lost, it may never be made up.

WHERE'S MUMMY?
Playing the simplest game, such as peek-a-boo, can help to teach your baby complex skills, namely that something is still there even if she can't see it.

Bookworm

Research bears out the importance of reading books to babies at an early age because they can stimulate a baby's development. There are now government schemes to give free books to babies, with local authorities giving out books and bookbags at varying ages. Your baby is also entitled to join your local library from birth, but you will probably want to buy a few of your own at this stage because most of them will be chewed as well as read. You may initially feel a little foolish choosing books for a baby, but remember there is much to be gained for both of you, and you will be developing your baby's language and communication skills.

Books for babies lend themselves naturally to reading aloud and many encourage a range of rhythm and sing-song tones that your baby will respond to. There are various fabric activity books that have bright, clear pictures, as well as squeakers, dials, rattles, and mirrors to attract and hold her interest. Board books with realistic pictures are also ideal for babies.

Fully-fledged dad

You will feel comfortable and competent as a dad if you are fully involved with your family, rather than observing from the outside, so I would encourage all dads to get stuck into caring for their baby. If you never start, you will never learn, and you'll miss some magical moments. Do the day-to-day tasks such as changing nappies, but also do things that are special to you. If my daughter wouldn't settle after her late-night feed, I used to light a fire and sit up with her. At first I saw this as the short straw, but quickly came to realize that it was a magical time that would be over forever in a few weeks.

The trick is to do what suits you as a dad and both of you as a couple. We know a family with four children where the dad has never changed a nappy. His wife has always been very happy with this, though, since he plays endlessly with all the children, which gives her a break.

FATHER'S VIEW

Feeding your baby

Throughout these three months your baby will become more and more proficient at feeding from the breast quickly and efficiently. Mealtimes are more predictable, so it should make it easier for you to plan your day without feeds dominating the arrangements.

That said there will be times when your baby gets distracted during feeds, as she is starting to take more of an interest in what is going on around her. If you are finding it a problem, try feeding her somewhere quiet, if possible, away from any hustle and bustle. It can become more difficult to breastfeed discreetly as your baby breaks off from the breast regularly to grin at you or pulls at the bottom of your shirt.

COMBINED FEEDING
You may decide to start giving your baby bottles some of the time. If you want to fully breastfeed when you go back to work, you'll need to express.

By the time your baby is four months old you may be preparing to return to work, and lots of breastfeeding mums make the decision to switch to giving their baby formula feeds at this stage. You don't have to stop breastfeeding, though, as you can either express milk for your baby to have while you are out (see page 89) or wean her on to formula during the day and keep her morning and evening breastfeeds going. The Department of Health recommends breastfeeding for the first six months, so it will benefit your baby if you can still breastfeed her some of the time. If you are dropping some feeds, or stopping altogether, do it gradually, so that your body has a chance to adjust. This will minimize the risk of getting engorged, leaky breasts.

Sterilizing

If you are bottle-feeding your baby and have been sterilizing your bottles, you can stop when your baby is six months old. It remains very important, however, to continue to clean the bottles well to reduce the risk of gastroenteritis. If you are weaning your fully breastfed baby on to bottles, you will not need to start sterilizing at this point. I sometimes see parents sterilizing their baby's bowls and cutlery once they start to wean. This is totally unnecessary, as is the sterilization of plastic toys.

When to start solids

If your baby has started waking on the hour, every hour at night she may be hungry. However, the Department of Health recommends that babies are not given solid food before six months as generally their systems are not yet ready to cope with anything other than breast or formula milk. Having solids too early can increase the risk of coeliac disease, allergies, and food intolerance (see pages 278–279) in susceptible babies. If you think your baby may be ready for solids before six months, seek advice from your health visitor. Solids should definitely not be started before four months, and no wheat products should be given before six months.

Feeding concerns

▶ **I'm going back to work in a few weeks and I can't get my breastfed baby to take a bottle. What should I do?**

Start getting him used to the bottle as soon as you can, so you can take things slowly. Your baby has never sucked milk from a teat before, and this requires a different technique to the "milking" action of breastfeeding, so he will need to practise. You may need to persevere, and give him lots of encouragement as he learns.

Cuddled close to you, it is not surprising that he tends to reject the bottle in favour of your breast. I recommend leaving your baby with your partner for 24 hours if he refuses to take a bottle from you. This is a great opportunity for you

to get a complete break and it is good for dad to be in total charge of caring for the baby.

▶ **Does my baby need extra vitamins?**

In general babies do not need to be given extra vitamins before six months. Bottle-fed babies don't need supplements as long as they are having at least 500ml (1 pint) a day, as vitamins are already added to formula milk. If your baby is mainly breastfed, she will need drops containing vitamins A, C, and D after six months. Your health visitor can tell you if your baby needs these and where to get them. You must give the correct dose as taking too much can be harmful.

Once your baby is a year old,

your health visitor or GP may recommend giving your baby vitamin drops even if she hasn't had them before, especially if she doesn't eat a full range of foods, which is a common problem with young children. But, ideally, babies and children should get all the vitamins they need from eating a balanced diet.

In some parts of the UK there is a recommendation that all babies are given vitamin D, as there are increasing numbers of children with rickets. This condition causes soft, swollen bones and, rarely, seizures, and is due to a lack of calcium and vitamin D. Rickets is common in breastfed babies whose mothers have little exposure to sunlight and a diet that is low in calcium.

QUESTION&ANSWER

Sleep habits

Your baby's random sleep habits may be evolving into a reasonably reliable pattern. By around four months most babies will sleep 12–14 hours out of 24 and for twice as long at night (8–10 hours) as during the day, although this will not be unbroken if your baby is still waking for feeds.

When you are considering encouraging your baby to adopt more conventional sleep habits, you may be concerned about leaving her to sleep on her own to sleep in your room. Don't feel guilty about this – although it is recommended that your baby sleeps in your bedroom for the first six months, she will be fine going to bed earlier than you. You can use a baby monitor so you can hear what is going on and go to her if she needs you.

Remember that you don't need to rock your baby to sleep in your arms – it is a good idea for her to learn to fall asleep by herself. By this stage your baby is unlikely to need more than one night feed (although she may want them), unless she was born very prematurely and your doctor or health visitor advises it.

SLEEPING ALONE *To encourage good sleep habits, lay her in her cot when she's awake so that she learns to fall asleep without being held and rocked.*

When she is unsettled

Your baby is likely to make noises while she is asleep – we all do this and we all have brief awakenings during the night. Try not to rush to her at the first sign of a whimper. If you do, you may disturb her and actually prevent her from dropping back off to sleep by herself.

If you want to encourage your baby to sleep for longer and be more settled, you might want to consider sleep-training (see page 114). This approach is not about leaving your baby to scream; it is about letting her know that she is safe and that you are close by, but that at night she can expect minimal attention from you. If your baby knows that you are always there for her but doesn't come to depend on being fed and cuddled to fall asleep at night, she will soon learn to sleep through. I cannot over-emphasize the emotional benefits of having an alert, contented baby and relaxed, happy parents who have all had enough sleep.

"We sleep-trained our first baby at six months, the second at five months, and the third at four months. With three young children, we really needed our sleep and wish we'd trained them all at four months."

Sleep-training

Your baby won't come to any harm if you leave her to grizzle and there is plenty of evidence that over-tired, stressed parents are less able to offer their baby all the emotional support that they need. Babies who are usually having two-thirds of their sleep at night can be encouraged to sleep through with a reasonable chance of success even if they wake frequently. Essentially, the idea is to teach your baby that you are always there for her, but that this is night-time and therefore time to sleep. Some babies are simply not ready for this until they are a bit older, and first-time parents may not want to attempt sleep-training until their baby is six months old, but if you feel yours is ready – or you are desperate for a decent night's sleep – give it a go. A word of caution, though: it is important that you are willing to persevere, as it can take several days for your baby to get the hang of not crying automatically for you if she finds herself awake in her cot. After following a calming bedtime routine, try one of the following sleep-training methods –

■ **Gentle withdrawal:** put your baby to bed after her usual routine, kiss her goodnight, and stay next to her cot. If she cries, stroke her hand to comfort her but don't pick her up. Stay with her until she falls asleep. Once she can fall asleep with you next to the cot, move away so you are sitting in a chair across the room.

The next step is to be around as your baby falls asleep, popping in and out of the room tidying up or whatever, so she knows that you are close by but not always right next to her. This technique may take longer than rapid return (see below), but may be gentler for your baby and is certainly easier on your nerves.

■ **Rapid return:** after kissing your baby goodnight, leave the room. If she cries, go back and reassure her briefly that you are there – without picking her up – and then leave again. Many people suggest leaving increasingly

REASSURANCE

Sometimes your baby may just need to know you're there. If she becomes unsettled once she's been put to bed, go and reassure her. Don't pick her up or over-stimulate her.

Moving your baby into a cot

By around four months, your baby will have outgrown her Moses basket and be ready to move to a cot. When choosing a cot, the most important requirement is that it complies with British safety standards (currently BSEN716). Avoid using pillows, cot bumpers, and duvets until your baby is a year old. If you buy a second-hand cot, make sure the bars are not more than 6.5cm (2.5in) apart (so her head can't get stuck between the gaps), there are no gaps between the mattress and the cot sides, and the paint is non-toxic.

At some stage your baby will start to roll over in her cot. Turn her on to her back again but don't feel you have to keep checking on her all night. The Foundation for the Study of Infant Deaths (FSID) recommends that you always put your baby on her back at the start of any sleep time, but say that once she can roll from her back to her tummy, then on to her back again, you can leave her to find her own position.

long gaps between going back, but it is not necessary – your baby will eventually fall asleep, feeling secure because you always come when she is distressed. Slowly she will learn that at night-time you will come if she needs you but you are not going to feed her, chat to her, or play with her.

Be prepared to repeat this many times each night for up to a week, although for many babies it may only take two or three nights. If you have two or more children, you may find you become more robust about sleep-training. With our third child, I checked him once then left him to cry. He cried for an hour the first night, 30 minutes the second night, and on the third night he slept through.

Making it work

Whatever technique you adopt needs to be agreed upon by both of you. If one parent is unhappy about using a sleep-training method they will inevitably want to pick the baby up, and she will never learn to go back to sleep without a cuddle. If there is a thin wall between you and your neighbours, it is a good idea to warn them that you are planning to try a sleep-training method. I sent our three-year-old on her first sleepover whilst we sleep-trained our youngest. Any disruption to your routine, such as a holiday or your baby being ill, will probably mean you have to re-establish her sleeping pattern, so be prepared to tackle it more than once during your child's babyhood.

End of maternity leave

Deciding whether to stay at home with your baby or go back to work can be difficult, and for many new mums the choice has to be made when their babies are still very young. However, for lots of women, especially single parents, the decision is driven by financial considerations.

THE RIGHT CARER *Give yourself plenty of time to research all your childcare options. Knowing you've made the right choice will make you happier and more confident about returning to work.*

Returning to work

Some new mums can't wait to get back to work no matter how much they love their babies, and if you feel like this, be reassured that this is the right thing for you to do. The important factor is to make sure that it is right for your baby, too. Please don't feel guilty because you are keen to return to work and are worried that she may suffer. She won't, as long as you find childcare that both you and she are happy with.

If you are someone who needs to be at work, you will be excited to see your baby when you get home and will be able to give her good quality attention when you are with her. The downside, however, is that you may miss out on some aspects of her development, which in these early months is very rapid. Lots of new mums compromise by returning to work part time, or if that is not possible, taking some extra unpaid leave in addition to their statutory entitlement. Part-time work can offer the best of both worlds, although do beware the "part-time" job where you are expected to fit a whole week's work into three days and end up doing the rest at home, all for a part-time salary. Of course, these days it doesn't have to be mum who is the part-timer or the stay-at-home parent. Whilst not the norm, there are increasing numbers of stay-at-home dads. Options on paternity leave and more flexible ways of working are all part of this trend.

It is worth bearing in mind that at five months your baby will probably cope better with being left in childcare than she will at eight months or older, as she will become clingier in the latter part of her first year. So this may be the ideal time to return to work; by the time your baby goes into her clingy phase, she will already be familiar with her carer, making separation from you less of a problem.

Types of childcare

Whoever looks after your baby will need to be experienced, communicate well with you and your child, and share your views on childcare. Unless it is a relative, the person you employ should be trained and have references. One thing that can come as a shock to parents is the realization that their baby is growing to love her carer. This is a good thing and should be encouraged, as your baby has to develop a happy relationship with anyone who looks after her, but it can be hard for you if you feel that you are missing out while someone else is enjoying her.

The childcare you choose will depend on various factors, such as your finances, what is available in your area, and what suits your baby. Gut instinct is an important part of choosing childcare. I remember walking into a nursery and being put off immediately by the smell and by the fact that all the toddlers looked bored. If you are not happy with a carer or a nursery, even if you can't put your finger on why, don't use them. Even if they turn out to be okay, you won't be able to settle at work if you are uneasy about your baby's wellbeing. The main options are –

■ **Family member or friend:** if you have someone close who you trust to look after your baby, this can be a huge relief, especially if you are going back to work while she is still very young. Remember, though, that grandparents or other relatives might have very different ideas to yours about how to care for a baby, so discuss this in detail before coming to any arrangements. Family childcare that doesn't work out can make for a very difficult situation. Talk through what will happen in this instance at the start. Bear in mind that while close relatives can look after your baby without being registered, if a friend or neighbour regularly looks after your baby for more than two hours a day, he or she will need to register as a childminder.

■ **Childminder:** these are carers (often parents themselves) who look after children in their home. They must be registered with OFSTED (the Office for Standards in Education), and will be inspected annually to check they are following recommended guidelines. An advantage to having a childminder to look after your baby is

KEEP IT IN THE FAMILY
In many ways a grandparent is the perfect carer, but have proper discussions about all aspects of the arrangement to avoid disagreements.

that she will be in a family situation, most likely with other children of different ages, which will be interesting and fun for her. Childminders' rates vary, and how much you pay will depend on where you live and how many hours/days' childcare your baby has. A childminder can be registered for three under-fives at a time, but only one baby under 12 months (an exception can be made for twins or siblings who are both under one year, although this has to be approved by OFSTED).

■ **Nanny or nanny-share:** a nanny is the most expensive childcare option, but she will be able to live in or out, depending on what suits you, and will care for your baby in your own home in the way you want her to. This may work out to be cheaper if you have more than one child. Oddly, unlike childminders, nannies don't have to be registered, although some may hold a qualification, such as a NNEB (Nursery Nurse Examining Board) diploma. Because of the cost, some families prefer to share a nanny, so you could consider getting together with a like-minded friend.

■ **Nursery:** day nurseries that take young babies are flourishing but there is a huge variation in the quality of care on offer. A good nursery will welcome you at any time, will have a key worker for your baby so she can form a relationship with one person, will give you feedback about your baby's day, and will always discuss any concerns with you. Council-run nurseries are difficult to get into unless you or your baby has particular needs, so most parents use privately run nurseries. However, these all have to be registered with their local authority, so you can check up on them. The recommended ratio for staff to babies in a nursery is at least 1:3.

■ **Au pair:** these are young people from overseas who come to the UK for a year or so to experience living with a family in a different culture, and improve their English. An au pair is unlikely to be qualified, so won't be able to have sole charge of your baby while you are at work, but will be able to help with housework and childcare, and babysit sometimes.

"I went back to work when each of my three babies was little and it was absolutely the right decision for me. I can honestly say that I never, ever tire of my children and I appreciate every minute with them."

Staying at home with your baby

It may seem like the simpler option to carry on caring for your baby yourself, but stay-at-home mums tend to fall into the guilt trap just as much as those who work outside the home. If you stay at home with your baby, you may worry about not contributing to the family's income or feel that you can't take a break when your baby sleeps as you ought to be doing the housework. It will help to get out to baby groups or to meet other full-time parents as much as you can. Your baby will enjoy the experience and you will have company and support. This is especially important if you are a single parent, as it is easy to feel isolated when you are on your own.

Remember that caring for your baby is a full-time job, and one that you would pay someone else to do if you weren't doing it, so you are making a vital contribution. Every family is unique, and if this is your choice, don't feel that you need to fill your days with chores. I have a friend who looks after her baby full time and sees taking time off for a coffee with friends as a crime. If you were in an office, you would stop and talk to people, and take coffee and lunch breaks, as well as work a limited number of hours. So remember, if you are at home with your baby all day, you are entitled to take breaks, too.

Once you are settled into a routine, it can be stimulating to take on an evening class or home-study course to give you another outlet. Doing other activities can make time spent with your baby feel more special.

FULL-TIME MUM *As a stay-at-home mum it's easy to put your own needs second. It's really important to take breaks and, for your own sanity, have regular contact with other adults.*

"I sometimes feel judged by friends who returned to their jobs after having a baby, but I have no regrets about being a stay-at-home mum, even though it has been a struggle financially at times."

Supporting each other

Whether you return to work or choose to be a full-time mum (or dad), it is important to recognize that both roles have their stresses as well as advantages. What is important is that you and your partner avoid getting caught up with issues such as who works harder, or who has a more valuable role. If one of you is working outside the home while the other cares for your baby full time, it is important that whoever is out at work does their share of the childcare. Both Peter and I have been lucky enough to have some weekdays off on a regular basis while our children have been growing up. While it is great to be able to have that extra time with our children, as well as the challenges of jobs we enjoy, we are both pleased to have the help of the other parent at the end of the day when one of us has had a full day caring for the children on our own.

Your life as a couple

The likelihood is that before you became parents you were both working people who arrived home together in the evening. Now that one of you is at home all day and one at work, it can be a challenge to your relationship and it can take time to adapt. Suddenly, coming home requires you to help make supper, change nappies, and support your partner. No matter how tired you are, bear in mind that she's been working all day too, and will need a break. This is no bad thing. Coming back to your baby can be an uplifting experience and something to look forward to. The key is to be involved, be sensitive to each other's needs, and reprogramme some of your old expectations.

SEX? WHAT'S THAT?

For most men, new parenthood does little for their sex life other than to make it less available! For women, who have recently given birth, it is hardly surprising that sex is usually low on the list of priorities. This is a challenge as sex is a key way of expressing love and intimacy, so its apparent withdrawal can be hard to deal with. Conversely, if you are too physically remote from your partner she may feel that you are not interested in her. A good hug can work wonders.

Try to keep the dialogue going and express your needs while understanding and supporting your partner's. Cuddle your partner without expecting anything more – there will be a gradual return to being more intimate, even if it's not her number one priority now. Bear in mind that pregnancy hormones can affect a woman's libido for many months, and that breastfeeding and babycare can make her feel that her body serves different functions than before. As with many of the early strains of parenthood, this is just a phase, and within a few months your relationship (and her body) will be getting back to normal.

FATHER'S VIEW

Common concerns

▶ I don't want to go back to work, even though we need the money. Am I being selfish?

It's natural to feel like this and you're not being selfish, but you do need to talk it over with your partner and point out the benefits of you being at home. There is the obvious benefit to your baby of having continuity of care from the person she loves most in the world, and the fact that you won't need to help her adapt to being cared for by someone else. You will also be able to continue to enjoy your baby to the full. On the financial side, you might not be as badly off as you think. You won't have the associated costs of working, such as childcare, travel, and lunches. Depending on your line of work, you could also compromise by agreeing to go back part time.

▶ My friend's childminder has a vacancy and she's encouraging me to take it, but I'm not sure I'm comfortable with the carer. Should I give it a try?

In a word, no. It is essential that you are happy with your baby's childcare and it's important to

follow your gut reaction on this. Just because you're not comfortable doesn't mean there is anything wrong with the childminder, but she may not be the right person for you or your baby. Keep looking, and follow your instincts – it will be very difficult to return to work if you are worrying about your baby's wellbeing. Remember, too, if the childminder, nanny, or nursery you do choose doesn't work out, don't be afraid to change your arrangements.

▶ My friends at baby group seem to be taking parenting in their stride, but I'm not coping well. Is there something wrong with me?

Lots of mums feel like this in the early months, especially if they are exhausted, have a difficult family situation, or a particularly miserable baby. If this is the case, you may be feeling overwhelmed and upset that life with a baby is nothing like you expected it to be.

I had an emergency Caesarean with my third baby, which was a huge shock, and I was a physical and emotional wreck for several weeks. As a result, Eddie was incredibly cranky as a baby and

I couldn't wait to hand him over when Peter got home. Now, though, he's a cuddly and adorable child and it's hard to remember not being completely bonded with him. Please don't struggle on alone – the sooner you seek help, the faster you'll be able to start enjoying life with your baby. It is possible that your feelings are due to postnatal depression (see page 101) and whether or not this is the cause, it's important that you talk things through with someone you trust and who is trained to make that assessment. Your health visitor or GP will be able to offer support and refer you for counselling if this is appropriate.

QUESTION&ANSWER

Caring for your adopted baby

Whatever your reasons for adopting, the start of a ready-made family is likely to be both rewarding and challenging, and it is essential to ask for any information, advice, or support you need so that you can enjoy your baby to the full.

YOUR ADOPTED BABY

If you have adopted a baby, you will have many of the same experiences, joys, and concerns as biological parents. However, you might find that after a very long period of waiting, your baby actually arrives rather more suddenly than you expected, taking you unawares. You may be especially anxious about how you will cope if

knowledge that there is a genetic tie. Birth mothers also have their hormones to help them with early bonding, so if this doesn't happen straight away for you and your adopted baby, don't worry.

In the same way as any other parents, give yourself time to get to know her, talk to her, sing to her, care for her, cuddle her and the bond will

LEARNING TO CARE FOR YOUR BABY

Unless your baby was born through a surrogacy arrangement and is with you from the start, you are unlikely to be around for initial lessons in practical care immediately after her birth. Your health visitor can support you through learning the basics of nappy-changing, feeding, winding, and generally handling your baby. Don't panic if it

"Lots of people we met on our preparation courses saw adoption as a last resort after being unable to conceive a child. For us, adoption was absolutely the first choice."

your baby is older, has had a difficult start in life, or if you don't feel anything much for her at first. These anxieties are normal – try to find a support group as talking to others in the same situation will help. Many child psychiatry services have specialist help for adopted and foster children who have had a difficult start in life.

BONDING WITH YOUR BABY

The pressure to bond instantly is tough enough for birth parents, but it is made easier for them by the

start to grow. Be reassured that it will happen eventually and, however long it takes, it will be worth the wait.

MEDICAL CHECKS

If your baby was born in this country, there will probably be records of her first medical checks. You still might find it reassuring to have her looked over by your GP, not least so they can meet each other. If you have adopted your baby from abroad, she may need to have more extensive medical checks, depending on where she was born.

takes a while to get the hang of it – birth parents are novices, too, and usually find caring for a young baby just as daunting.

Your baby will be used to someone else's routines to begin with and may take a while to get used to yours. This doesn't matter – just show her how much you love her and want her and she will soon feel secure.

Most adopted babies are bottle-fed and will still thrive physically and emotionally. They may also have received some colostrum through early breastfeeding with their birth mother. It is, however, possible to breastfeed if you have adopted a newborn or very young baby, although it might be a struggle at first. Talk to your GP or a breastfeeding counsellor about stimulating lactation with a breast pump and, if necessary, by taking medication. You can also use a system to supplement breastfeeding, where milk is fed to your baby from a bottle via a tube that is taped to your breast. The baby has the tube in her mouth at the same time as your nipple so she gets as much milk as she needs, while, at the same time, her suckling

DEALING WITH OTHER PEOPLE

Everyone has an opinion about parenting – and adoptive parenting is no different. However, you may feel more vulnerable and defensive of your baby and your parenting style, particularly if you have been through a long and hard struggle to adopt.

Do seek help fast if you are feeling low at any point – your GP or health visitor will either be able to offer you

MEETING HER NEEDS *Babies need food, warmth, love, and one-to-one attention – as an adoptive parent you can provide all this.*

"Plenty of people believe that gay couples shouldn't be allowed to adopt and we had to consider how attitudes like those would affect our children in the long term."

will stimulate your breasts to produce milk.

If your baby has started life on a bottle and is used to a teat she may not understand how to breast-feed – the "milking" action is very different to the more passive sucking of bottle-feeding. Expert assistance is vital here and the practical help and moral support of a trained breastfeeding counsellor/advisor (see page 312) will be key to whether you succeed or not. If it doesn't work, at least you know that you tried.

counselling or refer you for more specialist support

If you are a single adoptive parent, or part of a gay or lesbian adoptive couple, you may also have concerns about society's response to you. Be strong – families come in all shapes and sizes and your child will flourish through your love and care.

TEAMWORK *Adopting a child together is a momentous decision, and you'll probably find that it strengthens your bond as a couple.*

YOUR GROWING BABY

1 2 3 4 5 6 **7 8 9** 10 11 12

MONTHS

THIS TASTES GOOD FROM THE AGE OF SIX MONTHS, YOUR BABY WILL DISCOVER THE DELIGHTS OF SOLID FOOD

YOUR CLEVER BABY HANDLING TWO OBJECTS AT THE SAME TIME IS JUST ONE OF THE MANY SKILLS DEVELOPED DURING THESE MONTHS

I WANT MUM YOUR BABY MAY BECOME PARTICULARLY ATTACHED TO YOU AND GET UPSET WHEN YOU ARE OUT OF HIS SIGHT

"As new skills develop, watching your amazing baby will become a favourite pastime."

Your skilful baby

Between six and nine months is a particularly exciting time as your baby constantly soaks up new experiences and develops new skills. Barely a week will go by without you noticing something else that he can do. The challenge for you will be to keep up with him, especially once he is on the move.

This period is a time of firsts as your baby learns to sit unaided, crawl (or use some other means to get around), and possibly even pull himself up to stand. He will enjoy his first taste of solid food and you may also see the first signs of baby teeth coming through. Enjoy each of his achievements as many pass all too quickly. No matter how wonderful each milestone, you will find that the next one always seems more fascinating.

Physical development

Many babies will be able to sit up unaided by 6–7 months and some will be steady enough to play with a toy without toppling over. Now, when your baby lies on his back, he will start to lift his head and shoulders. When placed on his tummy, he may pull his knees up or lie flat and use his arms to raise his upper body.

Most babies try to crawl, but don't be concerned if your baby doesn't; some simply scoot around on their bottoms instead or progress straight from sitting to walking. Others get across the room by rolling over and over, or drag themselves along on their tummy commando-style. However your baby decides to get from A to B, once he's on the move you'll need to be even more vigilant about safety (see pages 134–135).

Your baby may get a surprise when he starts trying to crawl as when he tries to move forwards he may travel in the opposite direction. This happens because at this age his arms are more co-ordinated than his legs, and so by pushing with both he will actually go backwards. He will find this frustrating at first, but will make progress eventually.

His fine motor skills are progressing and he will be able to take hold of a toy and pass it from one hand to the other. He will also learn to hold a

ON YOUR MARKS...
Pushing up is a key physical milestone because it helps your baby position himself to crawl. Encourage him by placing a toy slightly out of reach.

HANDLING SKILLS
As your baby's grip develops, he will learn to pick up tiny objects.

ON HER FEET *She will enjoy being held in a standing position and soon pull herself up.*

toy in each hand and bang them together to make a noise. By the time he is eight months old, he may have got the hang of deliberately letting go of something, which will be a favourite game for him but may become very tedious for you. He will also be able to pick up smaller items now, such as a raisin. While at six months he will use his whole hand to grab, by eight months he may start to use his thumb and index finger in a pincer grip, which is far more accurate.

Baby talk

At 6–7 months your baby will probably be repeating single consonant sounds, such as "bababa", and blowing raspberries. By the time he is eight months old, he might start combining sounds to form strings of babble, such as "ah-boo-lo", so that his babbling is more speech-like when you chat with him. He may also learn to shout to get your attention; lots of babies enjoy the sound of their own voices so much that they repeat sounds again and again.

Psychologists have found that most parents automatically use gestures when talking to their babies, such as pointing, miming actions (for example, pretending to eat from a spoon when telling a baby it is time for lunch), and nodding or shaking their head when they say "yes" or "no". You may also have decided to try baby signing (see page 133). These gestures, say researchers, accelerate a baby's language development and help him to understand more words than he would otherwise.

What he understands

Your baby's understanding is growing in leaps and bounds: he'll copy sounds that you make and love it when you copy him; begin to understand the tone of your voice and maybe start to cry if you are cross or upset; and become fascinated by your conversations with other people, turning his head as he listens to each speaker in turn.

He will learn to follow your gaze and look at something if you look at it. He now understands object permanence and if he drops an object he is holding, he will look for it rather than instantly forgetting about it. If you sit him in front of a mirror, he will initially be fascinated by the "other" baby he can see, but soon realize that he is looking at himself. Now, as well as enjoying a game of peek-a-boo, he may try to copy you and play it too. His repertoire of communication skills is blossoming and he will put out his arms to let you know he wants to be picked up. A few babies may begin to point – at first with their whole arm rather than a single finger –although for many babies this skill develops later.

Separation anxiety

One new development during these months is that your baby may become less relaxed with strangers. At six months, he may happily smile at anyone and go to them for a cuddle, but at seven months he may be more reluctant, and by eight months you are likely to be his firm favourite to the point where he becomes anxious and upset if you even leave the room. This is known as "separation anxiety" and it is an important stage in your baby's social and emotional development. It can be a trying time for you as you may suddenly find that he wants to be with you all the time, even when you go to the toilet.

"It was sweet when my baby became so attached to me, but it made it difficult to get the housework done."

Gradually, your baby will become less distressed at being separated from you as his experience tells him that you always come back when you leave him. Once he is mobile, he will be able to follow you if you leave the room and this will go some way to easing his anxiety. Meanwhile, keep him with you when you are able. Encourage other people to hold back and allow your baby to initiate interaction with them, rather than trying to coax him to respond.

Development concerns

Your baby's development won't be routinely checked at this stage, but if you have any concerns, even if it is a generalized, non-specific worry, do not hesitate to mention it to your health visitor. She will then arrange for the relevant tests to be carried out for the following –

■ **Hearing problems:** although all babies born in the UK should have a hearing check soon after birth, you should let your health visitor know if you have any concerns about your baby's hearing or if you think he may not have had a neonatal hearing test (see page 27). Also tell her if there is any family history of deafness and, if necessary, she can arrange for your baby to be referred to an audiologist.

■ **Sight check:** your health visitor or GP will check that your baby's eyes are moving together and that he reacts to visual stimuli, such as you walking into the room where he can see you.

■ **Growth and development:** if you are worried that your baby might be underweight or overweight, the health visitor will look at his diet with you and recommend how to adapt it if necessary. If he seems to be a bit slow in reaching certain physical milestones, she will assess his overall capabilities. If there are concerns about his speech or how he is interacting with others, the health visitor will assess whether he is babbling, making eye contact, deliberately getting your attention and engaging in turn-taking during your "conversations".

A new role for dad

This is an age of many transitions for your baby: starting him on solids, moving him to his own bedroom, and perhaps your partner returning to work and giving up breastfeeding. This, then, is an important time for dads as there are lots of ways you can help your partner and baby as they both adjust and settle into a new routine.

Because your baby doesn't associate you with breastfeeding comfort, he may cope better with his new bedroom or sleep routines if you are the one to settle him. He may also be much more willing to take his first bottles and first tastes of solid food from you.

It will undoubtedly be a bit tough for your partner if she is returning to work after being off on maternity leave, even if it is what suits your family best. You can help with choosing and organizing childcare, and by supporting your partner emotionally as she deals with being apart from your baby, and practically as she

adjusts to being back at work. As well as helping out with practical care, make time for play and fun as well. Your baby will respond positively to all this attention and you will marvel at how well he is developing.

FATHER'S VIEW

Common concerns

▶ **I am English and my husband is French and we would like our baby to grow up bilingual. Should we speak to her in both languages at this stage?**

Research shows that the best way for your baby to grow up bilingual is for you to interact with her in both languages from the start. So do encourage your husband to speak only French to your daughter. Some bilingual babies are initially slower to develop language skills than babies who are exposed to a single language, as they are processing more information, but this is nothing to worry about and they soon catch up.

▶ **My son and my niece are both seven months old, but my niece seems to be more vocal and more sociable than my baby. How can I help him?**

All babies are different so don't fall into the trap of comparing your son with your niece. A gender divide at this age is not uncommon, with baby boys developing physical skills faster and baby girls tending to be more advanced in language and social skills. However, this is not always the case. Babies tend to concentrate on one main skill at a time, so he may be mastering some physical milestone but will then have a burst of language development. My eldest son didn't say anything until he was two, while my friends' babies were performing nursery rhymes with all the actions for months before that. I wasn't worried because I knew he understood everything.

Chat with your baby as you go about your day together, leaving him spaces to "reply" if he chooses, and try to engage him in lots of social play, such as nursery rhymes and action songs.

▶ **My baby gets wheezy with colds. Could the fact that I smoke be affecting him?**

Wheezing is common in babies, but the fact that you smoke won't be helping at all and will increase the number of colds he is likely to get. Research has shown that children of smokers are more likely to wheeze than children of non-smokers. If you or your partner smoke, the single most important thing either of you can do is to give up. It is not good enough to just smoke outside as you will still have smoke on your breath and on your clothes.

▶ **My health visitor says my eight-month-old baby is very overweight. He seems to be healthy and happy, so does it really matter at this age?**

Although plump babies often look cute, it's advisable for a baby's weight to be in proportion to his height. Early obesity can result in long-term health issues, such as diabetes and high blood pressure, as well as short-term problems, such as a delay in learning to roll over and crawling.

If your health visitor feels that your baby is worryingly overweight, it's wise to assess whether you are giving him more calories than he needs. A baby having three meals a day needs no more than a pint of milk in total. Fully breastfed babies rarely become overweight and are less likely to become obese in adult life. There is no need to worry if a baby is only slightly overweight as they usually slim down once they are more mobile.

Enjoying play

Everyday objects and toys become fascinating to your baby from six months, and he will want to explore as many as he can get hold of and put them all in his mouth. He will learn more if you sit down and play with him and will benefit greatly from repetitive games.

Favourite toys

SURPRISE! Interactive toys become more rewarding as your baby learns how they work.

Cause-and-effect toys are often a big hit with babies from six months onwards. For example, if you wind up a jack-in-the-box and help your baby press the button you will find it keeps him happily entertained. Repetition is important to babies as they learn new concepts and new skills, so don't be surprised if your baby wants you to show him how the same toy works again and again. You still don't need to invest in lots of commercially produced toys for your baby – he will have just as much fun playing with household items, such as spoons, empty yoghurt pots, cardboard boxes, and keys, and undoubtedly want to get hold of anything you are holding or wearing.

Babies of this age love to rummage so fill a container with a few small toys and other safe items and simply let him explore. He still has a short memory so if you keep a small stash of interesting playthings hidden away and swap them over regularly, he will always have lots of "new" toys to discover.

He isn't able to concentrate on more than one task at a time yet, so if he has a toy in each hand and you offer him another one, he will drop the toys he is holding and reach out for the new one being offered.

Baby signing

Teaching babies non-verbal forms of communication to express their needs and feelings is known as baby signing. The idea is that if your baby can let you know when he is tired, hungry, or thirsty, instead of just crying, he will be less frustrated.

There are videos and books and baby-signing classes in some areas that teach babies simple signs for words such as "milk", "sleep", or "more". Signing harnesses your baby's natural desire to communicate with you and many families swear by it. If you want to try it, some babies will take to it from around six months, while others will be more interested a few months later.

Little and often is the key to baby signing, and remember you will have to show him many times before he will be able to catch on. Simply show him the sign for an object or need when it comes up in conversation – for example, the sign for "more" when you offer more food. Don't turn signing with your baby into a school lesson – it simply won't work. The danger is that it is easy to pressure a baby to "perform" in your interaction with him; if you both enjoy it, that is fine, but if you don't, it is not worth pursuing.

Everything your baby holds will go into his mouth to be explored, so it is essential to ensure he cannot get hold of any small items that could cause him to choke. Once his teeth begin to come through, he will also want to bite on toys, wooden spoons, and other hard objects. Like many parents, you may be concerned that this is unhygienic, but don't worry and don't try to take objects out of your baby's mouth. It is important to remember that "mouthing" is a part of your baby's normal and natural exploration of his world. You can invest in special teething rings or toys, but they are not essential, and wooden or soft plastic toys serve just as well if you want to give him something to chew on.

Making music

Music is thought to benefit babies in numerous ways – boosting language and communication skills, helping them to relax and sleep, and encouraging physical, emotional, and social development.

Your baby will enjoy all kinds of music, from home-made shakers to your singing (even if you're tone deaf!), and commercial CDs of nursery rhymes. While you don't have to restrict his listening to music that is designed specifically for babies, it is a safe bet that one of your most-played CDs in the car will be baby songs.

TEETHING *Your baby will find it soothing to bite on a hard toy once his teeth start to come through.*

Keeping your baby safe

There are many hazards for a newly mobile baby in the home, including stairs, tables with sharp corners, and small objects that he can now get access to and swallow. Once you've baby-proofed your home, you can relax and he can explore more freely.

GET CRAWLING

The best way to discover any danger zones is to look at a room from your baby's point of view: get on your hands and knees and crawl to gain a whole new perspective on your home.

ESSENTIAL SAFETY MEASURES

▶ Install smoke detectors and a carbon monoxide detector.

▶ As soon as your baby can crawl, use stair gates at the top and bottom of your stairs. Show him how to go up forwards and come down backwards, but stay with him as he is nowhere near ready to tackle them on his own. Also consider putting a stair gate across the kitchen door so that your baby can watch you without getting close to the cooker.

▶ Put corner covers on furniture that has sharp edges to protect him from bumps and grazes. Temporarily remove or secure any unstable furniture, for example free-standing bookcases, so that he can't pull it over when he is pulling himself up to stand.

▶ Cover low-level glass with safety film, and use a fireguard to prevent him getting too close to the fire.

▶ Keep cords on your curtains and blinds tied up out of reach as they can strangle a baby or young child.

BEWARE BABYWALKERS

Using a babywalker is not recommended. They consist of a plastic frame on a wheeled base with a seat suspended in the centre. Essentially they allow babies to whizz around at speed on their tiptoes, propelling them into all sorts of potential hazards. A babywalker can tip if it hits an obstacle, and allows a baby to reach dangerous objects, such as pan-handles and cooker knobs. They are not good for your baby's physical development as they encourage poor posture and toe-walking.

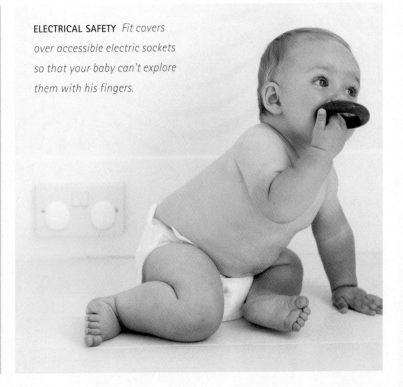

ELECTRICAL SAFETY *Fit covers over accessible electric sockets so that your baby can't explore them with his fingers.*

▸ Keep hot drinks out of your baby's way and avoid drinking them when he is sitting on your lap.

▸ Get a playpen (see page 159) so that you can safely answer the door, go to the loo, or check on the dinner without having to take him with you.

BATHROOM SAFETY

Be vigilant in the bathroom. Never leave your baby for a second, even if he is in a baby bath seat, as he can topple and drown in just a few centimetres of water. Run the cold water first so there is no danger of scalding him. Once he is able to sit in the big bath, use a non-slip mat.

CUPBOARDS

Use locks to prevent your baby accessing any drawers or cupboards containing potentially harmful items. Lock medicines, supplements, and chemicals well out of reach – even seemingly harmless products, such as iron tablets or mouthwash, are poisonous to babies. Consider giving your baby access to a cupboard of items he can safely play with, such as wooden spoons and plastic tubs. Tiny fingers can easily get injured by doors, so fit anti-slam devices.

OTHER PEOPLE'S HOUSES

If your baby is being cared for by a childminder, there should already be stair gates and other safety equipment in place. If he is looked after by a friend or family member in their home, make sure they have these – if necessary, you can buy a portable safety gate to take with you.

STAIR GATE *Once your baby is mobile, he will be determined to explore more of his home. A gate should be placed both at the top and the bottom of the stairs.*

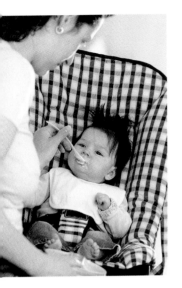

EASY FEEDING *When you first give your baby solid food, it will be easier to feed her in a bouncy chair than sitting on your lap. Once she is able to sit unsupported, she can progress to sitting in a highchair.*

Moving on to solids

Food is fun. Food is messy. Food is also powerful. As you want your baby to eat well, food is the most potent weapon he has at his disposal. If you show him how anxious you are for him to conform to your chosen eating pattern, he will rapidly learn how to use food refusal to his advantage.

First tastes

Once babies are six months old, the Department of Health recommends they move on to eating solid food, although their main sustenance will continue to come from milk.

Taking solids is a new experience, so let your baby gently explore the spoon with his mouth, rather than shovelling the food in. Try offering two or three teaspoonfuls twice a day to begin with. Be guided by your baby's appetite – he will let you know when he wants more. At first, new tastes will surprise him and he may pause before tasting more, or deciding that he has had enough. If he is not keen on solids, try giving him a small breast- or bottle-feed first, then offer a spoonful of food again.

Start off with some baby rice or a smooth vegetable purée, such as carrot or potato, mixed with formula or breast milk. Personally, I find baby rice on its own very unappetizing – it looks and tastes like wallpaper paste. If your baby spits it out immediately, try giving him food that has a more interesting flavour. Follow this with his usual milk feed.

Once your baby has got the hang of spoon-feeding, try introducing a different vegetable or fruit purée every few days to get him used to different tastes and textures. Good options are stewed apple or pear, carrot, sweet potato, banana, avocado, or swede. When he is used to a range of single foods, you can mix two or more familiar foods together – for example potato and carrot. You can use commercially prepared food or make your own, but don't add any sugar or salt. If you prepare your own food, you can freeze it in ice-cube trays, then store the blocks in freezer bags so you have tiny portions readily available. If you are using fresh produce, home-prepared food may be nutritionally better and tastier.

However, our babies had lots of meals from jars and packets and thrived, so don't feel you have to spend hours cooking and puréeing.

This can be an anxious time for you as a parent and you are bound to worry about whether your baby is having enough to eat. Remember that he will always eat what he needs – unless you allow him to use food to manipulate you (see below).

New textures

From around seven months, your baby will be ready to start trying lumpier foods containing more ingredients that are well-mashed, rather than puréed. He can start having three small meals a day, which can include food from a spoon and finger foods. Over the next few months your baby will need to gradually move on to a diet that includes foods from all the major groups: carbohydrates – from foods such as cereals, potatoes, and rice; fruit and vegetables; protein – from foods such as meat, fish, soya products, cheese, and legumes (lentils, beans, chickpeas etc); and fats – from foods such as milk, cheese, and yoghurt.

SELF-FEEDING *She will want to get hold of the spoon. Encourage this and don't worry about the mess.*

Handling food refusal

Some babies are little gannets from the start, while others take a far more leisurely view of it all. At first, all you need to do is introduce new tastes and textures and – crucially – avoid overreacting if he doesn't like them. However long you have spent puréeing carrots, if he closes his mouth or turns his head away, simply put the food aside and try again another day. This will make all the difference to whether he becomes a fussy eater or not later on. If you plead, coax, play aeroplanes with the spoon, then cook him another meal, he may well do it all over again. Your baby will quickly learn that this is a highly entertaining game and a great way to get your attention. Rest assured that a healthy baby will not willingly starve. Unless

FINGER FOODS

Encourage self-feeding by giving her pieces of small food she can handle easily.

they have a physical or mental disability that makes eating a problem, babies do not need to be coaxed to eat. If he doesn't want to eat the food on offer, fine. There will be more at the next mealtime, so end the meal and move on to a different activity. The moment you start cajoling him to have "just one spoonful for Mummy", you run the risk of drawing up lines for a battle that your baby will happily engage in for years to come.

Finger foods

You can give your baby finger foods as soon as he can pick them up and put them in his mouth. Try cooked pasta shapes, pieces of soft fruit, such as banana or melon, breadsticks, rice cakes, pieces of cheese, and pieces of cooked carrot, potato, or broccoli. If you give grapes, make sure they are cut in half because whole grapes are a choking hazard.

Never leave your baby unattended while he is eating in case of choking (see page 289), but do allow him to experiment, however messy the result. When you are feeding him, give him a spoon of his own to occupy one hand, and some finger foods to occupy the other. Encouraging this independence will pay off later on as he will be used to feeding himself. He will also be more likely to eat as much as he wants, then stop, thereby learning to listen to his appetite.

As soon as your baby starts to feed himself, things will get messy, so strip him down to a minimum and use a good bib. When he has finished, put him straight into the bath if necessary. Put a plastic sheet or newspaper underneath his highchair and site him well away from walls if possible. Banana is often a favourite finger food, but it is virtually impossible to wash out of clothes – it leaves a black stain – so an old bib or a least-favourite sleepsuit are the best options.

Organic and GM foods

All parents want to give their baby the best start in life and many choose organic food as one way to do this. Although there is little evidence that an organic diet significantly improves a child's health, there may be advantages: organic food is grown without the use of artificial pesticides or chemical fertilizers, and meat products are from free-range animals that are not given drugs to promote their growth. It seems sensible to avoid as many chemicals and additives as possible and it is also better for the

"My six-month-old baby didn't seem interested in eating solids until we sat him at the table with us at mealtimes. When he saw his big brother tucking in, he wanted some too."

environment to grow food organically as it promotes the growth of wild flowers and encourages the return of birds and insects. However, these foods are more expensive, and "natural" fertilizers may include dung that contains harmful bacteria because it hasn't been treated. So always wash fruit and vegetables carefully, particularly organic ones. GM foods have been genetically modified to avoid diseases or produce a better crop. There is currently no evidence that they represent any risk to your baby.

Drinks

The best drink for your baby to have with meals is plain water. By six months, he will be able to drink from a baby beaker and these come in a variety of shapes and sizes with soft or hard drinking spouts, and handles so he can pick them up easily. If you give your baby juice, dilute one part juice with 10 parts water and keep it for mealtimes only. The Food Standards Agency says that ordinary formula milk is fine for bottle-fed babies until they are 12 months old, when they can switch to ordinary cow's milk. You can buy "follow-on milks" for babies from six months, but it is not necessary to give these to your baby.

Foods and drinks to avoid

Leave these foods out of your baby's diet and check labels, too.

▶ **Honey**, which can contain bacteria that cause infant botulism.

▶ **Nuts**, which are a choking hazard. These should also be avoided if there is a family history of allergies.

▶ **Any drinks containing caffeine**, as well as other fizzy drinks and fruit squashes. Phenolic compounds found in tea interfere with the ability to absorb iron. Soft drinks contain sugars and additives.

▶ **Foods with added salt, sugar, and sweeteners** as these can be harmful.

▶ **Cow's milk** – avoid this as a drink until he is a year old, but you can use it in cooking and on cereal.

Everyday care

Your baby will experience a lot of changes in these months – such as moving to his own bedroom and having his brand-new teeth brushed. But his day-to-day care won't alter much; he will be familiar with his daytime and night-time routine by now and you should find he is more settled and secure.

A room of his own

The Foundation for the Study of Infant Deaths (see page 312) recommends that your baby shares your bedroom for the first six months, but after this age he can be moved to his own bedroom. There are several reasons for this – and an important one is that you will both feel more comfortable resuming your sex life without your baby being nearby in his cot. Being in his own bedroom may also help him to sleep for longer during the night. If he is a light sleeper, you may find that you disturb him (and he may disturb you) and that it is far harder to teach him to go to sleep on his own if he wakes and sees you there. It can be more tempting

Common concerns

▶ **My baby has a flat area at the back of his head. Is it true that he should wear a special helmet to reshape it?**
Many babies develop flat heads, partly as a result of being put to sleep on their backs. It does not affect growth or development. You can help improve it by giving your baby as much tummy time as possible and limiting the time he

spends in a car seat. Once he's spending less time on his back, his head shape will improve. Helmets are not recommended by British paediatricians or neurosurgeons.

▶ **My nine-month-old keeps banging his head against the cot bars. Should I be worried?**
While head-banging in older children may be a sign of emotional

disturbance, in a baby it is often a rhythmical comfort habit and your baby may find both the sensation and the sound it makes soothing. Occasionally, head-banging can be caused by pain or discomfort, such as earache, so if he seems unwell in any way, see your doctor. Otherwise, rest assured that he won't hurt himself by doing this and will grow out of it in time.

to cuddle him or take him into your own bed if he is in the same room as you.

You may find the idea of moving your baby into his own bedroom quite daunting, and worry about whether he will settle. This is understandable – lots of parents get concerned about not being near to their baby during the night. However, don't worry as this is not as big a step as it seems and frequently turns out to be easier than expected. Remember that your baby is excellent at picking up on your feelings, so try not to become too anxious. Placing a baby monitor in his bedroom will provide the reassurance you require that you will hear him when he needs you. As you will be moving his cot into his new room, his immediate surroundings will still have a very familiar feel.

If you do run into trouble, don't be tempted to give up too soon. It may take a couple of nights for your baby to settle, so do persevere. Reassure him if he is unsettled but try not to give in and move him back into your bedroom.

Bathing and dressing

At this age, bathtime is a part of your baby's routine that you will probably both enjoy. Once he can sit unsupported, he will enjoy playing with toys and splashing around, but you must still stay with him at all times. If you use bubble bath, choose products that are intended for babies, as those for adults and older children could irritate your baby's skin.

Once he is in the big bath, use a non-slip mat on the bottom of the bath to prevent him slipping. He can learn lots from bath toys with your help; for example, how objects float and sink, and how to pour. Kneel beside him as you may cause damage to your back by bending over the big bath to hold or play with him. Better still, bath with him and you can both have fun in the bubbles.

BEDTIME ROUTINE
Giving your baby a bath continues to be an important part of settling her at night.

PRACTICAL CLOTHES

Once your baby can crawl, clothes such as dungarees are very practical as they won't restrict his mobility.

There is a huge industry in baby clothes and it is quite usual for my children to look trendier than me. No huge expense is involved, however, because handing down clothes is an excellent way of recycling and my children are dressed almost entirely in other children's clothes. You will find no end of styles for your baby, but the crucial factors are comfort, washability, and ease of access for nappy-changing. Now that your baby is about to become mobile, consider practicalities and make sure he can get around easily. Stretchy fabric is easier than stiff denim, for example, and trousers are more practical than dresses when your baby starts to crawl.

Teething

Some babies get their first teeth very early on, while others are still toothless by their first birthday, but for most babies milk teeth start to emerge at around six months. Don't worry if your baby is showing no signs of teething yet as there is absolutely no connection between early dentition and intelligence, whatever your granny might tell you.

Signs that the first tooth may be about to make an appearance include dribbling a lot, a flushed cheek, slightly loose poos, and a desire to bite on objects. Offer your baby safe items to chew, such as teething toys, hard rusks, or wooden or plastic spoons. A large piece of raw carrot that has been chilled in the fridge (not the freezer) can make an effective teether, but stay close by in case your baby breaks a piece off – he may choke. You

What about shoes?

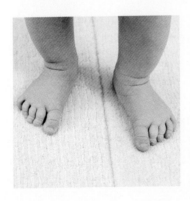

Your baby doesn't need to wear shoes yet. Even when he starts walking, he won't need them until he has been walking steadily and independently for several weeks.

His feet are still very soft and pliable so make sure that sleep-suits and socks are roomy and comfortable. If you feel that his feet need a bit more protection you can use soft fabric bootees or padders with plenty of growing room. Most of the time, though, it is fine just to leave his feet bare. If you do use soft padders make sure they don't have very smooth soles as these can be very slippery on shiny hall or kitchen floors.

can also soothe sore gums by rubbing them with a finger or by applying teething gel, which contains a local anaesthetic and is available from the chemist. Many parents tend to apply this liberally, but it does have a recommended dose, which you should always stick to. As always, infant paracetamol is helpful if your baby is in pain. Teething does not cause fever, vomiting and diarrhoea, excessive crying, listlessness, or loss of appetite, so if your baby seems unwell, see your doctor.

Your baby will eventually have 20 milk teeth, which usually come through in a particular order. The first ones to appear are the two incisors, which are in the centre of his bottom jaw, followed by the two above it, and he will probably have a complete set by the time he is aged around two and a half. Even if your baby has no teeth yet, his gums are hard enough to chew, so don't put off giving him food that has lumps and finger foods.

Tooth care

It is important to look after your baby's teeth as soon as they appear to keep them strong and healthy. Buy low-fluoride baby toothpaste and use a tiny smear of it on a baby toothbrush to clean his teeth. If he objects to having his teeth cleaned, sit him on your lap facing away from you with one arm firmly around him and use your free hand to clean them. A soft "finger cover" toothbrush may be easier to use. If you get him into the habit of teeth-cleaning morning and evening now, he will be less likely to protest once he reaches toddlerhood, as it will be a familiar part of his routine.

Like you, your baby's diet affects his dental health. Fruit juices and sweet puddings can cling to the teeth and damage the enamel, so keep these for mealtimes only as other foods and the saliva produced while eating will help remove the sugar. Never give your baby sugary drinks in a bottle. The worst sin of all is to send your baby to bed with a bottle of juice, as this will cause rapid tooth decay.

CLEANING HIS TEETH
Sit your baby facing away from you and gently use the same brushing techniques as you would on your own teeth.

Getting out and about

Increasingly, your baby will be finding other people fascinating and going to a baby group can be a great way to encourage his social skills, and also a good way for you to meet other mums. As well as going to drop-in groups, there are also more specific activity sessions aimed at young babies and their parents, such as baby massage or swimming. Whatever the activities involved, going to a group with you can enrich his play and your relationship, as long as you both enjoy it. If you feel shy about just turning up at a group, ask your health visitor if she can put you in touch with another local mum who already attends.

"Attending a baby group was a breath of fresh air – for both me and my eight-month-old daughter."

If going to a baby group doesn't suit you, you don't have to persevere – getting out and about to the shops or the park instead will also benefit both you and your baby. The park is a great place to meet other mums. Babies are good ice-breakers and other parents of similarly aged babies can be an important source of companionship and support. Hopefully you will soon meet some like-minded people. While it is great to swap notes on your offspring, though, try not to get drawn into competitive parenting. If you are so short of sleep you can barely speak, don't forget that your friend's little angel who is sleeping through every night may grow into a stroppy, whining teenager while your wakeful little nightmare may turn out to be a loving, considerate charmer.

Learning to say "no"

As your baby becomes more mobile and inquisitive you will increasingly need to set boundaries. It is important not to get cross if your baby repeatedly tries to do what he shouldn't – babies of this age have no concept of "right" or "wrong" and he won't understand that playing this good game he has discovered is being naughty. Nor will he be able to associate your shouting and punishment with what he has done. So stay calm, say "No" firmly, and then distract him with an activity. Reinforce the behaviour you want – don't try to punish him.

Common concerns

▶ **My baby is cutting a tooth and I'm scared she'll bite me when I breastfeed her. Should I stop?**

Don't worry, you can carry on breastfeeding your baby. When her first two teeth appear, they will be in her lower jaw and will be covered by her tongue when she feeds, so she won't be able to bite you. Once your baby's top teeth are through, if she does bite you, your instinctive response will probably be to yell – which may put her off biting again or may encourage her to try it once more to see whether she gets the same reaction. If she bites your nipple, take her off the breast

immediately and say "No". She will very quickly learn that biting means that she is taken off the breast and as long as you are consistent in your response, she will stop.

▶ **Every time I take my baby's nappy off, he starts playing with his penis. Is this normal?**

It is completely normal for both boys and girls to touch their genitals. Just as babies discover their hands and feet, they also discover their genitals at some stage and if handling them feels good, they will do it again. It is nothing to worry about and is best ignored.

▶ **My baby is always sucking her thumb. Should I discourage her from doing this?**

No. Your baby is rapidly learning that you are there for her and that you will come if she needs you, but you can't cuddle her 24 hours a day and sometimes she will need to comfort herself. It is normal for babies to suck their fingers or thumbs for comfort or become attached to an object such as a soft toy, cloth, or blanket. A thumb has a

distinct advantage over a dummy because it is always available and there aren't the hygiene problems associated with dropping a dummy on the floor.

Problems can sometimes arise if your baby is still sucking her thumb a great deal when her adult teeth come through as it can push them forward.

▶ **I'm a full-time mum and my baby seems to prefer his dad to me. What can I do?**

As your baby's main carer, he sees you all day and is secure in the knowledge that you're always there. Your very familiarity is what makes him able to take your presence for granted. His dad is out at work all day and is therefore a lively new companion to interact with when he comes home.

Encourage your baby and his father to enjoy the time they have together – but do make sure that you join in their play sometimes. Maybe try to redress the balance at weekends, too, so that your husband does more of the practical side of babycare and you have more of the fun.

First family holiday

By the time you have got used to being a family you will probably need a holiday. Many destinations are suitable for young babies, except those where infectious diseases are a problem. Also, a baby under three months is unlikely to cope well with a hot climate.

One of the great advantages of travelling with a young baby is that you can take him to most places and he will be happy as long as you are there. If you go overseas your baby will generally get a warm welcome as many cultures are more relaxed than the UK about babies and children being in social settings.

Your baby may be vulnerable to bugs in the recycled air on a plane in the first month, but after this age it is fine for him to travel by air. Having said that, boat and train travel is more environmentally friendly and you will be able to move around more easily during the journey. Under-twos can travel free on trains, ferries, and some airlines, although your baby will not get a seat of his own on the plane. You will be given an extra seat belt that attaches to yours so that he can be safely strapped in on your lap. You can book a sky cot for long journeys, but he will need to be on your lap for take-off and landing, which can be annoying if he is fast asleep in the cot. If you rent a car while on holiday, you will need to hire a suitable car seat for your baby. Don't take your own as it is one more thing to collect with your baggage. Some airlines let you take your buggy on with you; others make

PROTECTION *Sun cream of at least factor 30 can be used from six months. It's an essential barrier, whatever your baby's skin tone.*

TRAVEL TIPS

▶ **Baby products:** items such as nappies are on sale everywhere so you don't need to buy up the baby aisle of your supermarket. Just take what you need for the journey and for the first couple of days while you get your bearings.

▶ **Renting equipment:** if you are planning to rent items such as a cot and a highchair at your destination, check that they conform to current European safety standards. The cot bars should be no more than 6.5cm (2.5in) apart and the sides deep enough to stop your baby climbing out. The highchair should have a five-point harness or rings so that you can attach one.

▶ **Using a buggy:** for babies over six months who can sit up reliably, this is when a lightweight buggy, which you can fold or unfold with one hand and carry easily, comes into its own. Alternatively, ditch the wheeled option entirely and take a baby backpack carrier, suitable from around six months.

▶ **Take-off and landing:** your baby's ears may pop and feel uncomfortable when the plane takes off and lands. She will cry, which will equalize the pressure but you can pre-empt this by feeding her during take-off and landing, as sucking will have the same effect.

you put it in the hold. Keep it with you if you can as it is useful if your baby wants a sleep in the departure lounge – and for stashing your duty-free!

Even tiny babies need their own passport with a photo and this may take longer than you think to arrange. My daughter's photo was rejected three times by the passport office for various reasons, so I recommend having one taken by an experienced passport photographer.

FUN IN THE SUN

In warm weather, babies under six months should be kept out of direct sunlight. After this, your baby will still need plenty of protection and while high-protection sunscreens (factor 30 or more) are safe to use from six months, it is even better to keep him covered up with loose, light clothing. Sunhats with flaps at the back to protect his neck, long-sleeved T-shirts, and a sun protection swimsuit with arms and legs will all help to prevent your baby getting sunburnt.

Try to avoid being out in the sun with your baby between 11 am and 3 pm and make sure he has plenty of bottled water or very dilute juice to drink, to avoid dehydration.

MAKING A SPLASH *Many babies enjoy the freedom of movement and control of their limbs in water – something they don't yet experience on dry land.*

If you go to the beach, a blanket spread under a large parasol will offer shade and a safe place for your baby to play or sleep. A sheet draped over the parasol will create a makeshift tent and give him extra protection from the sun. There are also many baby-safe beach shelters on the market.

WATER BABIES

While it is fine to take your baby in swimming pools in the UK before their first set of immunizations at two months, it is best to be cautious abroad, particularly in countries where polio is still prevalent. Only take your baby swimming abroad once he has completed his initial course of immunizations at four months.

If your baby enjoys bathtime, he will probably love going into the water with you. Remember that whatever flotation devices he is wearing, you still need to hold on to him at all times. He will probably start to kick and splash gleefully once he gets used to being in such a large body of water. If he is frightened, though, don't pressure him. Instead, buy an inflatable paddling pool and put it under your beach umbrella for him to sit in. With water added, it is a fun-size swimming pool; without, it makes a great playpen for babies who are not yet on the move.

YOUR MOBILE BABY

1 2 3 4 5 6 7 8 9 **10 11 12**
MONTHS

IT DOESN'T FIT TOYS BECOME INCREASINGLY
IMPORTANT – STIMULATING YOUR BABY'S BRAIN
AND IMPROVING HIS HANDLING SKILLS

TICKLE ME ROUGH-AND-TUMBLE
PLAY WILL MAKE YOUR BABY SQUEAL
WITH DELIGHT, AND SHE'LL WANT YOU
TO DO IT AGAIN AND AGAIN

I'M OFF SOME BABIES TAKE THEIR FIRST STEPS BEFORE THEIR FIRST BIRTHDAY, BUT FOR MANY IT HAPPENS MUCH LATER THAN THIS

"Whether crawling or cruising, your baby is ready to be on the move, which means you will be, too."

Growing up

When you take a look back at the past nine months, the developmental leaps your baby has taken are quite remarkable. Nurtured by you, she has grown into a little person with social skills, who has begun to control her body and has a basic understanding of her world.

During the next couple of months your baby may take her first step or utter her first word, but even if she doesn't she will be making progress towards these important milestones. She will probably be sitting confidently by nine months and may be on the move by crawling, rolling, creeping on her tummy, or scooting on her bottom.

She will probably start to pull herself into a standing position, too, using anything that is convenient, such as the cot or playpen bars, any handy furniture, or your leg. Once standing, though, she will find it tricky to sit back down and may call for help until she learns to lower herself and fall back down on her bottom.

Once she has mastered the art of standing, she will at some point take a step while holding on to whatever she has used to pull herself up. This development is called cruising and she may soon be able to walk right round the room supporting herself on conveniently placed furniture and willing helpers. You can assist by walking with her, holding both her hands (if you hold just one hand she will feel insecure at this stage), or get her a sturdy toddle truck that has a low centre of gravity so that it is hard to tip up. A few babies decide to let go and take their first independent steps at around 10 months, but for most this won't happen until a few months later. Your baby will be able to manage going up the stairs soon, but won't be able to get down safely so stair gates remain essential.

In control

Your baby is refining her hand movements: she will start to point to things and rather than scooping things up using her whole hand, will use her thumb and forefinger in a pincer grip. You can encourage this new skill by

TAKING A STROLL *She will enjoy pushing a toddle truck once she's cruising. At first she may need a hand from you to keep it moving, and to prevent it from running away from her.*

offering her small pieces of food, such as raisins and cubes of carrot or cheese. Always stay with her in case of choking and remember that if she can pick up a raisin, she can also pick up a button, a pin or, especially dangerous, a tiny battery – she will still put these into her mouth, so it is important to keep them out of her reach.

Although at nine months your baby may still have difficulty letting go of objects on purpose, by 10 or 11 months she may begin to throw them. Food, cups, and toys are all good missiles and she will watch to see where they land, then wait for you to pick them up if she is unable to fetch them herself. Sooner or later you will get fed up with this new game, but remind yourself that she is still too young to be naughty – she is simply learning by playing and must do this to develop. If it is testing your patience, distraction is the best way to deal with it – for instance, find her a new toy or take her to look at something interesting in another room.

Learning new skills

Your baby is understanding more every week: she may start to turn and look when you call her by name and be able to follow a simple instruction, such as "Give Mummy the ball." Help her by keeping any instructions simple. For example, she is far more likely to respond if you say: "Wave bye-bye to Daddy," than she is to "Give Mummy the cup, then wave bye-bye to Daddy." Remember to praise success but to avoid reacting

LOOK AT THAT *She will begin to use her index finger to point.*

AREN'T I CLEVER? *If you clap, she may begin to copy you.*

BYE-BYE *Waving goodbye is one of her new social skills.*

negatively if she doesn't understand something. These new skills open up all sorts of play and communication opportunities, and make interaction much more fun and rewarding.

It can be very tempting to encourage your baby to show off her skills to assorted aunties, friends, and neighbours, but try to resist this unless she enjoys it. Like any other game, if she doesn't want to play, don't force her. Reaching milestones is not a race.

Emotional needs

Your baby may be affectionate and give you hugs and kisses, but it is not unheard of for babies to have their first tantrums before the end of the first year, when life begins to get frustrating. You will also notice that your baby's anxiety about strangers and separating from you becomes more intense. While at nine months she may be upset when you leave a room, it can become a real problem by 11 months, with the distress peaking at around the end of the first year. Don't worry, as this behaviour is normal, and you can help your baby cope by consistently reassuring her that you will return. This stage can be tricky for close family and friends, who may feel rejected by your baby's sudden refusal to go to them. It can also happen to a parent – it is common for a baby to become clingy to the main carer – usually mum – and refuse to be looked after by the other. It can be hurtful for the "rejected" parent, but this phase soon passes.

WHY HE CRIES *At this age, your baby may cry from frustration, especially if he is not quite as mobile as he would like to be.*

Party time?

If you want to have a party for your baby's first birthday, bear in mind that the celebration is for you, rather than her. Your baby may enjoy having some new toys and spending time with friends and family – a few at a time – but has no notion of what a birthday is about. She may turn out to be something of a party pooper if you try to get her to sit nicely and eat cake or play with gifts on demand. It can all become very overwhelming for a one-year-old and lead to tears of sadness rather than joy. If you invite other babies, they are likely to be bewildered, too.

You may be better off cracking open a bottle of champagne when your baby is fast asleep to celebrate a wonderful milestone for you, and the beginning of an exciting new stage of development for your baby.

So keep it simple and save your plans for the perfect party for future years. Introduce any presents your baby has been given over several weeks rather than all at once.

First words

Your baby's babbling is likely to be more sophisticated now, and you may even notice the occasional word in amongst her chatter. Whatever the sound is, it counts as a word if she uses it regularly with meaning. Encourage her by chatting to her, reading books, and naming the things that interest her.

RECOGNIZING OBJECTS

Your baby may not be able to speak yet, but he will understand the meaning of words. For example, if you say "Give me the keys," he will probably do it.

Your baby may say one or two words before her first birthday or they may not come for a few months – either way it doesn't matter because your baby's main communication will come from body language, gestures, and her own brand of "talking". If she says something like "dah" consistently to refer to her bottle, then it is a word. If she does have a made-up word like this, do not try to make her say the "proper" word. Instead, reinforce it in your response by saying, "Yes, that's your bottle."

During these months, you might hear your baby say "dada" and "mama" with meaning – although dada is likely to come first as your baby says "d" sounds before "m" sounds. A friend of mine wrote a list of her children's early words and expressions. I often wish we had done this as it is amazing how quickly you forget them. By 10 months or so, your baby's intellectual development has reached a stage where she understands that certain words you say refer to specific objects, actions, or people. She will know her own name and might even be able to say it by 11 months if it is easy to pronounce.

Whether your baby is deaf or has normal hearing, research has shown that she will "babble" with her hands if she has been exposed to sign language, and the early stages of language acquisition follow a similar sequence in both hearing and those with impaired hearing (see page 310).

Following instructions

Your baby's understanding is growing in leaps and bounds. If you tell her it is time for lunch, she may crawl towards her highchair or bounce up and down with excitement. If you pick up her coat, not only will she put her arms up to help you, but she may also look at her buggy or the door. She will probably kiss and hug you and wave goodbye to people reliably now and will enjoy the positive responses these social skills bring.

At some stage during these months, your baby may learn to shake her head to say "no", a skill she will practise frequently in the coming months and years. Although she is still easy to distract, this won't be as easy as it was a month ago; she is much more likely to protest if you try to take a toy away from her. However, she is still too young to feel possessive about her toys and won't be upset if another baby plays with them.

Baby books

Your baby will enjoy one-to-one time reading together and will probably have a few favourite books by now. She will enjoy the sound of your voice and may sit with you for several minutes at a time to look at a book. By the time she is 11 months old, she might even begin to point to some of the familiar images.

STORYTIME *Sharing books helps to develop language skills and is something many grandparents enjoy.*

She may be able to turn the pages of chunky board books, which means that a couple of these left in her cot at night may start to buy you a little extra time in bed in the morning. If you haven't already joined the library on your baby's behalf, now is a good time to do so, as this will give her access to a wide variety of books. Typically, a baby of this age will enjoy books that have clear, simple pictures, especially of familiar objects and situations; nursery rhymes; lift-the-flap books (although it will be some time before she can manage paper ones without damaging them); and books with concealed squeakers, different textures, and mirrors.

"My son's favourite is a board book of animal pictures. I talk about each one and when I make the appropriate animal noises, he tries to copy me."

Playtime fun

Your newly mobile baby is a true explorer and will want
to investigate everything. Intrigued and excited by her
surroundings, she will be into everything, although she will
be wary of strangers. She is likely to be interested in other
babies, but won't play with them for a couple more years.

Playing with you

You will notice that your baby's play is becoming more complex as she
acquires more skills. If you don't want to spend lots of money on toys
and feel as though you are drowning in a sea of primary-coloured plastic,
find out whether there is a toy library near you. This will give your baby
access to a wide range of playthings.

Babies of this age love incongruity and will find things like teddy
wearing Daddy's hat hilarious. They usually enjoy slapstick, too, and a toy
"falling over" may well be greeted with hysterical laughter. She will begin
to understand about turn-taking, so if you tickle her, she may well try to
tickle you back. Toys your baby may enjoy at this age include –

■ **Phones:** these are a source of fascination and she will enjoy playing with
yours, although she won't be too keen if you talk to a friend on it for ages.

■ **A ball to crawl after:** at nine months she probably won't be able to roll
it herself, but by 11 months she may. When she can, she will enjoy rolling it
to you and having you roll it back.

■ **Wheeled toys with string:** initially she will pull the string while sitting,
but these toys have a lot of mileage because once she is walking steadily
in a few months' time, she will be able to pull one along behind her.

■ **Anything she can drop:** once your baby learns to let go of things
deliberately and reliably, this will possibly be her favourite (and most
irritating) game! Avoid losing books and toys over the side of the buggy
when you are out by attaching them with clips. When she drops them, she
will be able to retrieve them – then drop them again.

■ **Stacking toys:** as well as light, easy-to-hold bricks, anything that stacks is
good at this age, for instance a set of beakers that fit inside each other or

STACKING TOYS

*A simple set of plastic
beakers teaches your
baby about colours,
shapes, and sizes.*

sit on top of each other to make a tower. These are also great for filling and pouring in the bath. A set of rings that fit over a pole contains several elements that are similar but different: the rings are the same shape, but different sizes and colours – and in some cases, textures. Initially, your baby will need help with stacking the rings (and some babies will be far more interested in biting them than stacking them) but as her problem-solving skills increase, she will be able to tackle it herself.

■ **Containers:** your baby will love putting things into a container and taking them out again. Shape-sorter toys are a good option as they offer more of a challenge. Show her how they work, but if trying to get the shapes through the holes is too tricky and frustrating for your baby at this stage, she can take the lid off and put them directly into the container.

Telly addicts?

Sitting with you to watch the occasional programme aimed at her age group (such as Teletubbies) won't do your baby any harm at all, but do not be tempted to use the TV as a babysitter. Some babies of this age will look at the screen intently, but have no way of making any sense of what they are seeing and will simply "zone out", mesmerized by the noise and action but not actually taking anything in.

Studies have indicated that towards the end of the second year short periods of viewing age-appropriate programmes may help boost language development, but this is not the case for babies under 18 months. As excessive TV viewing has been linked to growing obesity in toddlers, the couch potato habit is best avoided if you can, so try not to leave the TV on in the background while your baby is around. The radio can also add background noise which can block out sounds of speech, making it more difficult for you to communicate with your baby.

KEEPING BUSY *Your baby will be delighted with a container and a few small, safe objects or toys. He will put them in and take them out – again and again.*

OUTDOOR PLAY *Get outside whenever you can to widen your baby's play opportunities and offer a stimulating environment.*

Sand and water

While digging in the garden isn't a good idea if pets may have used the soil as a toilet, a covered sandpit will allow your baby to dig as much as she likes and explore the properties of sand. She will have lots of fun if she has a container of water nearby so she can play with them separately or together. Fill a bucket of water for her and help her pour it on to see the difference between wet and dry sand. She will enjoy feeling the texture of it with her fingers. Although she is too young to build with it, you can make sandcastles for her to squash, a game that will produce much hilarity. As she loves to fill and empty containers, a bucket and spade and some beakers are a great investment. Don't worry if she eats some sand – it will reappear in her nappy and won't do her any harm.

Out and about

The more you can get out with your baby the better for both of you. As your baby becomes mobile, play options are much more varied and interesting out of doors, for example during trips to the park to go on the swings and slides. As she is more interactive now, there is also great fun to be had from just being out and sharing the sights – ducks on the pond, other people's dogs, other babies, and the sights and sounds of a busy street. Parks offer plenty of opportunities for mobile babies to explore whatever the weather; she will be interested in scrunchy autumn leaves, laugh as you run through the rain with her buggy, and be amazed to touch snow for the first time. She will, of course, love to go on the apparatus too, but always be ready with a steadying hand, or to catch her if she tumbles. One important tip: in the park, watch out for dog poo, although most play areas are fenced off and dogs aren't allowed in.

When the weather is bad, you could also try your local soft play centre. Most of these have separate sections for babies and toddlers that provide a fun play space and soft landings for unsteady movers, and some run special drop-in sessions for under-twos. Your baby will be equally fascinated by what is going on at the shopping centre, but she may get bored if you shop for too long so take her out of her buggy occasionally or stop and talk to her. Try to stay alert and responsive to your baby as possible when you are out together – recent research found that some mothers were often "switched off" from their babies because they were listening to music on an i-Pod.

Playpens

Babies need freedom to explore, but as long as it doesn't become a place to contain her too often, a playpen can be a useful bit of kit. If your baby is cruising around the furniture, a playpen with upright bars can provide a great frame to hold on to, as well as a safe place to put her for short periods when necessary, either in the garden or the house. Now she can watch you garden or cook and you can get on with the job knowing that she is safe. Make sure there is a range of safe toys in there so she has something to occupy her. A playpen is also a great place to throw all your baby's toys at the end of the day if, like Peter, you want to convert your house quickly from toy-strewn chaos into some semblance of tidiness.

Playing with dad

Your baby is becoming more physically capable by the day and outdoor play and rough-and-tumble games are a great way to hone her new skills. But while she is very capable and remarkably resilient, it is important to remember that these skills have only just been acquired and it will be some time before she is competent and safe at using them.

There are two favourite dads' games at this age where a little caution needs to be exercised. One is throwing your baby into the air and the other is swinging her around by her arms. Both are usually met with squeals of delight, but each has its perils. In the first case, extreme caution needs to be exercised – it's a long way to fall if you drop her. In the second case, put your hands under her armpits. It is important not to swing her around or pull her up by holding her wrists as this can result in an elbow bone being pulled out of the socket. This is very painful and she will cry at the time, and then you will notice that she is not using the affected arm. However, a skilled clinician can "pop" the joint back in.

FATHER'S VIEW

Everyday care

Your baby will enjoy being part of family mealtimes and may be keen to try some more grown-up meals, which means that you can now cook for the whole family. At this age early morning waking can become a new challenge, but there are some creative ways to buy yourself an extra hour's sleep.

Eating habits

Family mealtimes are good for your baby's social development and she will probably take an interest in what you're eating, so try to avoid always feeding her separately even if it does mean you don't get to eat your food in peace. If her mealtimes don't yet coincide with yours, give her a snack of some finger foods so she can join in.

What you offer your baby to eat now will form the basis of her food preferences for life. If you give her sweets, biscuits, crisps, white bread, and processed foods, she will crave these as she grows, whereas if she has a healthy diet, she is more likely to make healthy choices later on. You're not depriving her by not giving her chocolate – she doesn't yet know what it is. Make it easier for her by eating a healthy diet yourself. She wants to copy you so this is the best way to encourage her to eat well. Shepherd's pie, chicken or fish with vegetables, couscous, noodles, pasta dishes, full-fat dairy products (your baby needs fats in her diet), and well-cooked eggs are

Typical baby menus at 9–12 months

▶ **Early morning:** breast or bottle.

▶ **Breakfast:** cereal with milk/ scrambled egg with toast/ yoghurt with fruit.

▶ **Mid-morning snack:** cheese/ raisins or rice cake/ little sandwiches.

▶ **Lunch:** hummus with pitta bread and vegetables/ baked potato with tuna/ pieces of cheese, tomato, and cucumber with breadsticks.

▶ **Mid-afternoon snack:** fresh fruit/ yoghurt/ fromage frais.

▶ **Dinner:** lamb or lentil casserole with mashed potatoes/ pasta with tomato and vegetable sauce/ meat, fish, or tofu with vegetables and a carbohydrate, such as potato or rice.

▶ **Bedtime:** breast or bottle.

all nourishing foods that you can offer your baby. These can be home-made or from jars, although it is still important to ensure that she doesn't have any added salt or sugar in her food. You can start to adapt your ordinary family meals for your baby (apart from finger foods, her meals still need to be minced, mashed, or chopped). Avoid adding salt until the end of the cooking time so that you can remove some for her before you season it. Alternatively, get the whole family into good eating habits and don't add salt at all.

How much food should she have?

The amount of solid food your baby eats will, in part, depend on how much breast milk or formula she is having. She only needs a certain amount of food a day and if she is having it as milk feeds, she won't be hungry for solids. As she gets used to eating at mealtimes, gradually cut back on her milk so that she only has one feed in the morning and one at bedtime. Start with a small amount of food at mealtimes (a couple of tablespoonfuls) so that she doesn't feel overwhelmed by the quantity – she can always have more if she wants. Try to remember that your baby may not be as hungry at certain times of day, or on a particular day. Our daughter used to eat happily at breakfast and supper, but was simply not interested in lunch. We just accepted it and moved on with the day and she has always been a happy eater when she needed to be. As long as your baby is growing well and gaining weight appropriately she is fine, no matter how little she seems to eat.

If you're concerned about her erratic eating habits, consider some famous early 20th-century research in which babies were allowed to choose their own foods from a healthy selection on offer. Their daily intake was extremely unbalanced, but over a period of months, each child ate a nutritious diet and all grew and developed well. So provide lots of variety, let her eat as much or as little as she wants, and try not to worry.

FAMILY MEALS *Your baby can begin to eat the same meals as you, but remember not to put salt in his portion.*

Your vegetarian or vegan baby

A vegetarian or vegan diet (vegan means no animal products, such as dairy produce, at all) is not necessarily a problem for your baby as she can get protein from tofu and legumes, and most dairy products can be replaced by soya. Babies need proportionally more protein and calcium than at any other time of life – this is no problem in vegetarian babies, but babies having a dairy-free diet will need to find calcium in soya products, green vegetables, and lentils. Iron stores can become low in babies by the age of six months, so it is essential to give iron-rich foods. Do be aware that a very restricted diet can lead to malnutrition, particularly in a baby. If you are in any doubt about your baby's nutritional requirements, ask your GP to refer you to a dietician who can ensure she is getting all the foods she needs for healthy growth. The Vegetarian Society (see page 312) is also a good source of information.

Early waking

I'M AWAKE *He may sleep through the night, but he is likely to want to start his day bright and early.*

Some babies tend to wake at sunrise, raring to start their day. If your baby consistently wakes up at this time, consider whether she needs a slightly later bedtime or shorter daytime naps – she is unlikely to sleep 12 hours a night at nine months if she has had a couple of three-hour sleeps during the day. Using blackout blinds in the summer may help, but if your baby is simply an early bird, provide some entertainment in her cot. Board books, a few small toys, and a favourite soft toy or doll may keep her occupied, while a safe baby mirror that attaches to the bars of her cot will give her someone to chat to. If she is a climber, make sure that whatever you leave in her cot can't be used as a step to clamber out. It is a good idea to have a low light on in her room – the soft glow from a 15 watt bulb won't disturb her but will mean she can see to play if she wakes up before dawn. If you are lucky, she won't call you for half an hour or so.

Travelling safely

Your baby will probably be ready to move on from her infant car seat, and it is vital that anyone who drives her around also has an appropriately sized and fitted seat in their vehicle. Car seats are designed for babies of a certain weight range, rather than a particular age, so your baby will be ready to move on according to her growth. The portable rear-facing infant seat that she has had since birth is intended for babies up to around 13kg (28.6lb), but to protect your back I recommend not carrying your baby in the car seat after three months. Second-stage seats, which are forward-facing, are designed for babies from around 9kg (19.8lb), or about nine months of age. These are fixed into your car with the existing seat belts or a fixing kit, and have their own five-point quick-release safety harnesses.

As with all baby equipment, there is a wide range of styles and prices, but the key thing here is that the seat you choose must fit your car correctly – not all seats will suit all models. As with infant car seats, if you use a second-hand seat for your baby, it is essential that you know its history and have the fitting instructions, otherwise your baby might not be protected in the event of an accident. Make sure everyone who is transporting your baby – grandparents, childminders, etc – knows how to fit her car seat properly.

Common concerns

▶ **My baby has rolls of fat on her arms and legs. Could she be eating too much?**
Babies of this age are designed to be chubby, and most will lose some of their fat as they start to become mobile. Talk to your health visitor about your baby's weight and growth – if she is gaining weight faster than expected, it might be a case of what she is eating and drinking rather than how much. She needs calories from lean meat and fish, legumes, dairy produce, cereals and fresh fruit and vegetables, rather than from processed foods such as biscuits and sweet drinks.

As long as she's eating healthy food and having her milk to drink according to her appetite, she's unlikely to be overweight.

▶ **How much milk should my 11-month-old have? He wants a bottle several times a day and then he won't eat his meals.**
As a rule of thumb, bottle-fed babies of this age will generally need around a pint (500-600ml) of formula per day. Most still have a milk feed in the morning and at bedtime. Your baby may be using his bottle for comfort and if this is the case try encouraging him to

have a different comfort object, such as a muslin, his thumb, or a cuddly toy. Babies shouldn't really have bottles after one year of age as they are bad for the teeth, so try giving him his daytime drinks in a lidded beaker. Some baby beakers come with specially designed soft spouts to help babies make the transition from bottles. He can have formula, water, or well-diluted juice at mealtimes, while plain water is best for drinks in between. If he gets used to a beaker during the day now, it will be easier to help him make the switch from bottles in a few weeks' time.

Childcare for your older baby

If you return to work towards the end of the first year, you and your baby may find it difficult to be apart to begin with. Look on the positive side – you have had 12 wonderful months together and, although you will always be your baby's number one, she will benefit from this new situation.

Try not to worry or feel guilty if you must return to work. Your baby will be fine if she is cared for in a welcoming, friendly, and stimulating environment. Research shows that babies whose mums go out to work generally thrive in good quality childcare. At this age it is often best to introduce new carers or environments well ahead of time and allow your baby to acclimatize gradually. If possible, stay with her during the first

Choosing the right childcare

Once you've established that you're happy with the environment, safety provision, and paperwork such as OFSTED reports and references, ask some specific questions:

NURSERIES

▶ Will my baby have a key worker? This is essential as your baby needs to build a relationship with one person at the nursery.
▶ Is the ratio of staff to babies the recommended 1:3?

CHILDMINDERS

▶ How many other babies and children are looked after and what are their ages?
▶ Will my baby be taken to the park and/or baby groups?

QUESTIONS FOR BOTH

▶ Is there a daily routine for meals, snacks, and naps etc.?
▶ What indoor and outdoor play facilities are available?
▶ What foods are the babies offered?

NANNIES

▶ Do you have formal training and/ or first-aid training?
▶ Are you happy to have a police check if you haven't had one already?

QUESTIONS FOR ALL

▶ What is your approach to behaviour and discipline?
▶ What happens if my baby is ill?
▶ How do you give feedback about my baby's day and is there a contact number I can call at any time?

couple of visits, then start leaving her for short sessions, building up to longer ones as she comes to know and trust her carer. It is natural for your baby to cry when you leave her with a new carer because of separation anxiety (see page 129), but the best way to help her cope is to say goodbye and let her see you go. If you don't, she won't be able to trust you not to slope off and will become more anxious and clingy. Hand her to the carer, kiss her goodbye, tell her you will see her soon, and leave. If you hover, it will be harder for both of you.

If you are worried, ring the nursery, nanny, or childminder to make sure your baby is okay. Most babies settle down happily, but if she is very upset day after day, or if she is crying for long periods after you leave, this may not be the right environment for her. If you feel the situation isn't working, talk to your baby's carer and if you are still not happy, drop in to see what is happening – a good nursery or carer won't mind at all.

QUICK GOODBYES
A speedy handover will be less painful for both you and your baby.

Common concerns

▶ **My mother cares for our baby a lot of the time, but the downside is that she is constantly telling us how to look after her. How can we handle this sensitively?**
Your mother is only trying to help and she may believe that your life will be easier if you take her advice. It's worth talking this through with her and explaining that you want to look after your baby in your own way, but that you value her help and understand that her relationship with her grandchild is important. Find something about which to ask her advice: it will make her feel better and she may well have a point of view worth listening to.

▶ **We'd love to go out more but are struggling to find a babysitter. What can we do?**
Ask your friends to recommend a babysitter, or you could join (or set up) a babysitting circle with other local mums where you take turns to look after each other's children. Bear in mind that young babysitters, even if they're being supported by a parent who is nearby and have been recommended to you as responsible, may not be able to cope in an emergency. The Royal Society for the Prevention of Accidents (RoSPA) (see page 312) recommends that you don't leave your baby with a sitter who is under 16. If you have any doubts at all about a babysitter, don't use him or her.

QUESTION&ANSWER

Your growing twins

If you have two or more babies, you may be starting to emerge from the fog of feeding, comforting, nappy-changing, and washing by now. The new challenge for you is chasing after your babies – often in opposite directions – once they are mobile.

MAKING LIFE EASIER

Caring for two babies instead of one is, of course, hard work, but the advantage with twins is that they have each other for company and comfort. This means they may be happy to sit together and watch for a while as you get on with your tasks.

Do be kind to yourself and keep chores to the minimum – clean only as much as you need to for basic hygiene.

TWICE THE CHALLENGE *A double buggy is essential as your twins grow, but it may be a while before you are adept at manoeuvring and storing it.*

That way you will have more time to enjoy this delightful stage in your babies' development.

A useful investment once your babies start to roll and move around is a playpen. Here they can both safely kick and wriggle around, giving you a few minutes to answer the door, catch up on paperwork, clean the loo or have a cup of tea and read the newspaper.

Supermarket shopping can be particularly stressful with twins. If you have a computer, make life easier by ordering a food delivery online.

YOUR COMMUNICATIVE BABIES

Each of your babies will enjoy one-to-one time with you or your partner so try to make a little space for this, even if it is just when you change one baby's nappy while your partner looks after the other. If you can share care of your babies with your partner, try to spend similar amounts of time with each baby so that you develop a good relationship with each of them.

Twins frequently develop language skills later than single babies. This is sometimes because twins are born prematurely and so will have later development in common with other premature babies. Parents have less time to interact with each baby individually, which is another reason why babbling and first words may take longer to appear. Another factor is the close rapport between your babies, which may mean that they have less incentive than single babies to develop their language skills; some babies even develop their own "language", which only they understand. At this age you need not be concerned if your babies are slower to vocalize than their singleton counterparts, but if you notice that they are a long way behind other babies of their age as they reach their first birthday (for example, they aren't babbling), discuss this with your health visitor as there are strategies that can help them develop their language skills.

INTO A ROUTINE

Meeting the needs of two different individuals takes time, but having a routine will help you to cope. If your babies generally feed and sleep at the same time, you will have a manageable rhythm to your days, whereas if they are on entirely different schedules, you may not get any time to yourself.

Whether your babies are breastfed, bottle-fed or a mixture, do try to continue feeding them simultaneously because if they feed at the same time there is more chance that they will sleep at the same time, too.

Research has suggested that twin babies who share a cot may be more likely to have similar sleeping and feeding patterns than those who have separate cots. Having said that, your babies will start to become more mobile during these months and so you may want to move them into separate cots in the same room, particularly if they are light sleepers.

It is worth making the effort to get out and about with your babies. You will all benefit from a change of scenery and fresh air and once you're confident about being out with your twins, you could try your local baby group where you will meet other mums.

SUPPORT FOR YOU

If you haven't already done so – you may not have had the time! – consider joining a support group for parents of twins (see page 312). If you can't track one down, your health visitor should be able to help you. Some groups offer support and advice online or over the

phone. Most of the people you know will have only had one baby at a time and it can be a lifeline to know that you can talk over any twin-related stresses with parents in the same situation as you.

TIME AS A COUPLE

Just as with parents of single babies, your relationship with your partner needs nurturing, too, and it is essential to get out together, even if it is only for a short while.

Now is the time to take people up on all those offers of help – you may need two grandparents or two friends at a time to hold the fort while your twins are very young. Arranging this childcare (regularly if possible) will ensure that you have some stress-free time to relax with your partner and much-needed time out for yourself.

PLAYMATES *Although babies still tend to play alone at this stage, twins will be so used to being together that they may interact earlier.*

THE 2ND YEAR

From dependent baby to independent child, between 12 and 24 months your toddler's development will be rapid. This is a time when the difficulties of tantrums and tears will be more than made up for by the magic of your child's inquisitive personality and the excitement of her beginning to walk and talk. Enjoy.

Contents

YOUR NEW TODDLER

"The toddler years are here, and your child's boundless energy will astound you."

PLAYTIME YOU WILL NEED TO GIVE YOUR TODDLER SPACE TO ROAM, SO USE THE PARK OR GARDEN WHENEVER YOU CAN

WHAT'S THAT? YOUR TODDLER MAY BEGIN TO ATTEMPT HER FIRST WORDS AND POINT AT THINGS SHE RECOGNIZES

CATCH ME IF YOU CAN
ONCE HE IS ON THE MOVE,
KEEPING UP WITH YOUR TODDLER
WILL BE A DAILY CHALLENGE

Into the second year

By the time your baby reaches his first birthday he will be into everything and may be a real little chatterbox to boot. You may understand one or two words by 14 months, but he will convey much of what he wants to say with his tone of voice, facial expressions, body language, and gestures.

Physical skills

Your baby's first steps are a real milestone and cause for celebration, but they will actually be more of a waddle. Legs apart, he will place his whole foot uncertainly on the ground with a rather stiff gait, and it will be some time before he walks smoothly with a heel-toe action. He may also start to climb, hence the need for stair gates early on, and soon progress to clambering on to the sofa. He probably won't be able to get down from it at first and will call for help, but you can show him how to turn on to his tummy and safely lower his feet to the floor. This is a good way for him to learn to come down steps, too, although he will need your supervision as this skill takes time to master.

Once your toddler starts walking independently, he will gradually become more competent at starting and stopping, and will soon be able to squat down to examine something interesting on the floor. Carrying something at the same time will take a bit longer, but once he is really confident, he may be able to pull a wheeled toy along on a string. Don't worry if your baby is still sitting firmly on the floor, though. As with all developmental milestones, babies acquire them in roughly the same order but at different times and some won't be walking for a few months yet. If your baby isn't cruising or even pulling himself up to stand by 14 months, talk to your health visitor or GP in case there is a reason for this – although the most likely cause is that he is simply not ready or interested yet.

At 12 months, he won't be able to dress himself, but he will be able to take some clothes off, such as socks, and will probably find it very funny if you get exasperated. Make a game of helping him to put them on again, then distract him before you get a repeat performance.

A HELPING HAND *Your baby will need some help from you as he begins to walk. Be prepared for him to take many tumbles at first – it is all part of the learning process.*

What he can understand

Babies of this age understand far more than they are able to say, and will respond with babble that has all the questions, commands, inflections, and cadences of "proper" speech. The chatting and interactive games that the two of you have enjoyed since your baby was tiny will have increased his understanding to a point where, as well as being able to follow simple verbal instructions to fetch something, he may also be able to cope with questions, such as "Where's teddy?" or "Do you want a drink?" – and reply in his own way. He may also be able to point to body parts now and you can help his understanding by talking to him as you dress him – for example, by saying "Where's your hand gone?" as you put his coat on, and then "Look, there it is!" You can also ask him to point to teddy's eyes, your nose, or a picture of a baby in his book.

All babies use signing to some extent as they make gestures, point, and clap, but if you have been teaching your baby specific signs for things (see page 133), this may come into its own now. He will be able to tell you if he is hungry or tired and this – in theory, anyway – will help to prevent some of the crying from frustration that is common at this stage.

Becoming a toddler

Your baby has reached a point where not only is he learning to walk and talk, but his view of the world and his responses to it are changing. Until now he has had very little control over his surroundings and his lack of understanding and skills have meant that he has needed you to do almost everything for him. Now you will see a new determination as he tries to be more independent. This is an exciting development, although his desire to manage by himself often outweighs his competence.

Your baby may or may not have launched into the mood swings that characterize this stage of development – some start at a year, others save tantrums for the end of the second year or even later – but let's just say that when it comes it will be great practice for when he becomes a teenager. So, why is your adorable toddler sunny one minute and screaming the next? Part of the difficulty for your toddler (and you) is that his understanding and desire to do things far exceed his abilities at the moment and so frustration sets in very easily. Experimentation and frustration are an essential part of learning and it is important to give your baby the opportunity to figure things out for himself, rather than always stepping in to help. There will be times when holding back will provoke tears, and so will intervening – but there is usually a point at which you can offer just enough help so that he can move on to the next step of what he is doing. For example, if he is trying unsuccessfully to turn the pages of his book and is becoming upset, lift the page slightly for him but then let him turn it himself. It is a tricky balance, though, so don't worry if you sometimes feel you can't get it right – this is a feeling shared by all parents and one that reappears frequently as children grow.

Me, myself, I

Throughout your baby's first year, he has largely perceived himself as part of you. This will have begun to change at around seven months with the development of separation anxiety, but as he

moves into his second year these feelings become more sophisticated and he will start to understand that he is an individual, separate from you. This is quite a difficult concept to begin to grasp, and it is very likely that your toddler will find such a major shift in his world-view unsettling. To understand that you and he are different people is a profound change in his life and thinking, and the uncertainties and confusions it can throw up are part of the reason behind tantrums and "the terrible twos". Whether this happens at 12 months, 14 months, or even later, as this new perception of himself begins to emerge, he needs to find out what he is capable of and how his actions affect you. Therefore he will start to test your boundaries. If he throws his cup of milk on the floor and you tell him off, he will probably do it again with one eye on you to

TAKING RISKS

As your toddler becomes more aware of his capabilities, he is likely to become more adventurous. Although he needs supervision, do try to step back at times and let him learn.

"I soon realized my son wasn't being naughty. He was just doing what toddlers have to do in order to learn."

IT'S NOT FAIR *Tears of frustration will be a regular occurrence as your toddler begins to learn an important lesson in life – he can't always have things his own way.*

see what happens. Remember that this isn't your toddler being naughty – he is simply learning about cause and effect, actions, and reactions. He is experimenting. Understanding this may help you to stay calm and make you more likely to respond by distracting him, rather than getting angry. Next time he leaves the cup on his highchair tray rather than throwing it, praise him and give him a hug.

At this age, his memory isn't good enough for him to remember what you don't want him to do, and his instinctive curiosity will get him into constant scrapes. But if you use positive reinforcement, such as praise and hugs, for behaviour you want to encourage, and do your best to ignore less desirable behaviour, your toddler will gradually understand how you would like him to behave.

Using distraction

You can help minimize outbursts (his and yours) by using the fact that he is still fairly easy to distract at the beginning of this year. Instead of saying "No" when he wants to watch his video again, take him to find a favourite game to play. Rather than telling him not to empty your handbag, find him one of his own to play with or ask him to help you empty the washing machine – and praise him for it. This way you are likely to enjoy each other's company far more.

Sharing

Your baby is learning about possessions. Whereas a month or so ago he would happily share toys, food, and even you, now he is less keen. Don't worry that he is becoming "spoiled" and selfish as this is just another stage he has to go through en route to understanding the world and his place in it. As he begins to define himself as separate and individual, then he is bound to be strongly possessive of his toys. It requires the next step in development for him to understand that it is safe to share things, and you can help him with this.

Keep going to your local baby group or try out a toddler group, where there will be a wider range of ages and different kinds of toys. The toys in a playground or toddler group are there for everyone, so this is a great way to start helping your child to understand the concept of sharing, and he will soon begin to learn.

Why smacking doesn't work

Your toddler's behaviour will sometimes frustrate you, and you may consider smacking him to "teach him a lesson". Before going down this road, ask yourself what you will actually be teaching him. If you smack him because he is not behaving as you would like, you are teaching him that if someone does something you don't want them to do, you hit them. Don't be surprised, therefore, if he hits another child who takes his toy or irritates him.

At this age, your baby doesn't understand about good or bad behaviour, so he has no way of learning anything from a physical punishment. As he gets older, it won't teach him anything useful either – and while he may behave well (when you're around), it will be to avoid a smack rather than because he wants to be "good".

If you smack him in retaliation for hurting you, to show him what it feels like, he will have absolutely no idea that the two incidents are connected: he is far too young to understand your feelings or motivations and will simply be distraught that you have hurt him. Some parents argue that there are occasions when they need to smack a child to warn them of danger. If you are close enough to smack your toddler when he reaches out to touch the cooker, you are close enough to lift him away with a firm "No".

VIOLENT BEHAVIOUR

Many people who routinely smack say it is the only thing that works and it never did them any harm. However, smacking is a form of violence and children who are smacked may well become aggressive as they grow up. Consider this carefully: if violence and hitting are unacceptable in the adult world (how would you feel if your boss hit you for doing something wrong at work?), why should it be appropriate for babies and children – the most vulnerable members of society?

Smacking can also escalate as your toddler grows older and more defiant. If you smack him and he just glares at you, you may then smack him harder next time to get a response. Stop. Babies and toddlers can be seriously injured this way.

If you do lose control and smack your child in anger, try not to be too hard on yourself. For most parents who smack it is an impulsive act and they feel terribly guilty afterwards, but we are all human and mistakes happen. If you do smack your child, hug him and apologize – after all, as he grows up you will want him to say sorry when he makes a mistake.

If you are so infuriated that you feel you might hit your toddler, make sure he is safe in his cot or playpen and leave the room until you calm down.

CAREFUL HANDLING *Getting on your child's level to calm her down is much more effective than smacking.*

Staying safe

Along with your toddler's growing physical skills comes a whole host of sticky situations he can get himself into. If you have already babyproofed your home, keep reassessing what is required to keep it safe, inside and out, as his skills and mobility develop.

YOUR INQUISITIVE TODDLER

While you want to protect your toddler, you don't want the house to be a sterile environment. Creating safe play areas will reduce the temptation for him to roam to other less appropriate ones. One room that has lots of appeal is the bathroom and your toddler may have no qualms about playing with the water in the loo. If it is difficult to keep him away, you can buy a simple toilet lock to prevent him from lifting the lid. If you are worried that your child could lock the bathroom door, you can either move the lock so that it is too high for him to reach or install a lock that can be opened from the outside if necessary. When my oldest son was a toddler he managed to lock himself in the bathroom while the bath was running. I was in a terrible panic but thankfully we had an au pair who calmly talked him through unlocking the door. I dread to think what might have happened if she hadn't been there and I certainly learned a lesson about vigilance!

OUT AND ABOUT

Ensure that you use the harness on the buggy as it is easy for your toddler to tumble out if he is not secured. Make sure that your baby's car seat is the

LITTLE FINGERS *It is natural for children to be inquisitive at this age, so create safe environments outdoors and indoors for him to explore.*

IN THE GARDEN

▸ Lock all chemicals and poisons away in a shed or strongbox.

▸ Lock sharp tools out of your child's reach.

▸ If you have a pond, either fill it in, put a high fence around it, or cover it with strong wire mesh or a grille that can withstand a child's weight. A fence must be designed so that a toddler can't climb over or under it, and the gate must be kept locked.

▸ Empty paddling pools, buckets, and other containers, turning them upside down after use, and ensure your toddler can't get into a rainwater butt.

▸ Watch out for unexpected choking hazards, such as small pebbles.

▸ Clip bushes with berries so they are out of reach, or even consider removing them. Check for other poisonous plants in your garden.

▸ Don't allow your child near electrical items, and ensure cables aren't placed where they can trip him up.

▸ Restrict his access to steep steps.

▸ Clear away any cat or dog poo straight away, discourage your baby from playing with the soil and, if he has a sandpit, cover it when not in use.

right size. He will need a second-stage seat (see page 163) and, if he is very dextrous, this is when problems can start. A second-stage car seat has a five-point harness, but for safety reasons it needs to have a quick-release mechanism. Once your baby works out how to press the button, he may do so frequently. All you can do is pull over, and strap him back in, as travelling unsecured can be lethal.

It is often a temptation if you are only travelling a short distance and are one seat short to either hold your baby on your lap or tuck him in the seat belt with you. Don't. Imagine a situation where you are travelling at 30mph and the car brakes sharply. If you are holding your baby on your lap, the effect of braking will multiply his weight many times and he may be ripped out of your arms to crash into the back of the seat in front or even go through the windscreen. Held inside your seat belt, your weight will simply crush him against it.

OTHER PEOPLE'S HOUSES

If you take your toddler to visit baby-free homes, beware of dangers such as accessible stairs, sharp corners, and flimsy furniture. Check, too, for

harmful objects. Houses with children just a few years older than your baby can be just as hazardous, as the living room is likely to be a treasure trove of objects that he could choke on, such as marbles and bits of Lego.

PET SAFETY

While your own family dog may be gentle and tolerant, never take the risk of allowing your toddler to clamber on

him or wind him up as he may bite if he is provoked too much. Always be wary around other people's dogs: ask the owner before allowing your toddler to get close, and be cautious – animals can be unpredictable. It is important to remember that dogs are pack animals, where a pecking order operates. Your child may be viewed as lower down the pack and be put in his place with a quick nip or worse.

INTREPID EXPLORER *He will love to climb stairs. Encourage this but supervise him carefully and teach him safe ways to go up and come down.*

Great games and toys for toddlers

One enjoyable development around this time is that your baby will be a more active participant in your games and is likely to hand you a toy as well as take one from you. Action games and songs still go down well and he might now be able to clap along and do some of the actions with a little help.

INTERACTIVE TOYS
He will become more skilled at handling and using his toys. A toy telephone is likely to be a firm favourite.

Your toddler will still be throwing, pushing, and clambering on things, but may also occasionally sit still for a few minutes, absorbed in a book or toy. As he will probably have received a lot of new toys for his birthday, it is a good idea to put some away so that you can bring them out at intervals over the coming weeks and months.

Your 12-month-old will be constantly on the go, and top of his list of games is investigating anything and everything so you will need to be vigilant. He makes no distinction between what you give him as toys and what he is keen to investigate, so he may be just as interested in the wrapping paper on his birthday presents as the most enticing toy inside, and everyday objects still make fascinating playthings – boxes, spoons, keys, and phones are just some of the items babies find irresistible. He will be keen to "help" you, too, so let him take the vegetables out of your shopping bag or put packs of pasta into the cupboard.

Be mindful of safety, though, and don't allow him to play with breakable, heavy, or small items that could injure or choke him. Don't buy him toys designed for older children, however innocuous they may seem – if they come apart, the pieces might be hazardous.

Toys that may appeal to your toddler at this age include –

■ **Ride-on toys:** a car that he can sit on and propel along with his feet will be a favourite. These sometimes have a handle at the back for pushing and many have a lift-up seat to stash bits and pieces inside.

■ **Cuddly toys:** your baby may become attached to a particular soft toy now and these are perfect for pretend play (see page 223).

■ **Construction toys:** a set of soft blocks, or a system of interlocking pieces that don't need to be aligned so he can easily push them together.

■ **Containers:** put interesting toys and safe objects inside and make sure it has a lid that he is able to manage.

Messy play

The chances are you have already discovered that your toddler enjoys playing with his food. He will have great fun exploring new textures – try filling a bowl with jelly or cornflakes and let him squeeze or crunch the contents through his fingers.

At around 12 to 14 months, your toddler may enjoy a first encounter with crayons and paint. Make sure that all the art materials you are using are non-toxic. Thick wax crayons are easiest for him to manage. He won't have much control over the crayon yet (most babies of this age hold crayons with their fist at first, and are unlikely to develop a mature grasp until they are three years old), and he will probably cope best with a large sheet of paper taped to the table or floor so it can't move around. Let him watch you draw something first, then see if he surprises himself by making marks on the paper too.

If he enjoys the crayons and you are feeling brave, try mixing up some thick paint for him, using children's powder paint with a little water to make a paste, and letting him experiment, either with a chunky paintbrush or with his fingers. The next step (literally) is to get him to put his foot or hand into the paint and make prints on the paper – cut out the best one later and you have a perfect home-made card for Granny. It is a good idea to run him a bath before getting started, to avoid the problem of containing a paint-coated toddler who is fed up with messy play and wants to clamber round the living room while you get his bath ready. His burgeoning abilities do not include common sense, so store crayons out of reach, unless you want your walls and furniture decorated, too.

I'VE GOT WHEELS *He'll love to be on the move and ride-on toys make this much easier.*

ARTISTIC FLAIR *Give her paper and chunky crayons to encourage early creativity.*

SNACK TIME *Your toddler's tummy is still very small and needs regular topping up, so he will need to eat healthy snacks.*

Everyday care

Your toddler is likely to become more wilful by the day and may express this at mealtimes, if he doesn't want to eat what is on offer, and when you are changing him, if he doesn't want to lie still. You will have to be firm when managing his everyday care, but remember that testing the boundaries is normal.

What should your toddler eat?

Even if your child has been happy to eat anything you put in front of him since you first introduced solid foods, you may find that he gets a bit more picky now. If he chooses not to eat something you have given him, that's fine – continue to offer it without making a fuss because babies adjust to new tastes gradually. You can offer him a good range of healthy meals without making him eat food that he genuinely dislikes, as long as it isn't a whole food group such as vegetables. If your child was previously a healthy eater and now shows signs of becoming fussy, remind yourself that if he misses a meal, or even several, he will not fade away and won't be harmed in the slightest, and that he will eat when he is hungry. If he won't eat what you have given him, remove the food after 10 minutes or so and get him down from the table. If you don't make an issue of eating, your toddler can't fight you over it.

If you are worried that your toddler hardly seems to eat anything at all, keep a food diary for two weeks and record everything he eats and drinks. You will probably find that he is eating more than you think. Keep offering small portions of healthy foods at mealtimes and healthy snacks, such as fruit, cheese, or rice cakes, in between and resist the temptation to offer him junk food "just so he has had something". If you offer him biscuits and sweets to encourage him to eat, you will be teaching him how to get you to give him these foods and soon they might be all he will eat.

It may be tempting to offer crisps and similar savoury snacks as these are easy finger food for when you are out and about and your toddler will definitely eat them, but they are best avoided except on rare occasions, as they are high in salt and fat, and have no nutritional value.

A small confession is appropriate here. My two youngest children generally eat only a small selection of foods. Nonetheless, they eat healthily, are growing well, are not overweight, and are getting all the nutrients they need, so we are relaxed about it. However, the rule is that if they don't eat what is offered then there is no alternative.

Milk and weaning

If you are still happily breastfeeding your baby there is no reason to stop, but lots of mums wean their babies from the breast at around this time. He can have cow's milk from 12 months onwards. The Department of Health recommends that you give full-fat milk until a baby is two years old, and then full-fat or semi-skimmed milk after that.

If your baby shows no signs of wanting to stop being breastfed, but you feel it is time to wean him, take it gently. If you are still breastfeeding during the day, gradually drop these feeds by offering him milk in a cup and distracting him if he wants the breast. This may be easier said than done if he is determined, but keep persevering. Once he is managing without breast milk during the day, you can replace his morning feed with milk in a cup. He probably won't protest too much as he will have lots of energy first thing in the morning and will want to get busy.

He (and you) may be more reluctant to stop the bedtime feed as it is a comforting part of the day. To help him cope, give him lots of cuddles as part of his bedtime routine so that you both still have this closeness.

Caring for your toddler

Now that your baby is becoming a toddler, sooner or later he will start to resist you when you try to wash him, dress him, and change his nappies. While this can be infuriating if you have a bus to catch in 10 minutes' time, remember that he is not doing it deliberately to wind you up. Trying to do things for himself and testing out new skills is all part of his normal development. One way to handle it

MOVING ON TO CUPS
Once your baby has reached her first birthday, she should have all her drinks from cups rather than from bottles.

Feeding concerns

▶ **My 13-month-old toddler keeps throwing his plate on the floor when he's had enough at mealtimes. How can I stop him?**

First of all, think about how you react when he does this. Toddlers of this age do drop and throw things and he will grow out of it, but meanwhile if he learns that doing this will get an interesting reaction from you, he will continue. Hard though it is, simply ignore it. He's finished his meal so wipe his hands and face and get him down. It might help to give him finger foods and put them on his highchair tray, rather than on a plate. If they stay put, praise him and he'll soon learn that keeping his food to himself gets him lots of positive attention whereas hurling it around the room does not.

▶ **My baby is 12 months old and since I've stopped giving her bottles she won't have any milk at all. I've tried giving her cow's milk in her beaker but she's not interested. What should I do?**

Don't worry too much about milk. She can get calcium and vitamins in other ways, such as from cheese, yoghurt, and fromage frais, all of which can be incorporated into meals. You can also give her soya-based products, which will help replace many of the nutrients she was having in milk. Do try to avoid giving her lots of juice to drink instead of milk, as too much juice can damage her teeth – stick to water as much as you can.

▶ **My partner thinks I should stop breastfeeding now that our baby is a year old. Is he right?**

Lots of mums stop breastfeeding at around 12 months, but it's perfectly okay to continue feeding if this is what you and your baby both want. With my own babies, I found that six months was about the right length of time to breastfeed, but it is down to individual choice. For me this coincided with going back to work and so it seemed natural to wean them from the breast. Other mums continue to feed throughout toddlerhood, or even longer, and enjoy the closeness that this brings.

My personal view is that breastfeeding beyond the age of two years is a little odd – this can lead to the spectacle of a child lifting up her mum's top to help herself to the breast whenever she wants.

Talk with your partner about how you both feel and why he thinks you should stop breastfeeding now, and decide what is best for all three of you. Your partner may have been looking forward to having you all to himself again and if that's the case it's important to get these feelings out into the open. As far as your baby is concerned, while she gets pleasure from breastfeeding she won't lose out nutritionally if you decide to wean her.

"My baby just decided to stop breastfeeding at 11 months. I'd been thinking about stopping at a year anyway, but to be honest it still felt like a rejection."

without too many tears is to let him join in as much as you can. The key is to make sure he feels involved –

■ **Dressing:** although your baby is too young to dress himself, if you set him the task of choosing between two T-shirts, or two sunhats, you may find that this distracts him for long enough for you to get the rest of his clothes on.

■ **Nappy changing:** however much you sing to him and jolly him along, your toddler may hate having his nappy changed by this age as he wants to be up and off, and will not be happy about being pinioned to the changing mat. He can't help with this task, but he can get the clean nappy out of the pack ready to hand to you at the right moment. If that doesn't work, a favourite toy that you keep just for nappy-changes might do the trick.

■ **Bathtime:** if he has lots of bubbles in his bath, he will get clean anyway so don't worry if he won't let you wash him with a face cloth. You can also try giving him a sponge or face cloth of his own to hold so that between the two of you he gets something approximating a wash.

■ **Hair-washing:** this can be a bit of a trauma if he is not willing to co-operate. He may be frightened of the water going in his eyes and ears and if this is the case, you can buy a halo-shaped shield to prevent it happening. Otherwise, keep hair-washing to a minimum and if you have to, just sponge his hair clean with the bath water.

BATHTIME FUN *She will treat bathtime as playtime, and may resist if you interrupt her with boring tasks such as a hair-wash.*

Sleep

Your busy toddler still needs plenty of sleep but he may be reducing the length and number of his daytime naps now. Babies vary in their sleep needs: while some sleep better at night if they have had substantial daytime naps that stop them being overtired and cranky, others are hypersensitive and won't go to sleep until midnight if they nap after 2 pm. If your toddler is one of the latter, it is worth getting out and about in the afternoon so he stays awake (although beware the soporific effects of the car or buggy).

You may notice that your baby takes longer to fall asleep as he gets older and sits or lies in his cot babbling away. Don't feel guilty if he is awake for a short time as he will soon settle and go off to sleep without your help. However, if it takes him a very long time to drop off, you might be expecting him to sleep more than he needs. At 12 months, he will need around 12–14 hours in 24. You might find it useful to keep a sleep diary for a week or so to see exactly how much he is sleeping, and may then need to consider putting him to bed later, having an earlier start in the morning or shorter daytime naps.

Your toddler can now have a low-tog, cot-sized duvet and a pillow, but keep a careful eye in case he learns to use it as a step to help him climb out of the cot. Adjustable cot bases should be at the lowest position now to foil your intrepid explorer and any toys large enough to be used as steps should be removed from his cot. If your baby keeps on escaping, it might be safer to lower the cot-side, or even place his mattress on the floor, thoroughly baby-proof his room and put a safety gate across the doorway.

Our cot was huge and our babies stayed in it until they were around three years old – and, thankfully, they never learned to climb out. This worked well for us as we were keen not to have our children climbing into our bed in the middle of the night.

Common concerns

▶ **My 14-month-old has just started walking but he falls over all the time. How can I help to keep him safe?**
Toddlers who have just learned to walk are usually unstable and will frequently tumble over. It's very rare for them to injure themselves seriously unless they encounter a hazard such as a flight of steps. Simply keep a watchful eye on him, use stair gates where necessary, and use protectors on furniture that has sharp corners. This phase is short-lived as your toddler will soon become steadier on his feet.

▶ **What can I do to stop my toddler hitting me?**
Firmly say "No, hitting hurts Mummy," and put her down or move away. This way, rather than giving her attention for hitting, you are removing attention. Similarly, if she hits another child, tell her it's not okay to hit, then give the other child your attention. On the other hand, when your toddler gives you a lovely cuddle without hitting you, hug her and tell her you love being with her and praise her for being gentle. This way she will learn that by not hitting you, she will get your loving attention. Toddlers hit when they are frustrated, to get attention, or simply to see what happens. It is common behaviour, but she will soon stop if you are consistent in your response.

QUESTION&ANSWER

First shoes

While it is absolutely fine for your toddler to be barefoot while indoors, as soon as he is ready to walk outside he will need shoes. His principal shoes are one item of clothing that should always be bought new. Because they mould themselves to the shape of the foot, another toddler's shoes won't fit your child properly. Make sure you go to a shop where the staff are specially trained in fitting young children's shoes. The fit, rather than the look, of the shoe is the most important factor, so while fashion shoes may appeal to your toddler, even at this age, stand firm and don't buy them if they are not the right shape for his feet.

That said, once you know your toddler's shoe size you can still use hand-me-downs for occasional wear. We have always carefully bought our children's main shoes, but we have used a variety of second-hand ones, too. If they appear to cause any discomfort or rubbing, simply discard them. Shoes can be very expensive and often only get a few months' use, so a common-sense approach is all that is required. Finally, pay attention to what the shoes are made of. Avoid footwear made of plastic – stick to leather and other breathable materials.

A "dirty weekend"

It's really important that you both continue to work at maintaining your relationship and find time to be a couple, as well as being parents. When your baby has reached his first birthday, it's a good time to think about taking this a step further than a night out at the cinema, if you haven't already. If you can afford it, consider having a weekend away at a hotel; if not, perhaps see if you can stay with some friends.

By now you're probably used to leaving your child when you go to work, or out for an evening, so concerns over separation should be easier to manage. Similarly, your baby will have become used to you being away for short periods, and provided he is with people he knows, he will be happy in your absence. This is where grandparents can be a real boon, as they will no doubt be really excited about having their grandchild to stay. Now he's older, he'll be easier to look after and he is likely to enjoy the different kind of attention he gets from his grandparents.

Take the time to plan your weekend carefully. Try to make sure it has a really romantic flavour – supper in a special restaurant, for instance – and that you have proper time to talk and share an experience as just the two of you again. It never ceases to amaze me when we get away together how different the conversation can be and how much we rediscover each other.

FATHER'S VIEW

Pre-term babies

The early years of parenting can be a little more complex if your baby was born prematurely. The stages of development are less straightforward, but it is important to try to put this difficult start behind you and care for your baby as normally as possible.

If your baby was born too soon, his development will have followed the same route as a full-term baby's, except that he has probably reached milestones according to when he was due to be born, rather than his actual birth date. So, for example, if your 12-month-old was born at 28 weeks, the chances are that he will be getting the hang of sitting alone, but his first steps might be some way off. Try not to compare him with full-term babies of the same age.

A TRICKY START

Your baby will have needed special care after the birth, making the early months even more challenging. Although neonatal units (see page 36) encourage parents to be involved with their babies, if your baby was very sick initially you may have found bonding difficult. Conversely, you may have bonded well, but may be very fearful that some harm could come to him.

If your baby needed to have medical support at home, such as oxygen or regular visits from a home care nurse, after being discharged from hospital, it was probably very stressful, but most parents do feel that it is a huge relief

to be able to care for their baby at home instead of in a ward.

During this first year, your baby will have had several assessments, including the normal developmental ones all babies have, and any major problems will most likely have been detected. Either way, having a baby who was premature is a difficult and challenging experience so don't be afraid to continue asking for support even this far on from the birth. While the first birthday is a major milestone, especially if your baby was very small and sick at birth, these issues, along with any physical and developmental problems he has as

"We were over-protective of our baby in the early months because of the difficult start, but we are learning to be more relaxed now that he's a toddler."

a result of his prematurity, may still be affecting all of you.

The earlier your baby was born, the greater the likelihood of long-term problems and most premature babies will have a very thorough check-up by their paediatrician at one year. This check will look at how he is progressing physically and developmentally, although he is still likely to be behind his full-term peers depending on how early he was born. Follow-ups after this will be as needed, or he may be discharged.

COMMON PROBLEMS

Unfortunately your baby's premature birth does put him at increased risk of some problems as he grows. These include respiratory infections, admission to hospital, reflux, and cot death. While these risks are not insignificant, your paediatrician, GP, and health visitor will all be aware of them and be ready to respond with the appropriate advice and treatment.

If your baby has chronic lung disease as a consequence of his early arrival, he is more likely to develop asthma in the early years but as he grows and his lungs mature, this will usually improve. Many pre-term babies will have caught up with their peers by the age of four or five, but some will need extra help at school and a handful will have significant problems, such as cerebral palsy (see page 308) and learning difficulties. A few will have problems with sight (see page 311) and all children who were born very early will have regular eye checks so that these can be detected and followed up as soon as possible.

YOU AND YOUR TODDLER

The early struggles can influence your relationship with your child as you may feel guilty or anxious about his health and growth. You are therefore more likely to indulge him over sleeping, eating, and behaviour. It is essential for your sanity and his healthy development that you avoid this, as your toddler needs boundaries just as much as any other child his age. It is understandable for you to be worried about his calorie intake if he was tiny and underweight at birth, but once your GP and health visitor feel that he is ready for solids, it is important that he has a healthy diet. The only way to achieve this is to be (or pretend to be) as laid-back as

possible when he spits out his lunch. Likewise with helping your baby to sleep; if you have spent several months worrying about his breathing, it can be difficult to encourage him to sleep on his own. You may want him sleeping in your bedroom for longer than you would have if he had been full term. Again, try to avoid this and follow the same advice as for a baby who was born full term.

A baby monitor will help to alleviate your fears and if your doctor feels that there is a risk of sleep apnoea (where a baby briefly stops breathing while asleep), you can be provided with a monitor to alert you to any episodes.

It will come as no surprise that the stress of having a pre-term baby and the subsequent worry about his growth and development can put a strain on a relationship. Keep talking to each other about how you feel, and don't feel embarrassed about asking your health visitor and GP for extra help and advice if you need it.

REACHING MILESTONES You may have to wait slightly longer for your pre-term baby to take his first steps, but it will be so rewarding when it happens.

YOUR LITTLE EXPLORER

"He is inquisitive
and hungry to learn,
and will look to you
to teach him."

I'M SHY THERE WILL
BE MANY SIDES TO YOUR
TODDLER'S PERSONALITY

LET'S PLAY INTERACTIVE GAMES WILL
BECOME A FAVOURITE, BUT BE PREPARED
TO REPEAT THEM AGAIN AND AGAIN

MUMMY'S HELPER HE WILL
ENJOY PRETEND PLAY AND WANT TO
BE JUST LIKE MUMMY OR DADDY

Your amazing toddler

Most children in this age range are continually attempting to push themselves beyond their comfort zone as they develop more and more new skills. If your toddler could clamber on to the sofa yesterday, he will try to get on to a kitchen chair today, so supervision is all important.

Your toddler will probably have mastered the art of walking by now, although some may take a little longer. Once he is steady on his feet and can toddle across the room without too many mishaps, he will add new variables, such as pulling something behind him. It is normal for some toddlers to be quite bow-legged at this stage – this will right itself in time.

Although your toddler will have his fair share of bumps and bruises as he tests his limits and strives to master his body, for the most part if you have taken safety precautions, he won't attempt something that is dangerously beyond him. If he can get up on to a chair but can't get down, he will call you to help him. Research by the Infant Studies Lab in the US has shown that by the time children are crawling confidently, they develop an instinctive wariness of heights. Babies in the study were unwilling to cross a transparent table-top that gave the illusion of crawling over a "cliff". Don't rely on this, though. Your toddler's instinct for self-preservation shouldn't be mistaken for common sense, which he doesn't possess yet. Be particularly aware of new situations and settings, and dangers that are not always present, such as an open window.

Toddler talk

During these months your toddler's language skills may accelerate: many (but not all) children will be able to say two or three single words by 15 months and some have quite a collection by 17 months or so. However, don't worry if all your friends' toddlers seem to be chatting away and yours still has just a handful of made-up words – or even none at all. If your child understands when you talk to him, can follow instructions, and communicates with you through gesture and babble, he is doing fine:

MULTI-TASKING *Your toddler may take walking for granted by now, and she'll love nothing more than a pull-along toy to keep her company on her travels.*

these are key steps on the way to talking. It is worth noting, too, that first-born children who have a full-time parent at home may learn lots of individual words early as they usually get plenty of one-to-one attention and are constantly having things pointed out to them. Second or subsequent children; twins, triplets and more; or those whose parents both work, often start to use words later but may put them together in sentences very quickly once they do begin to speak. Either pattern is normal. Having said that, if your toddler has no words by 17 months

"Being able to converse is great, although I'm the only one who can understand my toddler at the moment."

HAVING A CHAT *Your toddler may prefer your phone to his toy phone now, but be careful as he is quite likely to throw it when he gets bored.*

and also doesn't appear to understand or respond when you talk to him, discuss this with your health visitor. Some children have language delay for a specific reason – for instance, because of hearing problems – while others have a generalized delay in language and communication skills that could be due to a developmental problem (see page 299). Some are simply late starters, perhaps due to being born prematurely. If you have concerns about your toddler's development, do not hesitate to get him checked by your health visitor or GP. This way, if there are signs of a problem, it can be treated as early as possible.

Your toddler will most likely mispronounce words at this age. Letters such as "s" and "r" are particularly difficult to pronounce due to difficulty in coordinating the action of the lips and, particularly, the tongue. You don't need to coax him to pronounce the word correctly, as he will do that when he is ready. You can help him learn, though, by giving the proper pronunciation in your reply. So if he talks about his "doo", you can say, "Yes, those are your shoes." You can help him develop both his understanding and vocabulary if you expand on what he says to you when you are having a conversation. If he sees a dog and says "'oof, 'oof", you could answer, "Yes, it's a dog and look, he's chasing the ball."

Aim for toddler-level clarity as much as you can. If you ask him if he is too hot, he may look at you blankly (if he is not already grizzling because he is uncomfortable), but try asking him, "Shall we take your coat off?" and he may understand and reply. It is also easier for your toddler, both emotionally and cognitively, to cope with positive instructions, rather than negative admonishments, so saying, "Please would you put your cup on the table" is more likely to get the result you want than saying, "Please don't throw your cup on the floor."

Fun times

Not only does your toddler have boundless energy, he also has lots of love and affection to give and will frequently lavish this on you. Despite the frustrations of this age, toddlers are delightful company for much of the time, and many have a great sense of humour – except when things aren't going their way of course (we are all a bit similar in this respect).

Your toddler is beginning to be able to see what pleases you and what makes you cross, and while any attention from you will do, your happy, positive response is what he thrives on. If he hugs you and you hug him back and tell him you love him, he will probably do it again. Likewise, he will be delighted when you laugh at his antics, although beware of laughing too much when he does something you don't want repeated. In psychology there is an expression called "double-binding". This is when you say one thing, but your facial expression or body language gives a different message. This can be confusing for toddlers.

Sometimes, all the fun can get a bit much, especially when you are tired. A positive approach works well in these situations. So rather than telling him off for being too boisterous, lead him into a quiet activity, such as looking at a book. It takes a little extra effort, but pays dividends in the end. By being proactive in engaging your toddler in this way, you will be giving him the positive attention that he loves, and avoiding much of the tricky behaviour that happens when he feels ignored. It also prevents you getting into a cycle of constantly saying "No", which is easy to do and which can result in him learning to get your attention by making you cross.

THE ENTERTAINER
He will thrive on your attention and repeat behaviour that gets a response. If he does something naughty that is funny, try not to respond, even though it can be difficult to stifle the laughs.

Girls and boys

Do boys and girls behave naturally in a certain way, or do upbringing and environment have an influence? The answer is probably a bit of both, although research has found that there are some differences in how babies and toddlers of different sexes develop.

RECOGNIZING GENDER

We have all grown up in a culture where gender roles are clearly defined, even if we choose to ignore them, and because gender is a strong element of identity it is important for toddlers to be aware of their sex.

Although parents tend to refer to their child's gender frequently – "Good boy", "He's a sleepy boy", etc – the most a child is likely to understand at 15 or 16 months is that this is a word that refers to him. Your baby boy doesn't yet understand that he is a boy and that the toddler next door is a girl. Although he will probably become aware of his own gender and that of his friends over the next few months, it may be a few years before his strong gender identity leads him to reject certain toys, clothes, colours, or kinds of play as "not for boys".

NATURE OR NURTURE?

Lots of parents try to avoid negative stereotyping, such as "big boys don't cry", "girls can't throw", "boys are not nurturing", or "girls are not strong". It is difficult, though, to determine the proportion of nature to nurture as we can give very subtle reinforcements to gender differences without realizing. For example, a boy who becomes aggressive during rough-and-tumble play may be treated very differently from a girl who does the same.

During the second year, boys and girls are generally indifferent to social conventions about gender-specific clothes and both sexes may enjoy dressing up in any "grown-up" clothes, so don't be concerned if your little boy wants to wear dresses. Parents are often inclined to speak more softly to their daughters and play more boisterously with their sons. Even when you intend to avoid treating your child in a gender-specific way, you may find you balk at dressing your baby boy in pink, although most people don't have a problem clothing girls in blue.

GENDER DIFFERENCES

Broad generalizations that can be made about gender differences include –
Physical development: boys are heavier than girls at birth, and tend to grow faster, although conversely they are more likely to be miscarried, more vulnerable while in the womb, have a higher incidence of congenital problems at birth, and are at greater risk of cot death.

Boys are often more interested in learning to build towers, like construction toys, and will play with anything that has wheels, whereas girls may be more likely to engage in pretend play with teddies and dolls at an earlier age. But how much of this is due to parental expectations and how much is inbuilt remains uncertain.

"My little girl loved nothing more than dressing up in her lacy dress and angel wings at home, but when we went to our local toddler group she made a beeline for the 'boys' toys'. So we decided to put cars and a train set on her Christmas list."

Social skills: girls seem to develop social skills faster than boys and are generally aware of other people's feelings at an earlier age. Whether this is because that is what is expected of them or whether their brain development is responsible for the difference is open to debate, but it seems as though there may be a physiological element.

Recent research shows that the more testosterone there is in the amniotic fluid surrounding the fetus (whether it's a boy or a girl), the more "male" the social skills will be.

Boys are also more likely than girls to be diagnosed with developmental disorders that impact on social skills, such as autistic spectrum problems, attention deficit disorder (ADD) or attention deficit hyperactivity disorder (ADHD) (see page 301).

Language: a baby girl may start chatting earlier than a boy of the same age, and this could be linked to her greater social and interaction skills. It could also be because girls are more likely to be engaged in "conversation" by adults from a very early age, while people naturally engage boys in more physical, boisterous play.

CHOOSING TOYS *All toddlers like pretend play, and many little boys enjoy playing with prams, pushchairs, teddies, and dolls.*

Play: even if you buy dolls for your son and toy cars for your daughter, preferences for gender-specific toys among older children are so common as to be almost universal in our culture. You can encourage an interest in a range of toys, though, as your toddler will enjoy any sort of play with you.

Both sexes will get lots of pleasure from books and if looking at books with you is a normal part of their routine, there is a good chance they will grow up with a love of reading. As boys frequently find it harder to sit still with a book or toy as they get older, this is a good time to get yours hooked.

An emotional rollercoaster

One minute he will be a compliant, snuggly baby and the next he will be howling his outrage to the neighbourhood when you try to put him in his buggy. This can be hard to deal with but don't worry – you haven't produced a superbrat. He just needs a little more time to manage his emotions.

EVER CHANGING MOODS

Your toddler is more likely to get upset and frustrated if he is over-tired. Try to pre-empt this by calming him down with some quiet time.

This stage of development is just as frustrating for your toddler as it is for you. He has clear likes and dislikes, and knows what he wants but often he can't express this clearly and, even more often, what he wants is not allowed. For example, he may love cars with a passion, but no amount of screaming will induce you to let him play on the road. He doesn't yet understand this, however, so will keep trying until he realizes that it is never going to be permissible.

While it is very important to set firm boundaries for your toddler, as he will feel insecure if your limits are unclear, it is also important to be flexible about the little things sometimes. For example, if your toddler is unwell or tired and he wants to watch the TV for longer than usual, it won't matter if you let him on this occasion. Equally, if Granny has baked a fabulous chocolate cake, it won't hurt him to have some even if you don't usually give him cakes and biscuits.

It will also help your toddler to feel more in control if he is able to make some choices, although at this age it is important that these are simple, such as whether he wants toast or cereal for breakfast, or whether to wear the blue T-shirt or the red one.

Your toddler's personality

Most toddlers have big personalities and your child may frequently show many different facets of his character. His moods can be mercurial, to say the least, but try not to label him as "shy", "loud", or "stroppy", for instance. Labels can stick and affect the way your child sees himself (and even behaves) as he grows up.

Often in the space of one day, toddlers can be all of the following –

■ **Shy:** many toddlers are still very attached to their main carer and your child may continue to be wary of strangers. Don't force him to speak to strangers in shops, or even to unfamiliar relatives, but praise him when he does manage to say "hello" to them.

■ **Loving:** your toddler loves you and may lavish you with affection, but if he doesn't, don't force hugs and kisses on him. Just follow his lead and respond when he wants it so that he feels loved and cherished.

■ **Attention-seeking:** he craves your attention and while he would far rather have your positive attention, for instance playing, chatting, and cuddling, if he doesn't get this, he will go out of his way to get any attention at all, even if he has to make you cross to get a response.

Handling your toddler's fears

Along with your toddler's growing understanding may come seemingly irrational fears. These may be of the dark, of spiders, of his bath, or even of your perfectly harmless next-door-neighbour. This development is very common and may well be based on your own irrational fears. Try to be sympathetic while, if possible, showing that you are not afraid of whatever is frightening him.

If he is terrified of the bath, don't force him – give him a wash instead.

Similarly, if he is afraid of the dark, use a night-light in his bedroom; if he is afraid of your neighbour, let him see you speak politely to her, but don't try to make him be sociable.

This is not about giving in to a phobia or adding to it. It is important to remember that your toddler can't rationalize his emotions, but with your support he will grow in confidence and maturity and these normal and common childhood fears will fade away naturally.

■ **Playful:** toddlers learn about their world through play and, like all baby mammals, they love romping around. As your toddler's social skills develop, he will enjoy being silly to make you laugh – watch for the playful gleam in his eye as he does something he knows you don't want him to do.

■ **Oppositional:** all toddlers engage in battles of will at some stage, but some are more stroppy and stubborn than others, answering "No" automatically to any suggestion and screaming whenever they are frustrated. When dealing with this behaviour, try to stay calm and use distraction techniques. Avoid being drawn into battles and don't start screaming and shouting yourself. He will grow out of it eventually.

■ **Busy:** it is in your toddler's nature to be inquisitive and he will be constantly on the go and fiddling with whatever he can get his hands on. Sometimes this gets him into hot water as his urge to explore is stronger than his desire to do what you tell him, so give him lots of safe things to explore to satisfy his inquisitive nature.

■ **Loud:** toddlers are noisy, whether they are shouting, singing, or throwing or banging things. You can join in with this sometimes by singing together or banging a saucepan alongside him, but your child will also benefit from some quiet, calm time, too.

■ **Babyish:** your child is still a baby in many ways and will frequently revert to babyish behaviour, for example, wanting an occasional bottle, especially if he is unwell or unsettled. Don't panic that he is regressing – this is entirely normal behaviour, so let him be a baby when he needs to be.

■ **Reactionary:** toddlers generally like things to stay the same, which may actually help you keep life under control. The downside is that he may eat only cereal for three weeks in a row and want to wear the same T-shirt day after day after day.

■ **Exhausting:** spending a whole day alone with your toddler is likely to make you long for the moment your partner comes home and for a well-deserved glass of wine.

"My 16-month-old is a joy to be with – we have our difficult days when there are many tears, but these are easily outweighed by the fun and rewarding times."

YOUR INDIVIDUAL CHILD *She may still be tiny, but your toddler is a person in her own right and there will be many facets to her personality – shy, cheeky, loving, serious, playful, and inquisitive. Even without language she'll express much of what she's thinking in her gestures and expressions. One thing is certain – life with your toddler will never be dull.*

Play and your toddler

Although play has always been crucial to your child's development, during these months he will really begin to learn about his world through toys and imaginative games. He is likely to concentrate for longer periods, but will still rely on you and other adults or older children to be his playmates.

IMAGINATIVE PLAY *Toys such as train sets are stimulating. He will learn more from them if you play with him and help him discover how the different elements work.*

Pretend play

If your child has begun to enjoy pretend play, you can encourage this by helping him to feed teddy, bath dolly, and "prepare supper". He needs props at this age, though, and won't yet be able to drink from an imaginary cup or eat from an imaginary plate. Just as you did when he was a baby, let him take the lead or initiate these games if he wants to. So if he pretends to drink out of a cup, you can join in and have "tea" with him.

If he seems a bit nonplussed by these toys, you can play with them and see if he will join in. If he is not interested, don't try to force it. At 16–18 months, some toddlers are too young for symbolic or pretend play, but if your child has no interest by the end of his second year, talk to your health visitor who can help assess whether this is simply a lack of interest or whether it indicates a possible problem (see page 299).

Small worlds

By this age, your toddler can begin to explore small toys, such as animals, people, houses, trains, and cars (although make sure they are safe for under-threes). Some of these toys can be expensive – if you haven't done so already, join a toy library so that your toddler can try them out.

Small toys are good for your toddler's development in several different ways: they will help develop his hand-eye co-ordination and dexterity, encourage him to use his imagination, and give him early practice in collaborative play with you. He won't be ready to play these games with another toddler yet, but older siblings, cousins, and friends can be pressed into service as alternative playmates when you are too busy to join in. You can help his understanding and extend his vocabulary by pointing out the names of different objects and their colours, shapes, and sizes. For example, show him the cow and talk about what noise it makes, put the big cup next to the little cup, and group all the red bricks together. He will understand more than you realize as his cognitive skills will be well ahead of his language skills. At this age, your toddler may use one word to describe entire groups of things. For example, every large animal that he sees might be a "horse", even if it is a cow, and every wheeled vehicle may be a "car". This is a normal step in the learning process – the world is a complex place and it will take time for him to make sense of it, but playing all kinds of sorting games will help.

Getting out and about

Once your child is walking with a reasonable degree of competence, he will love a wide-open space where he can toddle without encountering any obstacles. He will also enjoy playing alongside other children. Some parks run toddler groups, or "one o'clock clubs", with indoor and outdoor play facilities, on a drop-in basis. These are great opportunities for your toddler to venture away from your side and be with other children.

Daddy's home

Daddy's arrival home from work is a major event for your toddler. As always with moments of great expectation coupled with end-of-day fatigue, it can easily go wrong.

Your toddler, excited at your return, will neither understand nor care that Daddy is exhausted. It is a really wonderful experience to have someone so completely enthused to see you, but if you are feeling frayed at the edges it can seem like an overwhelming demand on your energy when you were looking forward to slumping with a beer and the paper. It's easy to get caught in a negative cycle, which can make coming home stressful even when you've had a good day. However, a few minutes of happy greetings and proactively engaging your toddler in his favourite game really is worth the effort. It is far more likely to result in the few minutes' peace you'd hoped for, and prevents you getting into a habit of shouting at him to calm down.

Also, spare a thought for your partner if she's been at home all day. This is not all coffee, croissants, and chat – caring for a toddler is a full-time job and she'll be looking forward to adult conversation and a hand with the childcare and chores. Mutual respect for each other's roles and sharing the load is the key to keeping your family balanced – and this of course also applies to Mummy's homecoming if Daddy is the child's main carer.

FATHER'S VIEW

Everyday care

Your toddler is likely to be eating a wider range of foods by now, but if he isn't, try not to worry. A relaxed approach is more likely to get results. If you and your partner have rather erratic lives, be aware that your toddler will benefit from some semblance of a routine.

If you continue to offer your toddler healthy meals and snacks and he turns up his nose at them, don't despair. Children of this age are particularly resistant to change and your toddler will be even more adept at using food to manipulate you if you let him. Keep giving him a range of foods at each meal that includes both familiar and unfamiliar items. That way he will always have something he is happy to eat, but has the option to try the new food. If he doesn't try it, don't make any comment, but if he does – even if he just puts it in his mouth and takes it out again – praise him for being adventurous. It is still important to avoid the temptation to coax him to eat, as he will seize the opportunity to do battle with you if you show him that you are concerned about his eating. He can now eat everything you eat so try to include him in your meals when possible.

Many toddlers love simple meals such as pasta and tomato sauce with vegetables, and low-salt beans on toast (this is surprisingly healthy, and the beans just about count as a vegetable portion), followed by slices of fruit and milk or water to drink. Don't be surprised, though, if he sometimes has a change of heart – just when you think you have found a range of healthy foods that he will eat, however limited, he may decide he is going to refuse to eat something that he has always loved.

Encourage him to feed himself by cutting food into small pieces and not worrying about whether he uses his fingers or a spoon. Many toddlers will try new foods, such as soups or hummus, if given some bread or celery to dip in.

REFUSING FOOD *Your wilful toddler will definitely let you know if he doesn't like what's on the menu, but don't get drawn into mealtime battles.*

Snacks and mealtimes

Your toddler's tummy still needs refilling more frequently than yours, so snacks are important and he might want to "graze", rather than have three larger meals a day. If you are struggling to get him to eat meals with the rest of the family, time three of his snacks to coincide with when you would like him to eat breakfast, lunch, and supper. This way, he will be hungry enough to sit in his highchair to eat something and still be joining in with the family meal.

Gradually, you can decrease the amount your toddler has for his snacks, and this should mean he will be hungrier at mealtimes. Try giving him slices of fruit with a high water content, such as apples or melon, rather than more filling carbohydrate or dairy foods. Watch out for how much your child is having to drink between meals, too – if he has a couple of beakers of milk during the morning, he will be unlikely to want much lunch.

HEALTHY EATING *Rice cakes are a healthy snack for your toddler, but if she doesn't like them try giving her a low-sugar dry cereal instead.*

Additives

When you read food packaging there is often an alarmingly long list of additives and this frequently takes the form of "E" numbers. These lists can be deceptive, though, as some of them refer to innocuous or natural ingredients that are harmless. For example, E101 is vitamin B2 and E300 is vitamin C, both essential dietary components. Others, though, have been linked to health and behavioural problems in toddlers including E102, which is a food colouring called tartrazine that has been associated with hyperactivity (see page 301) in susceptible children. The sweetener aspartame, also known as E951, has been rarely associated with headaches and giddiness, as has monosodium glutamate (MSG), a flavour enhancer, which has also been linked to asthma and allergies. Check the label on the product and, if in doubt, don't buy it. The easiest way to avoid additives is to buy fresh ingredients and prepare food from scratch. This doesn't have to be complicated and will be healthier for your child than prepared food.

Salt intake

We all tend to eat far more salt than we need and the Food Standards Agency recommends that toddlers have no more than 2g of salt per day. Even if you don't add salt to your child's food, most processed foods, including bread and cereals, contain at least some salt so it is important to check the label to see how much has been added.

Convenience foods are usually very high in salt unless the packaging states otherwise. It is okay for your toddler to eat them occasionally but it is better to opt for child-friendly brands that don't have added salt, sugar, and artificial sweeteners. Among the worst foods with a high salt content are crisps, which can contain up to 0.68 grams of salt per pack – one-third of your toddler's daily allowance.

"I stopped adding salt to food once my toddler shared our meals. We all got used to it surprisingly quickly."

Do routines matter to toddlers?

Many toddlers feel more secure when their daily life is familiar and expected. If, for example, you have established a bedtime routine for your toddler, he may be affronted if you skip a stage by cutting short his story and cuddle time. The very sameness that bores you will help your toddler to wind down and go happily (usually) to bed. Even toddlers whose parents have a nomadic lifestyle generally thrive best where there is some pattern to their life. That said, there is no right or wrong way to do this, and how you organize your days with your toddler will depend on what suits you and him best. If having a routine goes against the grain for you, there are some positive sides that are worth considering –

■ **More sleep:** you are more likely to get an uninterrupted night's sleep if your toddler is used to being put to bed at a regular time, and you will also have more time to yourself in the evenings.

■ **A better eater:** your toddler may become a good eater if his body clock is used to regular meals and snacks.

■ **Good behaviour:** over-stimulation, over-tiredness, and a lack of routine can make even the sunniest child hard to live with. A calm rhythm to the day can improve matters enormously.

Common concerns

▶ **My child seems to have a sweet tooth, but is it wrong to add sugar to his food?**

Your toddler doesn't need added sugar. There are sugars in fruit and vegetables, and some other foods, such as milk, are naturally sweet. If you can keep refined sugar (such as table sugar) out of his diet at this age, you'll be setting the precedent for good habits that will help him develop a taste for healthy food. Yoghurt and fromage frais can be sweetened with fruit purées and desserts can be made with apple juice as an alternative to refined sugars. It is safe for him to have honey from 12 months, but this is just as bad for his teeth as sugar. It's easy to get caught out by cereals, some of which contain a massive 38 per cent sugar.

▶ **Our 17-month-old seems to get a second wind just before I put her in her cot. How can we calm her down in the evening?**

Consider how the timing of your toddler's bedtime fits in with the rest of your day. If you try to put her to bed soon after one or both of you arrive home from work you may end up with a disastrous combination of her excitement at your return and your guilt at putting her to bed shortly afterwards. So try to set a bedtime that is realistic and that gives your toddler some time with both of you before the end of her day.

Ensure you're not trying to put her to bed too early – if she's not tired enough, she's unlikely to settle. Conversely, if she is over-tired, she may find it hard to get to sleep, and many toddlers become manic and out of control once they go past the point of being able to wind down. If this is the case, a longer daytime nap or an earlier bedtime may help.

Avoid boisterous games just before bedtime as she may find it difficult to calm down afterwards. It may help to be more specific about her bedtime routine, even to the point of reading her the same story every night, so that she gets the message that it's now time to sleep. The aim is to help her wind down with a regular sequence of events – bath, story, song, sleep. The techniques for helping toddlers to go to sleep on their own are the same as those for babies. The difference with your toddler is that she'll be more practised at engaging you in chat or play with charming behaviour! Stand firm: return if she needs you or is upset, but become rather boring once she's in her cot. Once you've tucked her in and kissed her goodnight, the message is that you're there if she needs you but that after bedtime you're very dull and aren't going to be any fun until tomorrow.

▶ **My parents are a great help in looking after my toddler, but they let him snack on chocolate and biscuits. Should I stop them?**

I think this is one issue where it's important to be tactful, but firm. If you don't want your baby to have chocolate and biscuits, discuss this with your parents. They may enjoy indulging their grandson with these treats, but you can suggest other snack foods he will also enjoy, such as toast fingers or breadsticks with hummus. Explain that you're trying to get him used to eating healthy food so that he has good eating habits from the start, which will benefit his health now and as he grows up.

Getting through difficult times

Not all new families come through their child's babyhood intact. This is often due to a breakdown in communication or hard-to-reconcile differences about parenting and family life. Always try to keep the lines of communication open and, if necessary, seek professional help.

For some parents, a baby may have been an unwanted addition to the relationship. For most, however, if the partnership itself is strong, once the initial shock of having a baby is over, the relationship grows – nature has a wonderful way of ensuring that babies melt even the most resistant hearts. In some families, one partner may have wanted a baby more than the other and even if both partners very much wanted to become parents, the reality of a baby can become the cause of a rift.

If you are having difficulties resolving conflicts in your relationship as parents, it may help to consider the following –

■ **Relationships need nurturing:** if your new baby seems to be causing a rift between you due to jealousy or different expectations of where your lives should be right now, then it is very important to find the time to talk things through. Don't neglect your relationship as a couple; you need to make space to do things together like you used to. Life won't ever be quite the way it was, but with planning you should be able to get out regularly and have some baby-free time together. If you are finding it hard to communicate or your discussions always seem to end in conflict, consider

"We split up because we couldn't agree on how to bring up our one-year-old daughter. It all started with little disagreements but because we didn't discuss them, things just got worse and worse."

getting professional help. A counsellor can play a vital role in finding middle ground and helping you listen to each other's needs and ideas rather than the conversation degenerating into arguments and blaming.

■ **Accept that your natural parenting styles may be different:** the way you raise your children generally reflects your own upbringing. You will probably want to emulate some aspects of how your parents brought you up, although there will be other aspects that you feel were not ideal and that you want to avoid (this means that you will probably have the occasional disagreement with your baby's grandparents, too).

If your partner had a different upbringing to yours, he or she may have radically different ideas about parenting, especially when it comes to disciplining your child. If you are against any form of physical punishment and your partner believes that "a short, sharp smack never hurt me and certainly made me behave", you are heading for trouble unless you can find a way to resolve your differences. Like it or not, you will find yourself unwittingly quoting your parents – particularly in times of stress – and emulating some of their most annoying habits, even when they seem irrational.

■ **Be aware of how disagreements affect your child:** we all know that small disagreements can quickly become heated arguments when we are tired and stressed. While some differences of opinion are inevitable and won't traumatize your baby, if he witnesses these frequently and is living in an atmosphere of screaming rows or brooding, resentful silences, this won't be good for him.

If you can, try to talk any problems through before they get out of hand – long-standing resentments can be extremely corrosive to your relationship. It is best to wait until the heat of the moment has passed and then discuss the problem away from your child. Try not to apportion blame but rather understand the seeds of the problem and therefore how you might deal with it, and work on finding a solution together.

TEAMWORK *Raising a family is easier if you are on the same side. Agree what is important from the outset and always present a united front.*

When conflict goes too far

If you feel that your partner's behaviour is physically or emotionally abusive towards your baby, it is important that you protect and support your child. As a parent, you have a duty to do this, so do not hesitate to talk to your GP, health visitor, or a social worker. Do not let feelings of guilt and shame prevent you from doing this.

If your partner is abusive towards you in any way, you should seek help, both for your own sake and for your baby's. In this instance, it may be appropriate to say that domestic violence is a factor. This term covers psychological, economic, and emotional abuse as well as the more obvious physical. Domestic violence is a silent epidemic, with research showing that it can affect up to one in four women during their lifetimes. It is more common after the birth of a child, and while in the majority of cases it happens to women, men can also be victims.

Studies show that in families where domestic violence occurs, up to half of the children may have been hit, but these environments are poor for a child even if they aren't being directly abused. Seeing and hearing their parents arguing, and in many instances witnessing violence, is damaging. Don't suffer in silence. It is best to seek help early when perhaps professional support may bring resolution rather than to allow things to drift and become worse.

■ **Present a united front if possible:** consistency over boundaries is very important for children and it will make your toddler feel secure if you at least appear to agree on major issues. As he grows, your child will test your boundaries. This is part of growing up but be warned – just as your baby could tune into your emotions from his earliest days, your toddler will learn to use any rifts between the two of you for his own ends. If, for example, you ban all sweets but Daddy allows them if he is nagged for long enough, your toddler will soon work out who to go to when he wants chocolate. This may seem innocuous enough, but it can be extremely undermining for the parent who has set the boundary in the first place.

Issues like this can become common areas of conflict between both you and your toddler, and you and your partner. If you are to find a way to work together as parents, it is important that you don't exclude your partner when you make decisions about key parenting issues such as childcare, bedtimes, food, behaviour, and discipline.

■ **Parenting classes:** ideally, all new parents should attend these enlightening classes, whether or not they are experiencing difficulties with their child. The classes prepare parents for each step, help them

Common concerns

QUESTION&ANSWER

▶ **My friend finds being a mum very stressful and often shouts at and smacks her toddler when he gets on her nerves. What advice can I offer her?**
None, if you want to stay friends. If your friend is finding life very stressful you could offer to look after her little boy for an hour or so to give her a break, or ensure that you're there for her if she wants to talk. Maybe you could babysit one evening so that she can go out. All toddlers push their parents to the limit at times, and it's easy to become completely exasperated. Although it's best not to offer unsolicited parenting advice to your friends (or anyone else) unless you're asked, the exception is if you see a parent do something that is clearly abusive towards a child, in which case it's your duty to intervene. If you're worried that a child may be at risk, you can phone social services or the NSPCC (see page 312) anonymously and discuss your concerns.

▶ **We have a 16-month-old and I would love to have another baby, but my partner is adamant that one is enough. I'm tempted to flush my contraceptive pills down the loo, but know it would be wrong. How can we resolve this?**
You're right to resist the temptation to deceive your partner as that's not a good basis on which to bring a new baby into your family, and he would rightly be devastated if he found out. It's important to talk things through together and find out why he feels so strongly about this. He may have found becoming a parent a huge upheaval and could be afraid that a second child would cause even more havoc to your relationship. For many men, financial considerations also cause a great deal of pressure, especially if he has become the sole breadwinner. If this is the case, it may be that you could reach a compromise and return to work part time.

As your little girl gets older and parenting is not quite such hard work, your partner may be willing to reconsider. Meanwhile, keep the lines of communication open. And remember, many couples are making the decision to have just one child. Be reassured that there will be opportunities for your child to meet other children, so she won't lose out as much as you think.

understand their child's perspective, and help give them strategies to deal with challenging situations. Contact Parentline (see page 312) for more information on classes.

■ **Always try to keep your sense of humour:** if you can lighten up and laugh when things don't quite go to plan, you can save yourselves considerable angst. I remember saying to my youngest child, "I love you so much," whereupon he replied, "And I love Daddy!" It would have been easy to find this hurtful, but instead of feeling miffed, I had a good laugh about it – and it was good to hear how attached he was to Peter.

YOUR BUSY TODDLER

GROWING INDEPENDENCE
YOUR TODDLER WILL BE MORE DETERMINED TO DO THINGS FOR HIMSELF AND BEGIN TO BECOME ATTACHED TO HIS POSSESSIONS

LET ME HELP HE LEARNS BY DOING AND WILL BE KEEN TO GET INVOLVED IN EVERYDAY TASKS

PHYSICAL SKILLS SHE WILL HAVE PROGRESSED FROM WALKING TO TACKLING STAIRS, AND MAY EVEN BEGIN TO RUN

"Her concentration levels will improve, and she is likely to become preoccupied with certain toys."

Your little communicator

Your toddler is making physical, mental, and emotional leaps forward. As well as being fascinated by her surroundings and what people are doing, she will make the most of her growing communication skills – even if she doesn't talk much yet – to build on her relationships and learn to interact.

Physical skills

Virtually all children can walk by 18 months, and the most proficient may start to experiment with going backwards. Once she is walking confidently, she will soon progress to running – although this will be a bit ungainly at first. Some toddlers attempt to kick a ball by 20 months. When your toddler starts to run, you will notice that she doesn't have very refined brakes so keep her away from obstacles and hidden steps, and low walls and water in the garden. She may be able to get up and down the stairs (coming down backwards or on her bottom) with minimal assistance.

She will be increasingly dextrous as well as mobile and, while at 18 months she will be able to take off easy clothing such as socks, by 20 months she may be able to undress herself with your help.

Language and understanding

When they are around 18–19 months old, some toddlers have a plethora of single words at their disposal and some may be putting two or more words together to make phrases by 20 months. These phrases may be something your child has heard you say, such as "all gone", or they may be entirely of her own making, such as "shoes on", "Daddy car", or "yotta (lots of) yotta bird" (from a 20-month-old). If she has many single words, she may have a big language boost during these months, as research has shown that once a toddler's word count reaches around 50, her language tends to accelerate rapidly, enabling her to speedily acquire 200 or more words.

However, if your 20-month-old is still pointing at the cat and saying "ah-ba", she is in good company, as some children – including very bright ones – don't come up with any "proper" words during this year. Speak to

LITTLE DRIBBLER *Once he is steady on his feet, he will develop new skills such as running and playing with a ball. Some toddlers begin to kick and throw at this age.*

"At 18 months, my toddler hadn't taken a solo step. Then one day she let go of the sofa and virtually ran across the room. I've learned to take each stage as it comes now and be content for her to do things in her own time."

your health visitor if you are worried and want to rule out a developmental or other problem, such as hearing difficulties. However, you probably don't need to worry: stories abound concerning toddlers who don't speak at all, then come out with a complex sentence at the age of three. Albert Einstein was reputed to have held off talking until his fourth year.

At 18 months your toddler may still use one word for everything in a group – for instance, she might think of all furry creatures as "cats". A few months later, though, she may know better and understand the joke if you point to a sheep and say "miaow". However well your toddler is able to communicate, by the time she is around 18 months old she may deliberately choose to ignore you at times, which is a skill that most children perfect over the years.

During these months, your toddler's memory will be improving. For example, she may begin to look in the cupboard for her shoes, search for the cat (who will be sensibly hiding as far under the bed as he can get), or rummage in your shopping bag for the biscuits she knows you bought at the supermarket. While it is still possible to distract her, it is not as easy as it was a couple of months ago because out of sight no longer means out of mind. The ability to remember is an important step forward in your toddler's learning and one that should be celebrated, although it may not always seem that way when she persists in trying to get the biscuits you don't want her to have and, instead of being diverted by an interesting game, hits the deck screaming in fury.

Music and development

If your child enjoys music, you may see her start to dance by jigging on the spot from about 18 months and, by 20 months, she might even be able to step in time or run round and round when she hears her favourite tunes. She will enjoy making her own music with toy instruments or simply by banging a spoon against a saucepan. Music helps to boost your toddler's intellectual development, too – we humans seem to be programmed to respond to tunes, rhyme, and rhythm, and research has indicated that singing or playing music to your toddler will help develop her memory.

Music also has a more immediate, practical use, as you may find that your toddler is more likely to co-operate when you sing songs to get her through nappy changes, washing, and dressing. Try making the song appropriate – "This is the way we put on our socks/brush our teeth/wash our face" to the tune of her favourite song – and encourage her to join in with you. Singing a song helps to reinforce the routines that toddlers find comforting and may help to avoid her becoming upset and stroppy over everyday necessities.

Seeking attention

Your toddler's desire for your attention will feel all-consuming at times, and she will do whatever is needed to get it – throwing things, shouting, or pulling the dog's tail. Try to understand her motivation, while explaining why she mustn't behave in this way. However, if she always misbehaves when you are on the phone, for example, try to see things from her point of view. She can see you and hear you but can't get your attention and she doesn't understand that you are talking to another person. Aim to save long phone calls for when she is in bed.

If you are writing a shopping list, your toddler might pick up a crayon to "make a list" too. If she does this on a piece of scrap paper, you are likely to be amused and praise her, but if she does it on an important letter, you will probably be cross. Again, try to understand what is behind her actions – she was trying to please you and be like you, and she doesn't know about important letters yet. Next time, make sure she has her own piece of paper to scribble on.

MUSIC MAKER *He will appreciate simple musical instruments – a guitar to strum, a drum to bang, or maracas or a tambourine to shake – the noisier the better.*

EMOTIONAL CARE

At this age, your toddler sees the world as revolving entirely around him, and he needs your love and approval to feel secure.

I want to be like you

Whenever possible, let your toddler join in with what you are doing: for example, give her a small trowel so that she can dig alongside you in the garden; some toys to slosh around in a bowl of water when you are washing up; and something safe to stir or some pans to play with when you are cooking. Your toddler may also enjoy toy versions of household items and appliances, such as a pretend toolkit, an iron and ironing board, a tea-set, or a vacuum cleaner.

It is never too early to encourage your child to have a go at genuine household chores, and she will probably enjoy it, especially as it enables her to imitate you. Give her a sponge and let her help you clean the car or wash the kitchen floor; see if she can pick out all the socks from the pile of clean washing (later on, she will be able to match them into pairs, which can be very helpful); and a cloth so she can join in with the dusting.

You will also notice that wherever you go, she will come too. Be prepared for no privacy in the loo for the next year or more, but think positive – if she decides to copy you, it may make potty training a lot easier.

Your toddler's self-esteem

Try not to undermine your toddler's self-esteem. If she does something naughty, aim to criticize the action rather than the child, so rather than saying, "You're a very naughty girl to empty the rubbish all over the floor," try, "That was a naughty thing to do – let's see if you can help Mummy clear it up". If she does help you, praise her. It is important to avoid saying anything to your toddler that could deeply upset her, such as "I hate you," or "You're stupid". If you find yourself shouting at or slapping your toddler in frustration, take a deep breath and a step back. If you say or do something you regret, explain that you didn't mean it and that you are sorry, and give her a cuddle. So often when children are driving you mad by whingeing and being difficult, all they really want is a big hug from you. With our youngest child, in particular, all sorts of situations were and still are resolvable in this way.

"Small boys are like puppies – they need lots and lots of love and a good run every day!"

Common concerns

▶ **My 20-month-old never stops running around, and won't listen to me or concentrate on anything for more than a few minutes. Could he be hyperactive?**

Like all toddlers yours seems to have boundless energy, but this doesn't mean he is hyperactive. It certainly can be exhausting trying to cope with a lively, defiant toddler, whether or not he has a diagnosable condition, but there are several things you can do. To begin with, keep life as calm as possible and stick to a routine. This will help your son feel secure and make it easier for him to concentrate. When he does listen to you, praise him – and when he doesn't, try to engage his attention. Give him plenty to do as this can help reduce aimless running around.

Take him out for a daily run-around in the park – toddlers have lots of energy that pushes them out of control if it's not burned off. Some parents swear that their toddlers become hyperactive after eating sugary foods. While it's good to avoid lots of sugar for various reasons, there is no scientific evidence that it is responsible for

hyperactivity. Usually lots of sugar is associated with treats and children's parties when children are bound to be excited anyway.

It is unusual to diagnose hyperactivity, known as attention deficit hyperactivity disorder, or ADHD (see page 301), in a very young child. If, however, your toddler sleeps very little, is prone to tantrums and seems to be more defiant and/or restless than other children his age, speak to your GP or health visitor about your concerns. You can also contact the Hyperactive Children's Support Group (see page 312).

▶ **My 18-month-old seems reluctant to mix even with people she knows well, and if a stranger approaches her she freezes and hides her face. How can I help her overcome this shyness?**

We all have different personalities and toddlers are no exception. Some people are naturally more shy or introverted than others, and your little girl may still be struggling with separation anxiety (see page 129). Rather than trying to force her to socialize, try to create situations

that aren't too overwhelming for her. For example, have a toddler she knows round for tea with her mum, or spend time with close family members in a familiar setting. Give her time and she may gradually come out of her shell.

▶ **My little boy is very sociable, but he doesn't say any understandable words. He has had several ear infections and I'm not sure he can hear me properly. What should I do?**

It's usual for toddlers to have spoken their first words by 18 months or so, but the range of normal development is very broad and he may simply not be ready yet.

However, as your little boy has had recurrent ear infections, it's important that he has a hearing test. Toddlers who are prone to ear infections can develop glue ear (see page 267), which affects their hearing. This condition is treatable, so it is important to take him to your doctor. If his hearing is fine, your GP or health visitor can assess his development with you and arrange for him to have further tests if necessary.

QUESTION&ANSWER

YOUR ACTIVE TODDLER

Ball pools are a safe environment for your toddler to play in. Physical activities are essential to help him let off steam.

Fun and games

You will probably be able to get your toddler to focus on activities for short periods, although her concentration span is still likely to be short. Encourage her to play on her own some of the time because that way she will learn to enjoy her own company and become more self-sufficient.

Your toddler will gradually become more competent at managing crayons, paint, sand, and water. She may begin to make deliberate splodges of paint on paper, scribbles with crayons and chalk, and be able to fill a bucket with damp sand, although you will still have to help her turn it over, tap it, and lift it to reveal her sandcastle.

If your child enjoys painting, try making butterfly pictures with her. These are very simple and have an instant wow factor that appeals to toddlers. Fold a piece of thick paper in half and cut out a simple butterfly shape. Open it out along the fold and get your toddler to daub thick blobs of different-coloured paint over one half of the shape. Then fold it in half, press firmly, and open it up again to see a gorgeous butterfly.

Your toddler may enjoy playing with playdough. Initially she will probably just hold it, poke it, and generally experiment with its squishiness. She may try to taste it, too, so make sure that it is either a non-toxic product or make your own (see box, right). Once she has got used to the feel of the playdough she can roll it into a ball, squash it flat, make handprints, cut out shapes, or press it into moulds. While she is unlikely to even think of making anything representative for some time yet, she will enjoy watching you be creative.

"I find creative play with my toddler so rewarding. The first time I did butterfly prints with him, we unfolded the paper to reveal the butterfly and the look of wonder on his face was priceless."

Playdough recipe

125g (4oz) plain flour

60g (2oz) salt

1 tablespoon oil

2 teaspoons cream of tartar

250ml (8fl oz) water

Food colouring or non-toxic paint

Heat all the ingredients gently in a saucepan, stirring constantly until the dough becomes stiff. If it is too stiff, add more water; if it is too sticky, add more flour. Allow the dough to cool and knead it – this makes it smooth and pliable and also ensures there are no hot spots. You can keep the playdough for a few weeks in an airtight container, plastic bag, or wrapped in cling film.

Let's pretend

Pretend play is an important way for your toddler to make sense of everything that goes on around her. As her sense of self becomes more sophisticated, she will play at being other people and imagine how it is to be someone different. Using her imagination in this way also helps her language skills develop, as these games give you both plenty to talk about. At this age you may still have to initiate and join in a lot of her pretend play and she may copy you or invent her own contribution, but gradually, with help from you, her ability to play imaginatively will flourish.

To start with, she will enjoy playing at everyday situations, such as pretending to eat, drink, and sleep. Reading books, having pets, visiting a farm and going on a train will all help to fire her imagination. She may well enjoy being a cat, a cow, a train, or a plane, and will love it if you join in too, for example by copying the noises and actions. Many toddlers simply want to play at being mum or dad.

Once she is completely steady on her feet, a shopping trolley or toy buggy (with a doll or teddy to go in them) will help her to recreate

LOOK AT ME *Dressing up gives your toddler the opportunity to be both creative and independent.*

everyday situations – and if you give her an old scarf, hat, or pair of shoes she can be whoever she wants to be. Dressing up is very popular for both girls and boys. You will find plenty of props for this kind of pretend play around the house – for example, a sheet over a clothes airer can be a tent, a house, a shop, a cave, or a tunnel. A crawl tunnel that collapses for storage is a versatile toy that will last your child for years as it can graduate from being a simple tunnel to crawl through (or for you to pop out of if your toddler is a bit nervous at first) to a prop for all sorts of complicated games of make-believe right into the early school years. Hang on to some old boxes and packages that can become special "presents" to wrap and give, goods in a "shop" or even, with your help, the basis for her very first forays into junk modelling.

Sometimes games can switch from fun to scary very quickly – if you are being a big, friendly dog chasing your toddler or you are playing a tickling game, she might suddenly find it overwhelming. Be sensitive to this and stop as soon as it starts to become too much. She will learn from this that she can say "no" and expect to be listened to, which is a valuable lesson for life.

Toy people, animals, houses, and cars, and pretend food and kitchen sets are great for imaginative play. Over the coming months she will start to play out elements from real life and familiar stories. This will help to

Do toddlers need classes?

In many social circles there is fierce competition to be the perfect parent. This manifests itself in many ways, but often involves enrolling babies and toddlers in a variety of group activities from an early age in order to maximize their development. These groups are more structured than the informal drop-in baby or toddler groups that lots of mums attend for company and a change of scene, and may involve music, singing, drama, or gym. These classes often involve the parents enthusiastically joining in while their babies sleep, watch in a bemused fashion, or scream. Brave fathers who attend these groups rarely do so more than once. As your child grows these classes may progress to ballet, swimming and Suzuki violin, and before you know it she will have moved on to brownies and karate. While classes are great if they are enjoyable and benefit you and your toddler, don't fall into the trap of feeling she's missing out if she doesn't do them. What is most important is that she is ready for classes and is enjoying them.

develop her intellectual, social, communication, and language skills, and the small size of the toys will help improve her fine motor skills, too. As she begins to concentrate for longer periods, she will become absorbed in these games and, when she is ready (probably not for at least another year or so), will learn to include other children in her imaginative play.

Being her playmate

It can be hard to know how much time to spend playing with your child one to one. Symbolic play with a toddler can be mind-numbingly boring and I do recommend encouraging your toddler to play on her own for at least short periods of time. If this is your second child you will probably find that she is happy to watch her older sibling and will be far easier to occupy.

Days out

Depending on your child's personality and the kinds of things she enjoys, there are all sorts of outings that may engage her interest now. Most toddlers enjoy a visit to the zoo, and child-friendly farms, where they can see, touch, and maybe even feed, animals. Do, however, be scrupulous about handwashing to avoid tummy upsets or more serious infections.

Build on the kinds of expeditions you have already tried; now that your toddler is slightly older they can be much more varied with more opportunities for her to get involved. Paradoxically, though, expect progress to be slower as she will insist on walking some of it and doing lots of things herself. Doing things her own way, and taking the time to explore different environments and absorb different experiences fully, is a vital part of her development so follow her lead to some extent. For example, if she finds the sleeping rabbits on the farm interesting, don't rush her on to see the pigs feeding. Give yourself plenty of time, however frustrated you become, and take the time to point things out to her.

IMAGINATIVE PLAY

A kitchen set, complete with pretend food, is a great toddler toy. It enables her to be just like mum and dad and prepare "a meal" for those she loves.

Everyday care

Having a routine will help your toddler feel secure but, conversely, she may also resist it to test the boundaries of what is possible. A reluctance to get out of the bath and an unwillingness to stay in her own bed are a couple of the problems you may face, but there are ways to tackle them.

Sleep sense

Once your toddler is mobile, even the most co-operative sleeper may try a few tricks to get your attention at bedtime. She may try to involve you in more prolonged rituals, but try to stick to the routine you have established and resist her requests for just one more story, cuddle, drink, or whatever. If she gets up during the evening or keeps on calling for you, settle her back down firmly and consistently and avoid getting involved in any play or discussions.

If your toddler is in her own bed rather than a cot, she may get up during the night and get into bed with you. If you are too sleepy to take her back, it can be all too easy to snuggle up together. Before you know it,

"Our toddler had always settled well at night, until she realized she could get out of bed. It was quite cute the first time she did it, but we soon nipped it in the bud."

this will have become a habit and it will be you or your partner who decamps to the spare bed or sofa. Once you have more than one child, the possibilities are endless – and exhausting.

These bed-hopping antics are absolutely fine if they suit your family, and if both parents are happy with it. Plenty of parents are relaxed about their children joining them at night; a child psychologist I know always advised against bed-sharing with children until he had his own and loved it so much that he bought a bigger bed. If, however, one of you welcomes bed-sharing and the other doesn't, this can cause conflict so it is important to talk it through. If you are in this situation, perhaps you can compromise by being firm about your toddler staying in her bed at night, but allow her to join you in bed each morning to start the day with a cuddle.

Mealtimes

By around 18 months, many toddlers are able to tackle their food using a child-sized fork and spoon, although not all are willing to do so as eating with their hands is more tactile, fun, and efficient for most children of this age. If you supply her with the right equipment, she can at least have a go. Try not to make an issue of eating nicely – she will attempt to copy you at mealtimes as well as she is able to at this age. If she is particularly dextrous, you might be lucky enough to see a decrease in the amount of mess at mealtimes but, for many, things will get worse before they get better. Try to be relaxed about this rather than making an issue of it.

USING A CUP *By 20 months your toddler may be able to manage a cup without a lid with relatively little spillage. Give just a little at first and let him practise with water, rather than milk or juice.*

Continue to ensure that she joins in with family meals and give her the same food as you are eating whenever possible. Making separate meals for toddlers is tedious and it is good to encourage her to try a variety of tastes and textures. Never force-feed your toddler, and do allow her to have some dislikes without getting away with omitting whole food groups, such as vegetables, which isn't acceptable and can be overcome (see page 246). When you take her out to a restaurant, choose family-friendly places that have highchairs and a relaxed attitude. If you are worried about mess or breakages, take along a plastic plate and a plastic pelican bib with a trough to catch dropped food and let her eat with her fingers.

Keeping clean

A combination of running around all day and exploring means your toddler is likely to need a bath by the end of most days. This can be a lively evening event and an extension of her playtime, so you may find you

NEW SKILLS *As your toddler becomes more dextrous, he will be able to have a go at teeth-cleaning and doing up his shoes. But he still needs your help most of the time.*

have trouble getting her back on to dry land. Try to see it from her point of view; she is having a lovely time playing in the bubbles and has your full attention (she is still far too young to be left alone in the bath), so she is unlikely to want it to end. It may help to entice her out if she knows there is a story and cuddle coming before bed. If you try to lift her out of the bath without warning, she will probably object, but if you let her know it is nearly time for a big cuddle in a warm towel, followed by a favourite story, it will hopefully do the trick.

Teeth-cleaning can be a bone of contention and, as with a younger baby, if your toddler really won't co-operate, try sitting her on your lap facing away from you with one arm firmly around her and brush her teeth with the other hand. If you give her a brush of her own, with a tiny dab of paste, you might not need to resort to this as she will love being grown-up and brushing her own teeth. While it is good to encourage her to use the toothbrush, she will not be skilled enough to get her teeth properly clean at this age so it is important that you brush them, too.

Introducing a potty

If your toddler takes an interest in the toilet, mainly by following you there, this may be the time to introduce a potty. Simply start by putting it in the bathroom next to the loo or in her bedroom, where she can play at sitting her doll or teddy on it. When she does, comment on how grown-up teddy is getting – and leave it at that.

Your toddler will start to use the toilet or potty when she is physically and emotionally ready, so try not to make a big thing of how she will be a "good girl" when she does. Otherwise she may feel that she is doing wrong by not using it and may resist it when the time comes (see page 250). Having said that, if she wants to use it at this early age (and a few toddlers do), make the most of her interest and enthusiasm.

Getting dressed

When your child's developing motor skills allow, try to let her do some things for herself when you have time. It can take an age for her to put her shoes on, and she will need you to help fasten them, but there is something incredibly endearing about your toddler standing there with her wellies on the wrong feet and her coat on inside-out. It is also important for her growing independence and self-esteem that she is given plenty of opportunities to try out these fledgling self-care skills.

Your toddler will be able to take clothes off before she can put them on and it can be immensely frustrating if you have just managed to get her dressed and she decides to strip off again, especially if you are in a rush. Be patient and if it becomes a real problem, use fastenings that she can't yet undo, such as buttons. This, of course, is only an option until you begin potty training when quick removal of clothing is essential.

Common concerns

▶ **My toddler gets filthy every day. Should I use antibacterial products?**

It is important for your toddler's development that he has the opportunity to explore safely without you worrying about whether he'll get dirty. Having said that, some kinds of dirt are worth trying to avoid, such as earth or sand that pets might have soiled, or dropped bits of food that may have gone mouldy. These exceptions aside, it's good for your toddler to encounter germs as it will help strengthen his immune system, which protects him from harmful bacteria. It's fine to use an antibacterial cleaner on his highchair tray, where bugs can multiply rapidly on smears of room-temperature food, but if you use antibacterial soap on his hands

you'll strip away healthy as well as harmful bacteria. If you use antibacterial cleaners around your home, you'll create a sterile environment that will prevent your toddler building up immunity to germs. So you don't need to be too fastidious. I've never knowingly bought an antibacterial product other than bleach to use in the loo.

▶ **My daughter's back teeth are coming through and she's really miserable. How can I help?**

The larger back teeth, or molars, can cause discomfort while they are coming through so try to be sympathetic and give her lots of cuddles. Infant paracetamol or teething gels may help your daughter through the worst of it. If she's off her food temporarily don't worry as the pain won't last long.

▶ **My little boy is 20 months old and I've noticed that his skin has an orange tinge. Why is this?**

Over the course of my career I've seen orange toddlers brought to me by parents, who are worried their child has jaundice. But in most cases this is nothing more than the effects of their diet. If your little boy eats lots of orange foods such as carrots, sweet potatoes, and satsumas, this is probably responsible for his colour. Children whose diet is heavily weighted towards these can develop an orange tinge. If you have any other worries about his health, check with your GP but if this is the only symptom your child has, try introducing a wider range of similarly healthy foods of different colours into his diet and watch his skin return to normal.

QUESTION&ANSWER

Expecting another baby

Although you have an idea of what to expect this time, you will be juggling this pregnancy with caring for your first child, and perhaps work as well. Don't underestimate how challenging this can be and accept all offers of help.

At first, your toddler is likely to be completely uninterested in the idea of a new sibling. However, she might become intrigued later on when it is easy to feel the baby moving around. No toddler will understand the concept of waiting months for a baby to arrive, though, so it is worth keeping everything low-key until much later in your pregnancy.

When you do talk to your toddler about the baby, story books on the subject are a boon. If you can, let her spend time with other families where there is a toddler and a new baby, so that she can get used to the idea of having a brother or sister, and some experience of a newborn.

The natural tiredness and queasiness of early pregnancy can quickly become exhaustion and hard-to-manage sickness, which you have little time to alleviate. Toddlers are adept at picking up on moods: signs that Mummy is not coping may make her uneasy and anxious, and she may respond by testing you with difficult behaviour. This is the last thing you need when you've been throwing up all morning, so be kind to yourself and don't try to do too much. Make any changes to your toddler's routine well before the new baby arrives and have a dry run of your arrangements for the actual birth if possible. Someone your toddler is familiar with, such as a grandparent, should be on hand to care for her, unless your partner is not intending to be with you during labour. Try to arrange for the carer to spend some time with your toddler before the birth, to allow her to get used to them.

AFTER THE BIRTH

When you see your toddler after the birth, greet her with open arms and give her a big cuddle while someone else holds the new baby. Show her how

---

HOW DAD CAN HELP

Dads can play a key role in helping a toddler cope with the prospect of a new baby. It's important to make sure you're involved with tasks like putting your child to bed before the baby arrives so that you can play a fuller part in her care after the birth, and so that your child doesn't see the baby as the cause of change. While supporting your partner in the early days you will often be able to involve your first child in helping you – passing the baby wipes for nappy changes, for example. This will help her come to terms with her new sibling, as well as build your identity as a family. This is a challenging time as you attempt to be all things to all people – working dad; support to your partner; and the person who fills the small gap in your first child's relationship with her mum. Try to understand how difficult it may be for your toddler to cope with this new sibling. As her parents, you represent her whole world of love and security and any intrusion on this is hard for her to cope with. Be prepared for unexpected twists, too. By the time our new baby arrived I had become our daughter's "favourite". However, once Su finished breastfeeding, our daughter switched her allegiance back to mum – and I was left holding the baby!

"When I became pregnant my toddler was at the height of his tantrums and I struggled to cope. Rather than trying to be a supermum, I asked for help. It was fairer on all of us."

JUST THE TWO OF YOU *As the arrival of your second baby approaches, make the most of the one-to-one time you have with your toddler.*

thrilled you are to see her. Some parents swear by giving the toddler a present from their new sibling.

Despite your best efforts, your toddler may react negatively to the baby, but if you can give her one-to-one time when the baby sleeps, this will help her to cope. You may be surprised at how quickly your toddler bonds with your newborn, and you can foster this by pointing out that the baby loves to watch her, and by getting her to put her finger in his palm so he grips it tight. She doesn't know about

newborn reflexes and will simply be delighted that her new sibling wants to hold her hand.

HOW YOU MIGHT FEEL

You may worry about whether you can possibly love anyone else the way you love your firstborn child, but you will find that you have more than enough love to share between them. Your new baby will be a unique little individual, and the way you respond to him may be very different from the way you are with your toddler. This helps you to

love them equally but to have a different relationship with each.

As for coping with both children at the same time, you will get the hang of it and find that a lot of your toddler's activities and routines can go on as normal, while your baby feeds, sits in his bouncy chair, or snoozes in the sling. Try to line up some post-baby arrangements for your toddler – perhaps an afternoon at his grandparents or a day out with your partner – so that you can have an occasional break in the early days.

YOUR INDEPENDENT CHILD

13 | 14 | 15 | 16 | 17 | 18 | 19 | 20 | 21 | **22 23 24**

MONTHS

GOODBYE TO NAPPIES YOU MAY WANT TO INTRODUCE A POTTY IN THE COMING MONTHS

FUN AND GAMES YOUR TODDLER WILL START TO INITIATE PLAY AND MAY HAVE FAVOURITE TOYS

PLAYMATE HE MAY BEGIN TO INTERACT WITH OTHER CHILDREN TOWARDS THE END OF HIS SECOND YEAR

"From baby to little boy,
he will become more skilled
and capable by the day."

Growing up

You and your child have learned so much together and, as well as all the hard work and stress, there will have been a great deal of joy in these first two years. She will be a real companion by now as she uses phrases to chat to you, helps you with tasks, and takes her place at the table at mealtimes.

Moving on

By 21 months, your toddler may be able to climb more confidently and if she is a steady walker, she might try to balance – walking along a low wall holding your hand is likely to be a favourite game. By 22 or 23 months she may be able to walk downstairs, although she still needs your supervision and will put both feet on each step as she descends. By the time she reaches her second birthday, your toddler may be more adept at running and may be able to throw a ball overarm.

Becoming sociable

At this stage your toddler will still play alongside other children (known as parallel play) rather than with them, but she will gradually begin to interact. You or another adult will have to support and facilitate this social play for some time yet, but by making sure she spends time with other children you are laying the foundations for her to be able to share her toys, games, and imagination with friends of her own making in the future.

Your toddler has a mind of her own, and while she is still self-centred, she is also learning to empathize with others and take turns. By their second birthday, many toddlers are interested in other children and how they behave, play, and even feel. If your toddler sees another child crying, she may be curious or even sympathetic, but it will take time for this interest to blossom into an ability to make friends. You can, however, help her learn to share by turn-taking with her and praising her when she manages this. You are her role model, and if she sees you sharing, praising, and saying "please" and "thank you", it will help her acquire the social skills she needs to interact with other children as she grows.

THE ADVENTURER *Your toddler will love to climb, jump, and run. Your instinct will be to protect him from harm, but try to give him the space to learn.*

Her collection of words may be growing almost too quickly for you to keep track of them and by 23 or 24 months, some children's two-word phrases have expanded to three words or more and might include the occasional verb – for example, "no go bed", "all gone juice", or "teddy eat apple up". However much or little she speaks, she continues to understand much more than she can say. As well as chatting, she may

Reflections on the past two years

This is an excellent time to draw breath and reflect back on the journey that you and your new family have taken. You started it with a little bundle in a Babygro and blanket (that you could barely believe had been created from the two of you) and you now have an independent person who is able to express opinions and communicate with you, walk and run, feed herself and even boss you around. If you're a dad for whom the appeal of a small baby was a bit of a mystery, this is the beginning of a wonderful journey into increasingly interesting and interactive development and play.

I remember mixed feelings at this stage, as I felt something akin to mourning for the loss of my beautiful, innocent, helpless babies, yet this was outweighed by the thrill and wonder at all the new things my children could do and the excitement of all their new discoveries.

It's also a good time to reflect on your own journey and your own meteoric development as a dad. While your toddler has gone from a primitive grasp reflex to precision-lifting of even the smallest objects, you have progressed from fumbling at nappy tapes to being a master of small buttons and poppers; and while her language has gone from random noises to simple words or phrases, your conversational offerings have also

mushroomed, with such gems as, "He sleeps through the night now – so we don't get woken till 6am" and "Darling, has Johnny done a poo yet?". Your technical skills, too, have multiplied; while your toddler has mastered complex tasks like walking and making a brick tower, you can open a buggy with one hand or even manage the complex arrangement of a five-point car-seat harness without the help of your partner. Both of you are a credit to your family – well done!

FATHER'S VIEW

even begin to sing and will love nothing more than copying you in an action song or rhyme.

While your 21-month-old still needs you (or another familiar adult) close by, she can cope better with waiting a few minutes for your attention. But by 22 or 23 months she may be rather bossy, issuing orders such as, "story now", "no talk, Daddy", or "stop". She has reached a stage where she is using language in a more abstract way – asking you *not* to do something rather than asking *for* something is quite an intellectual leap – but she still has limited verbal skills. She also wants to test out her power and control over you. Handling this is a fine balance between responding to all your child's interruptions when you are busy, or ignoring her completely. Try explaining that you need her to play alone for a few minutes and that you will be able to join in after that. Remember to tell her how pleased you are with her if she gives you a few moments' peace, but don't expect miracles.

Me, me, me

As your toddler's sense of self becomes ever stronger, this will become evident in her body language and her speech. Watch her beaming with pride in all her achievements or stiffening with annoyance when another toddler encroaches on her territory. Phrases such as "Ellie shoe" or "Ellie cup" will be common pronouncements as she learns to label her belongings. A few children will start using first person pronouns at this age so you might hear "my teddy" or "me do it". Her tone of voice will speak volumes, too, and there is no mistaking the difference between a conversational "Ellie chair," when she is chatting to you at home, "Ellie chair!" when she shouts as a rebuke to a visiting toddler who is about to sit in it, and "Ellie chair?" when you lift her towards an unfamiliar highchair in a restaurant.

PLAYING GAMES *She will have progressed from playing peek-a-boo to hide and seek, but as she will want you to find her she is unlikely to be very well hidden.*

Toddler fun

As your toddler becomes increasingly skilled and dextrous, she will be able to master such things as building a tower of bricks or finding the right hole for her shapes. These little triumphs are sources of wonder to your child and an important part of developing her confidence and independence.

MAKING THINGS *Boost her confidence by showing her how she can create something with stickers, paints, or crayons.*

On the move

Now that your child is becoming more physically able and agile, she may enjoy a greater range of ride-on toys. Little tricycles with no pedals, which she pushes along with her feet, are ideal as few toddlers can pedal at this age. If she is able to pedal, she will enjoy a traditional tricycle, and a few children may be able to manage a toddler-sized bike with stabilizers by the time they reach their second birthday.

Toddler-powered cars that have a door and a roof are hugely popular with this age group. If you go to a one o'clock club or toddler group, you will often find that these toys cause the most arguments among the children. They can be used indoors or outdoors and are great for pretend play, too, especially as many have a parcel shelf that is big enough to accommodate a teddy or doll. It is worth going to local groups that have plenty of play space as it will give your child the opportunity to try out these large-scale toys and for you to see whether she enjoys them.

Creative play

Some toddlers may enjoy new kinds of creative play, such as collage, towards the end of this year. You will need to help her put the glue on to the paper at first, then provide a selection of pictures, bits of fabric, and glitter to stick on, and see what she makes of it. If she likes playing with stickers, you can try using star charts to encourage desirable behaviour. For example, if you are trying to get your toddler to allow you to brush her teeth, put up a chart in a conspicuous place and let her choose a sticker to put on it every time she lets you. As she is still very young, give her the sticker whether she makes a fuss or not – as long as you have managed to brush her teeth. This old-fashioned method of rewarding children really does work, even when they are very young.

Quiet activities

As long as she watches programmes with you (and you switch off when they have finished), television can be a good learning experience. Programmes that are made for this age group will give her plenty to think about and talk about and can help her learning. If your toddler enjoys books, she may be able to follow a simple story by this stage and you may see her pretending to read to her toys, just the way you read to her. Toddlers do vary in how much quiet play they can cope with but yours may find activities such as puzzles, books, and building blocks absorbing for increasing lengths of time, especially if she has your full attention.

Sharing

Many children won't fully grasp sharing until after the age of two, but there is no harm in gently teaching her. Encourage her by playing different games with her where turn-taking is important, such as rolling, throwing, or kicking a ball to each other. Practising these desirable social skills now will help to smooth the way for her when she begins to play more independently with other children.

LEARNING TO SHARE

THAT LOOKS MORE INTERESTING... *Your toddler is highly likely to want a toy if another child has it.*

YOU CAN'T HAVE IT, IT'S MINE... *Being possessive of toys is normal at this age and is not naughty behaviour.*

WOULD YOU LIKE THIS INSTEAD? *Most toddlers learn to share given time, encouragement, and praise.*

Your almost capable toddler

Your toddler is growing up, but in many ways she is still a baby, and still sees herself as being the centre of the universe. This means that while she is driven to become independent, she cannot be expected to be selfless and her behaviour will often reflect this.

LETTING THEM LEARN

Although it can be difficult when you are in a rush, try to be patient. Toddlers need time to learn new skills.

If your toddler pushes you away, this is not thoughtless – it is just that she has no idea of how this will make you feel, or even that it will make you feel anything at all. When babies are born they are self centred because it is essential to their survival, but rest assured that if you model caring, thoughtful behaviour, your child will learn as she matures to take others into consideration. By the same token, whatever your child sees you do will be normal to her as she has no other yardstick with which to judge life. So if you shout at her or smack her regularly this is the world you will develop in her mind. Remember that children learn their social skills and behaviour from their parents. If they grow up in an atmosphere of aggression, shouting, and swearing, they will think of this as normal human interaction. Good manners are eventually more likely to come naturally to children who witness caring adults around them.

Self-care skills

Your toddler will want to try to do many things for herself, which is a very positive impulse but not always convenient when you have little time. Consider starting to get ready early to allow extra time for your child to have a go at washing, teeth-cleaning, and getting dressed. To make things easier, keep her toothbrush and flannel where she can reach them, put her clothes on a low shelf and make sure there is a sturdy step by the wash basin. If standing by while she struggles to put her legs into her trousers drives you crazy, try thinking of it as another game she is learning to play. In the same way that you should try not to intervene if she is attempting to fit a shape through a hole in her shape sorter unless she asks or is becoming upset, try to give her time to learn these new skills of dressing and face-washing, too. If you are in a hurry, try and compromise – for example: "I'll get you dressed quickly so you have time to put your own cereal out for breakfast." For hygiene reasons, it is a good idea to supervise hand-washing carefully, especially before meals and if she has started to use the potty or toilet.

Little helper

Toddlers love tasks that they are able to master and she will feel very grown up if she can help you around the house. For example, give her a small, lightweight jug or watering can to water the plants; let her help you put clean clothes away into drawers and her dirty clothes into the washing basket; encourage her to tidy away toys, which is especially easy if you have containers to sling everything into. It can be a lot easier to get jobs done if your toddler isn't feeling left out as well as setting a great precedent for sharing household tasks between family members.

TODDLER JOBS *Helping you is great for your child's self-esteem. She is fascinated by what you do and joining in makes her feel important.*

Further afield

When you are out of the house, your toddler will want to be independent, although there are times when this is simply not possible. It is worth thinking ahead about potential problems so you can steer around them. If she spends ages climbing on to the bus without help while a queue of passengers tut loudly behind you, you will end up having to carry her on while she probably screams. However, if you lift her on, asking her where she would like to sit, she will be busy deciding while you pay the driver. However well she is walking, your toddler has no road sense yet, so even if she appears capable, be very careful around roads, hold on to her or put her in the buggy when necessary. Using reins or wrist straps can also be reassuring when you are near busy roads.

Handling tantrums

Some children sail through the early years without so much as a stamped foot and their smug parents can't understand why other people have so much trouble with their toddlers. If this sounds like you, beware – your next child may more than make up for the first one, and you may eat your words!

Why toddlers have tantrums

BEFORE... *When your toddler is having a tantrum, she will act as if her world is coming to an end.*

Your child is completely dependent on you for support and security. As she explores her separateness from you, she needs to test your boundaries and also ensure that even when she pushes you to the limit, you will still love her. Frequently, the power and confusion of her emotions – the tension between needing you and discovering the lure of independence – can become too much for your toddler, and this can result in a tantrum.

Toddlers also encounter frustrations at every turn. Your child may want to do things but be unable to because she is not allowed, or because she doesn't quite have the skills yet. Or she may be overtired, hungry, or upset and unable to explain this to you because she doesn't have the self-awareness or language skills. All these things can lead to a tantrum.

Nipping tantrums in the bud

We all get tetchy if we are tired, anxious, bored, or hungry and toddlers are no different. You can sometimes avert a tantrum by dealing with potential triggers before they get out of hand. Offering a snack and drink can help, and these are also good diversions as they will give your toddler something to do. At this age don't expect her to be able to walk far, especially if an outing coincides with her usual nap time – always take the buggy or a back carrier unless you are prepared to carry her as well as all the shopping. A toddler who is gearing up to throw a wobbly will often become suddenly oppositional – saying "no" to holding your hand or getting in the buggy, for example. You will probably learn to recognize a change in her tone of voice, pitch of cry, or posture, which will alert you to an impending storm. At this point, distraction is your best option – and let's face it, singing a song, making silly faces, or skipping down the pavement are all less embarrassing (and more fun) than coping with a tantrum in public.

What you can do

Handling tantrums involves resisting the urge to have a tantrum yourself. Many, many parents have marched out of supermarkets, playgrounds, and family weddings with a furious, screaming toddler held rigid under their arm like a battering ram. Or had to try to stuff a flailing, kicking dervish into a buggy in a public place. Mortifying though this is for you, remember that it is worse for your toddler, who is totally out of control and very distressed. Be reassured that most onlooking parents of older children have been in the same situation at one time or another and are probably simply breathing a sigh of relief that it is not happening to them.

When I was in the supermarket recently, there was a toddler having a tantrum in a trolley. Her father was (or appeared to be) unperturbed and calmly carried on with his shopping, and eventually she stopped screaming and smiled at him. My immediate thought was, "There's a dad who's in control", swiftly followed by, "That must be a second child". It is rare for tantrums in a first child to be handled as effectively as that, but staying calm and not making a fuss really does work. So, if at all possible (and it isn't always easy in a public place), do nothing. Ensure that your child can't hurt herself while she is flailing around, then remove your attention

AFTER... *Although she may have pushed you to the limits, give your toddler time to calm down and then cuddle her and reassure her that you are still there for her.*

"My toddler calms down if I stay nearby but leave him alone, so I pretend to read the paper. This way he can't see I'm cross, and it also helps me resist the temptation to tell him off and make things worse."

EARLY DISCIPLINE
When dealing with behavioural issues, always get down to your child's level.

until the rage passes. You can't reason with her while she is having a tantrum as it simply won't work, and trying may make things worse.

While her tantrums may make you angry, especially as they are often irrational, try to remember that her behaviour is not calculated or malicious. Having said that, if you give her lots of attention when she has a tantrum, or give in to whatever triggered the tantrum, this can encourage her to do it again next time she is thwarted. If this happens, your toddler will soon learn that it is worth screaming and shouting to manipulate you, and may start behaving this way deliberately, which is something to be avoided at all costs. The following may help –

■ **Be consistent with your boundaries:** don't try to stop your toddler's tantrum by giving in to her demands, even if you are somewhere public like the supermarket.

■ **Resist the urge to argue:** at the height of her tantrum she will be out of control, unable to listen, and giving her attention will feed the flames.

■ **Be patient:** no child will scream for long if no one is listening and she will soon learn that she gets your attention once she calms down.

■ **Try distraction:** sometimes a new game can stop a tantrum in its tracks.

■ **Handle it well afterwards:** as soon as her screaming begins to subside, pick her up and give her a big hug to reinforce the acceptable behaviour.

Breath-holding tantrums

Your toddler may work herself up into such a state of fury and distress that she stops breathing. This will be terrifying for you to witness, as she will go silent and turn grey-blue in colour. She will usually start breathing again after around 15 seconds or so.

Your child cannot hurt herself by holding her breath. This is because long before she can do herself any

harm through oxygen deprivation, she will lose consciousness – and the moment she does, she will start breathing again. If your child is prone to these breath-holding (cyanotic) episodes, the best advice I can give is to ensure she is in a safe place – not at the top of an ungated flight of stairs or anywhere she can bash her head when she falls – then try your best to ignore her (or at

least pretend to). Thankfully, most children grow out of these episodes before they reach school age.

A few children have a far rarer condition called reflex anoxic seizures, which is where a breath-holding episode results in a convulsion and if this happens, you should seek medical advice. There is a good support group called STARS (see page 312).

Behavioural concerns

▶ **Every time we go out with our toddler, he seems to have a screaming fit. Taking him to the supermarket is embarrassing. How can we handle this behaviour?**
The trouble with tantrums is that the more they wind you up, the more likely your child is to throw one at a time when it will cause maximum upset because he'll sense your tension and anxiety. For the time being, see if someone can look after your child while you do the supermarket shop, or buy your groceries online, while you work out ways of handling his tantrums in the privacy of your own home.

The technique of rewarding positive behaviour and ignoring negative behaviour works much of the time, so if he's behaving beautifully, try to praise him and give him good, fun attention. If he screams, take no notice and get on with something nearby (or pretend to). It is possible to do this in the supermarket if you're brave and have the courage of your convictions, but it's best to practise at home first. Once you do take him shopping again, praise him for any good behaviour during the trip.

▶ **My toddler is 23 months old and won't go into his buggy without a fight. The trouble is, he won't walk far either – he just wants to push it like a toddle truck. How can I persuade him?**
This can be infuriating when you're trying to get somewhere on time or you just want to walk at a normal pace in a particular direction. The chances are that ordering your toddler to sit in the buggy will lead to tears, tantrums, and possibly one of those awful situations where you end up strapping him in by force, which is a horrible experience for both of you.

The aim is to get him to want to ride in his buggy. It can help if he is into a routine of having one of his favourite snacks to eat while sitting in his buggy. But make sure you don't use this as a bribe once the argument starts, otherwise he'll learn that throwing a strop brings him a snack. Knowing there is something interesting to play with in the buggy will also make him keener to use it. If he has to spend a long time in the buggy while you're out, try to make time for him to amble a bit on the way home.

I must confess that I've used firm handling on occasion to get my toddlers into the buggy, as sometimes no amount of reasoning will convince them, and you simply need to go ahead and strap them in despite the struggles. It's often surprising how quickly they stop struggling when they know you're not going to give in.

▶ **My little girl is very cheeky and I know I don't help as I find her antics very cute and funny. My mum says I'm the cause of her naughtiness. Is she right?**
In a word – yes. Toddlers have strong personalities and your little girl's cheekiness is all part of her character. She wants to please you and because you find her antics cute, she keeps behaving this way to get the positive attention – so you're encouraging her to be cheeky. It's unfair if you then suddenly get fed up and tell her off for something that made you laugh half an hour ago. It's important that your child understands your boundaries, and that you're consistent about how you would like her to behave.

QUESTION&ANSWER

Everyday care

Your previously happy eater may become more picky about food at this age, especially if she is testing your boundaries, but remember that she won't starve and try to stay calm if she refuses food. As she needs less sleep during the day, you may find her bedtime routine and sleep patterns alter slightly, too.

Food fads

ROLE MODEL By taking the time to sit down and eat at the same time as your toddler, you can teach him about healthy food and good manners.

If your toddler is a fussy eater, the message remains don't worry and, above all, don't let the kitchen table become a battlefield. Nothing terrible will happen to her if she misses a couple of meals. If you are offering a range of healthy food that includes at least some fruit and vegetables, you are doing a good job. Baked beans (low-salt variety) and sweetcorn are acceptable to many toddlers and if you add a cup of juice and some raisins, you have succeeded in giving her four out of the recommended five portions of fruit and vegetables a day. If you are looking for inspiration, try these healthy versions of toddler favourites –

■ **Potato slices:** brush slices of potato with olive oil and dry-roast them. These are tasty and healthier than chips.

■ **Home-made pizzas:** buy individual bases to make your own pizzas – once the tomato sauce and cheese have gone on your toddler can help you arrange vegetables to make funny faces.

■ **Home-made burgers:** make your own burgers by shaping lean beef mince into small patties.

■ **Grilled chicken:** instead of giving her nuggets, try drumsticks, or cut grilled chicken into bite-sized pieces.

If you don't keep junk food in the house it is easier to avoid the temptation to give in to your toddler if she refuses a nutritious meal or snack.

Visiting the dentist

It is important to take your toddler to the dentist regularly so that any problems can be identified early and treated if necessary. Preventative care is the best way to avoid fillings and your dentist can advise you on diet and tooth-cleaning.

The British Dental Health Foundation recommends taking your child to the dentist as early as possible, to get her used to the environment, sitting in the chair, and all the new sights, sounds, and smells of the surgery. You will need to make this appointment yourself. I saw a child in my clinic with terrible tooth decay; his mum had never taken him to the dentist because she was waiting to be sent an appointment.

Many adults are frightened of going to the dentist, as they associate visits with painful treatments they have experienced themselves. Things have moved on considerably and dental check-ups won't hurt your toddler, so try not to convey your fears to her. You can read books about dental visits together, and tell her about the "magic" chair that goes up and down and the special mirrors for looking inside her mouth, so she can treat it as yet another adventure.

I'm constantly amazed by parents who tell me that their child eats nothing but chips and biscuits; if this sounds familiar, ask yourself who is in charge in your family and who does the shopping. For incredibly stubborn toddlers who appear to eat nothing, a food diary can help reassure you that she is not actually living on thin air. Also beware the toddler milkoholic – more than a pint a day will suppress her appetite.

Bear in mind that your toddler won't yet be able to last through a chatty meal with family and friends. Once she has eaten as much as she wants, you can avoid tears by either getting her down from the table to play or giving her some small toys and books to occupy her at the table for a little while longer while you eat.

Sleep problems

Some toddlers resist going to bed with all their considerable might. If your child is one of them, it is important to try to discover why this might be happening. There are many reasons for sleep troubles, including –

■ **She is not used to going to sleep alone:** if this is the case, the suggestions on the next page should help her drop off without you. Try not to get disheartened by having to repeat methods you used before – it is quite normal and this time you can be confident they will work.

■ **Her routine has been disrupted:** if she has been ill or you have been on holiday, you may need to help her back into a sleep routine.

■ **She needs a later bedtime:** at the end of your child's second year, she probably needs around 12–13 hours' sleep, including daytime naps. If she sleeps a lot during the day, she will find it hard to sleep at night.

■ **She thinks she is being left out:** if your toddler feels excluded when you put her to bed, try to be patient. It helps to ensure she has had enough of your positive attention before bedtime so she is not feeling as though she has missed out on time with you.

■ **She is thirsty:** leave a spouted beaker of water within reach, but don't fall into the trap of having to refill it several times each night.

If all else fails, keeping a sleep diary for two weeks can be very helpful. Simply record your toddler's sleep patterns – day and night – for this period and note events like the amount of time spent playing or cuddling at sleep time. This will give a clear picture of what is really happening, rather than what you perceive to be happening. Keeping this diary also allows you to agree on a joint approach.

Settling your toddler

Once she has had her last story and goodnight kiss, let her know that it is time to sleep, but you are nearby if she needs you. Even if she doesn't have a comfort object, a soft toy in her cot may keep her company and help her settle. Tuck her in and promise to return in a few minutes if necessary. When you do, keep it brief and boring. If she cries, go back and comfort her with minimal contact. You may have to do this a number of times at first until she settles, but if you are consistent in this checking technique, your toddler will eventually learn to settle on her own because she knows you will come if necessary, but that you won't get her up unless she is ill. Once she gets the hang of it, you will be able to relax, knowing that all is well because you have checked on her – and if you stick it out, you will have some time to yourselves in the evening.

Night fright

Nightmares, or waking up feeling frightened, are very common in young children and at this age your toddler may not have the words to explain how she is feeling. She will need you to calm and reassure her, as she won't be able to settle back to sleep until the anxiety has passed. If it helps, leave a night-light on for her so that she can see her familiar things if she wakes up. Try to leave her with something happy, and unscary to think about as she drifts back to sleep – for example, talk briefly about going to the park tomorrow, or about a favourite story that you know she loves.

Your toddler may be frightened to go to sleep if she is having nightmares. Reassure her that you will always come if she needs you and try to get to her as quickly as possible if she has a bad dream. Avoid scary stories or high-action videos before bed, and keep her bedtime routine as calm as possible.

Night terrors are different to nightmares as your child may appear to wake but won't know where she is or who you are and may scream, shout, and behave strangely. This can be unnerving and distressing for you, but your child is not properly awake and is unlikely to remember it in the morning. These episodes rarely last more than half an hour and all you can do is be there as a reassuring presence until she falls back to sleep. We don't know exactly why night terrors happen, although they seem to run in families, but thankfully children do grow out of them. Night terrors won't harm your toddler, although it is important to prevent her injuring herself if she is flailing or running around, but if they are happening frequently, or your child seems under stress, see your doctor. If they occur regularly at a particular time of night, you can sometimes prevent them by waking her before that time to disrupt that particular stage of sleep.

BEING UNSETTLED *He may become anxious at night if he has bad dreams. A favourite toy can help him settle.*

"My toddler developed a fear of 'monsters' and started having nightmares. I reassured him straightaway each time and gradually he woke up less often. We also make a game of checking under his bed."

Giving up nappies

Girls are often ready for potty training earlier than boys, and most (but not all) children are clean and dry by the time they are three. Don't worry if your toddler turns out to be a late starter. There is no point in forcing your child to abandon nappies before she is ready.

WHEN TO POTTY TRAIN

Most parents approach potty training their toddler with some trepidation but, if you manage to time it right, it really doesn't have to be too difficult.

Toddlers vary wildly in this area of their development. There is no "right" age, but somewhere between 18 and 30 months is a common time to begin. There are huge cultural differences in potty training: in developing countries where washable nappies are the norm, babies are encouraged to sit on a potty after feeds from an early age and many are trained by one year. This saves a lot of time and effort and I sometimes wonder if we'd be more motivated to potty train earlier in the UK if we didn't have disposable nappies.

IS SHE READY?

Even though life may be easier with nappies, don't put off potty training if your toddler is showing signs that she is ready to start. These include:
▶ Telling you her nappy is wet or dirty.
▶ Showing an interest whenever you go to the toilet, and perhaps wanting to copy you.
▶ Awareness that she is about to do a wee or a poo – she needs a bit of advance warning before she can successfully use a potty.

HOW TO START

It is easier to potty train in warm weather as your toddler can be outside and wear minimal clothing – and patios are far easier to clean than carpets. Having said that, if your child is ready during the winter, go ahead. If you don't have a potty already, take her out to buy it as she is more likely to sit on one she has chosen.

Show your toddler the potty, explain what it is for and ask if she would like to have a go. If the whole idea upsets her, leave it, as this isn't a skill you can force her to learn. Your role is to encourage her once she has begun to develop some control over her bladder and bowels, while avoiding making her feel bad about accidents. Pressure is counterproductive and can make the whole process take far longer.

If she is happy to use the potty, take off her nappy and let her sit on the potty to see what it feels like. Some toddlers tend to wee when their nappy is removed, and if this happens, you can praise the positive result whether it was intentional or not. This will leave her keen to repeat the experience. If she doesn't wee, try again a little later. If you leave your toddler's nappy on, or use pull-ups (absorbent paper pants that can be removed in the event of an accident), this will protect your floors and furniture but it may not be very helpful in raising her awareness of her toilet needs. If you put her in normal pants, or leave her lower half naked, she will inevitably make a puddle. This gives you the opportunity to suggest that she uses the potty next time. You can also sit her on it regularly if she is willing, and she will probably be keen to produce a wee. If she does, praise her. When she has an accident (there will be many), avoid making a fuss.

Some toddlers find the sensation of doing a poo in the potty or toilet distressing and may prefer to have a nappy on to poo even though they are happy to wee in the potty. If your toddler feels this way, put a nappy on her, so she doesn't hold the poo in and become constipated. With encouragement, you may be able to get her to poo on the potty if you line it with a nappy – a sort of halfway house. Give her time and don't worry – she will get there in the end.

HELPING HER *Learning to use a potty should be a positive experience. Introduce the idea of it gradually and when she shows an interest in sitting on it, praise her, whether or not she uses it.*

"I suddenly realized that my little boy wouldn't become potty-trained automatically – I would have to make the time to teach him."

POTTY-TRAINING TIPS

DO

▸ Spend time with other toddlers who are using a potty – peer pressure can work wonders.

▸ Have a spare potty for teddy to sit on as this may encourage your toddler.

▸ Let your child use the toilet if she prefers – you can buy seats that fit over the loo and steps to allow for the height difference.

▸ Remind your toddler about the potty as she won't remember by herself at first.

▸ Use pull-ups for trips out and naps until your child is reliably dry when she is awake at home.

DON'T

▸ Tell her off for wetting herself.

▸ Allow potty training to become a battle, or an issue that distresses your toddler. Simply go back to nappies for a while.

▸ Buy new sofas before embarking on potty training. We did, and bitterly regretted it.

▸ Try to leave her nappies off at night, however reliable she is during the day. Many toddlers are not ready to stop using nappies at night until they are at least aged three.

HEALTH
CONCERNS

Contents

In this comprehensive health section you will find valuable information on a wide range of common childhood conditions, with advice on what you can do and when to call the doctor.

When your child is ill

You are bound to be worried if your child is ill, but he may pick up on your anxiety so try to stay calm. A liberal dose of tender, loving care is one of the best medicines of all, and in our household a kiss works wonders for minor ailments.

A cold is the most common childhood illness, but babies and young children also get other respiratory illnesses, leading to a runny nose, coughing, and possibly wheezing; rashes, which may be caused by infections; allergies, such as asthma or eczema; diarrhoea and vomiting; and ear infections. As a parent it can be difficult to know when to worry. With any illness, it is normal for a child to go off his food, but make sure he has plenty of fluids (see box, below). A good rule of thumb is that if your child becomes very distressed, dehydrated, or is having difficulty breathing, seek medical advice. A baby under three months with a fever should always be checked. If there is a rash, tell your doctor. He will also ask if your child is feeding, how long he has been unwell, and whether he has been in contact with an infected child.

The interaction between mind and body is particularly important when your child is sick. If you are confident and reassuring, you will help him through each illness and may speed his recovery.

When your child is dehydrated

Sick babies and toddlers can become dehydrated quickly, which can cause further problems. Signs include:
▶ Dry lips and tongue.
▶ Dark urine.
▶ Sunken fontanelle (see page 42).
▶ Lethargy and not seeming himself.
▶ Fewer wet nappies than usual.

WHAT YOU CAN DO
▶ Seek medical advice straight away if your baby is under six months, and within 24 hours if he is older.
▶ Keep offering him liquids, including the breast or bottle. If your toddler won't drink from a cup, you might find that he will lick an ice lolly.

▶ Offer rehydration drinks, which are available in sachets from your pharmacist and will help your child's body absorb fluid more efficiently. Offer small sips every few minutes; your child shouldn't take large gulps of fluid as this can cause vomiting.

Common baby symptoms

You know your child best of all and will be the first to notice if he seems unwell or is not himself. This chart outlines some common symptoms in babies and toddlers, and their possible causes. Do not hesitate to seek medical advice from your GP if your baby is ill or if you are worried about his health in any way.

SYMPTOM	POSSIBLE CAUSES
▶ Coughing	The most likely cause is a cold, also known as an upper respiratory tract infection (URTI) (see page 264). A cough can also be caused by the mucus from a runny nose running down the back of the throat, by asthma (see page 279), bronchiolitis (see page 266), croup (see page 265), whooping cough (see page 274), or pneumonia (see page 266).
▶ Diarrhoea	Loose, runny, and sometimes explosive poos are common. They can be caused by gastroenteritis (see page 274); or food allergy or intolerance (see page 278). Your toddler may have diarrhoea (see page 278) due to an immature digestive system.
▶ Difficulty breathing	This is common in babies because their airways are tiny. It may be due to asthma (see page 279), bronchiolitis (see page 266), croup (see page 265), or pneumonia (see page 266).
▶ Earache	This is usually caused by middle or outer ear infection (see page 267). Babies or toddlers with earache will often pull at their ear.
▶ Excessive crying	Most babies who cry excessively do not have an illness (see page 98). Medical causes include conditions that result in tummy ache and, more rarely, bone pain, including fractures (see page 292) and bone infection. In general, ill babies become quiet, not noisy.
▶ Fever	This is usually a sign of infection, which can be caused by bacteria or a virus. Take steps to reduce the fever as getting too hot can occasionally lead to febrile convulsions (see opposite).
▶ Fits (convulsions)	Fits (see opposite) are extremely frightening for parents to witness but if they are caused by a high fever they are rarely serious. Other causes are epilepsy and "fifth-day fits", where seizures occur for no particular reason in an otherwise healthy newborn.
▶ Rash	Rashes have a whole host of causes including infectious diseases (see pages 269–274), allergies (see page 279), eczema (see page 280), and skin infections (see page 282).
▶ Tummy ache	Constipation (see page 276) is a common cause of baby and toddler tummy ache. Seek medical help quickly if there is severe pain. It can also be caused by intussusception (see page 278) and gastroenteritis (see page 274). Tummy aches caused by anxiety can affect a toddler.
▶ Vomiting	Can be caused by an infection, including gastroenteritis (see page 274), a UTI (see page 268), food poisoning, or a structural problem such as reflux or pyloric stenosis (see page 275).

Seek urgent medical help if your child is unusually drowsy or irritable, has a headache or stiff neck, has a seizure, refuses fluids or can't keep them down, has a persistent high fever (see opposite) despite anti-fever remedies, or has a non-blanching rash (see page 270).

Fever

A normal temperature is 36.5–37°C (97.7–98.6°F), but children's temperatures are prone to fluctuate and a temperature as high as 38.5°C (101.3°F) is not necessarily a cause for concern. Fever is the body's normal response to an infection, but the actual temperature is not as important as your child's general state. For example, there is no need to worry if there is an obvious cause, such as a cold, and your child seems settled when the fever drops. Often we see hot, cross kids turning up in A&E whose parents are embarrassed because they are suddenly much better. This is because simply taking their child into the fresh air has cooled them down.

The time to be more concerned is if your child is irritable or lethargic, or if his temperature fluctuates to 38.5°C (101.3°F) or more for more than four hours, despite your attempts to bring it down. A fever should be brought down as quickly as possible particularly if it is over 39°C (102.2°F). A child with a fever may look flushed and feel hot (although his hands and feet may be cold), and he may refuse food. The best way to diagnose a fever is by using a thermometer (see page 260).

What you can do:

The aim is to cool your child down. This is one time when you must ignore well-meaning Granny who wants you to wrap your child up nice and warm when he is already boiling hot.
■ Give him paracetamol or ibuprofen in the recommended dose. It is better to give medicine regularly than to wait for the fever to return.
■ Remove his outer clothing so that he is wearing his vest and nappy or underwear.
■ If the fever is very high or you don't have any paracetamol or ibuprofen, sponge him down with lukewarm water. Avoid letting him shiver, as this will raise his temperature further.

Call a doctor if:

■ Your child's temperature won't stay down for four or more hours.
■ A fever comes and goes for five days or more.
■ Your baby is under three months old.

Febrile convulsions

For a significant number of children (about five per cent) aged between six months and five years, a high temperature can result in a fit, or febrile convulsion. This causes the limbs to stiffen, uncontrolled, jerky movements, and loss of consciousness. Be aware that it is often when the temperature is rising rapidly at the beginning of an illness that the fit happens. On the whole, febrile convulsions are harmless, are not related to epilepsy, and cause no long-term problems for the child. They can, however, be extremely distressing for the parents; many say they thought their child was going to die.

What you can do:

Lay your child on his side in the recovery position (see page 287) so that he doesn't choke. Never put your finger or anything else in his mouth. Call an ambulance and, if possible, time how long the fit lasts. Most are short-lived, but time passes very slowly when you are watching your child in distress. The fit will probably have stopped by the time the ambulance arrives, but if he is still fitting he may be given medication, usually rectally or intravenously. Rarely, if the fit won't stop, he may need an anaesthetic and have to go to intensive care for a short time.

If the fit is over before you have a chance to call an ambulance, take your child to your GP for a check-up. Most children sleep for a little while after a convulsion and don't remember anything afterwards.

Will it happen again?

Approximately one-third of children will have further febrile convulsions up until the age of five, so aim to keep your child cool if he has a fever (see page 259). If he has a convulsion on another occasion, you won't need to call an ambulance unless it lasts for more than five minutes. Call your doctor as he may need to see your child to diagnose the cause of the fever. If your child has convulsions that last for longer than five minutes, you may be given diazepam in suppository form (see right). You will be advised when to give this medication – it is usually when the convulsion has lasted for more than three minutes.

Fortunately, febrile convulsions are rarely serious. When he was two years old our youngest son had a convulsion, which was entirely our fault. He had a high fever and was miserable, so we brought him into our warm bed with us and went back to sleep. We were awoken by jerking movements that lasted about a minute. He has been fine ever since and has never been allowed to overheat like that again.

Taking a temperature

Most of us judge fever according to how hot the skin feels. However, it is better to be a bit more scientific. The most effective way to take a baby's or toddler's temperature is to use an electronic ear thermometer. This only takes a few seconds and causes minimal fuss. The tip of the thermometer is placed in the child's ear and then the temperature is shown on a digital display.

Digital thermometers are used in the armpit or mouth. They are effective, but it can be difficult to get a baby or young child to stay still for long enough to get an accurate reading. A fever strip thermometer is held against the forehead and changes colour according to the temperature. However, these are less accurate. Using a mercury thermometer is no longer recommended.

EAR THERMOMETER *The quickest and most effective way to take a baby's or toddler's temperature is to use an ear thermometer.*

Baby medicines

Many parents are wary of giving their children medication, but if they are in pain or have a fever it is worse to leave them to suffer. Always keep a supply of sugar-free infant paracetamol suspension and ibuprofen at home. If your baby is over three months old and has any cold symptoms and a fever (see page 259), give him one of these medicines and then wait for half an hour before taking his temperature again. You can give him paracetamol every four hours and ibuprofen every six hours (as long as you don't exceed the maximum daily dose for each one). Your child can have both, so alternate them. Don't hold back on giving your child these medicines if he has a temperature. Similarly, if your baby is in pain, give him painkillers regularly – it is better to keep the pain away than wait until he is uncomfortable again before giving each dose.

There are some over-the-counter medications, such as cough medicines, that don't actually work, but many parents use them because they like to feel they are doing something to help their ill child. The child may feel better, but this is often due to the placebo effect; if you say a medicine will make your child feel better, it will in at least one third of children. This does rely on a child having some understanding of language, though.

Types of medication

■ **Liquids:** most medicines for babies come in liquid form and the easiest way to give them is with a medicine syringe. Draw the medicine up until you have filled the syringe to the required

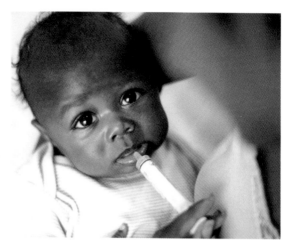

MEDICATION FOR BABIES *To give liquid medication to your baby quickly and easily, and with minimal spillage, use a special medicine syringe.*

number of millilitres and encourage your baby to suck the end of the syringe while you gently squirt the syrup in, aiming for his cheek rather than the back of his throat so that he doesn't gag.

If you are confident and hold him securely, your baby will probably swallow the medicine happily. Failing this, try putting the teat from a bottle into his mouth and squirting the medicine through that. You can use a spoon but there is a high chance of the medicine spilling.

If you are having difficulty getting your child to take prescribed medicine, talk to your doctor who may be able to find one with a better taste or one that is given less frequently.

■ **Suppositories:** lay your baby on his back or side and take off his nappy. Slide the suppository, which is bullet-shaped, into his anus rounded side first. Hold his buttocks together for a short time afterwards to make sure it doesn't come shooting straight back out.

■ **Drops:** putting drops into a baby's or toddler's eyes or nose is easier if you have someone to help you. To give eye drops, wrap your baby in a towel to prevent flailing arms and lay him in your lap. Hold his head steady and pull his lower lid down slightly. Place one drop into each eye behind the lower lid. Repeat if he blinks and you don't think the drop went in. To give nose drops, tilt your baby's head back and place a drop in each nostril and, if he is old enough to understand, ask him to sniff. A spray may be easier to use – you simply place the nozzle in each nostril and squirt, and your baby can remain upright.

Over-the-counter medicines

This is a chart of medicines that you can buy without a prescription. Seek advice from a pharmacist or GP if you have doubts about giving a medication, and check it is suitable for a child under two years old. Keep medicines out of the reach of children. For more details on how to use specific medication, see the relevant sections.

MEDICINE	WHAT IT IS FOR	HOW IT IS GIVEN
▶ Paracetamol	Fever and pain	Orally (by mouth) or rectally (as a suppository)
▶ Ibuprofen	Fever and pain, and inflammation	Orally
▶ Cough medicines	Different types of cough (dry, chesty, etc)	Orally
▶ Antihistamines	Acute allergic reactions, hay fever	Orally
▶ Oral rehydration solution	Acute gastroenteritis and any other illness with a risk of dehydration	Mixed with water as a drink
▶ Saline nose drops	To clear blocked nostrils	Nasally
▶ Infant Gaviscon	Treating gastro-oesophageal reflux	Mixed with milk
▶ Lactulose	Mild constipation	Orally
▶ Senna	Moderate constipation	Orally
▶ Steroid creams	Inflamed eczema	Rubbed into skin
▶ Emollients	Dry skin and eczema	Rubbed into skin
▶ Teething gel	Painful gums	Rubbed into gums
▶ Nit lotion	Head lice	Applied to scalp
▶ Worm medicine	Threadworms	Tablet or syrup

WARNING Never give aspirin to a child under the age of 16 unless it is prescribed by a paediatrician. Aspirin is associated with a rare and potentially lethal disease called Reye's syndrome.

Infections

It is easy for your child to pick up infections, especially if he goes to nursery. Scrupulous handwashing can help to prevent tummy bugs, but a cold will always get passed around.

Playgroups, nurseries, and (usually) child-minders ask parents to keep children with contagious diseases at home until they are no longer infectious. This is particularly important if a child has impetigo, diarrhoea and vomiting, or conjunctivitis as these are conditions that spread very easily.

■ **Viruses:** these tiny organisms cause the majority of infectious diseases in children, including colds, chickenpox, measles, and whooping cough. Viral illnesses get better without specific treatment and viruses do not respond to antibiotics, which is why your GP won't give you antibiotics for your child's cold.

■ **Bacteria:** these larger organisms may cause illnesses such as pneumonia, urine infections (UTIs), and some types of tonsillitis and meningitis. Bacterial infections may be treated with antibiotics and it is crucial to have the right one (see box, below). Your GP may take a swab from your child, or a urine sample, before starting treatment, and prescribe the antibiotic that is most likely to be effective. A different course will be tried if the sample indicates resistance to the antibiotic.

Reactive arthritis

Toddlers sometimes complain of a painful hip or knee following a viral infection. This happens when the antibodies produced to fight the virus go awry and set up a reaction in a joint instead. This will go away by itself, but your GP may recommend tests to rule out a rare, more serious infection called septic arthritis.

About antibiotics

To be effective, antibiotics must be taken in the correct dosage and the course must be completed. There may be side-effects, including tummy ache, nausea, diarrhoea, and thrush. If your child is allergic to the antibiotics, there will be an itchy rash all over his body. Antibiotics won't work if the bacteria have become resistant. Resistance to antibiotics is partly a result of their overuse in situations where the infection would get better on its own. A good example of this is ear infections where it has been shown that, even if the infection is due to bacteria, a child will get better just as quickly without antibiotics. Antibiotics also fail to work if the illness is caused by a virus or it is caused by a different bacteria to the one being targeted.

Colds

Most of your child's illnesses in the first few years of life will be respiratory infections, and the most common will be a cold. A cold is a viral infection that affects the upper respiratory tract. It causes all-too-familiar symptoms – runny or congested nose; sneezing; sore throat and croaky voice; cough; fever; and watery or sticky eyes. Children take years to learn to blow their nose so you may rapidly become the sort of mother you swore you never would be and simply leave your child's nose dripping for the whole world to see.

It is normal to have six to eight colds per year in childhood, and these are more common in the winter months. It takes a long time to build up any sort of immunity to colds because there are so many hundreds of viruses that cause them. Therefore, one cold every three to four weeks from October to March is to be expected. It is, however, a myth that a cold can be caught by getting chilly: the virus is spread in airborne droplets from coughs and sneezes or from people's hands. Make sure that all members of your household wash their hands after going to the toilet and before eating, as this will help to reduce the spread of germs.

Expect a cold to upset your baby's routine for a few days, particularly at night. If she doesn't settle back into a good sleeping pattern, you may need to sleep-train her (see page 114).

What you can do:

■ Give your baby plenty of fluids and lots of cuddles. Expect her to be clingy and to go off her food.

■ Treat the symptoms – such as fever (see page 259) and a blocked nose (give saline nose drops) and she should get better in around a week.

■ Treat (or better still, prevent) sore, dry lips by using petroleum jelly at least twice a day.

■ Try a decongestant rubbed on her chest or olbas oil sprinkled on a hankie tied to her cot.

■ A dry atmosphere makes it harder to inhale. Try putting a damp towel beside a radiator.

See a doctor if:

■ Your baby's fever is not settling and she is irritable.

■ She is wheezy, has difficulty breathing, or earache (babies with earache may rub or pull at their ears and will be very miserable).

■ She is not taking fluids.

FEELING POORLY *A cold may make your child miserable and a bit lethargic, but plenty of cuddles should help.*

Croup

This is a viral infection that affects the voice box, trachea (windpipe), and bronchi (the main airways below the windpipe). It causes inflammation and narrowing of the airways, which gives the child a hoarse voice, barking cough (like a sea-lion), and noisy breathing with difficulty inhaling.

What you can do:

Most children get better with no specific treatment, but you can try the following:
■ Keep your child as calm as possible as this will help to settle his breathing.
■ Steam helps because moist air is easier to inhale than dry air, and this is best achieved by sitting with your child in a steamy bathroom.
■ You could also try placing a wet towel close to a radiator or using a room vaporizer. Avoid sitting your baby next to a boiling kettle for safety reasons.

MOIST AIR *Sitting with your child in a steamy bathroom may help him to breathe more freely and ease croup.*

See a doctor if:

■ Your child is struggling to breathe. Children often respond quickly to a single dose of steroid, but the most severely affected will need observation in hospital. Rarely, croup can mimic a condition called epiglottitis – a serious infection of the flap of tissue at the front of the throat.

Tonsillitis

The tonsils are two round pieces of tissue at the back of the throat, which help to protect the upper airways from infection, but which sometimes become infected in the process. Symptoms include a sore throat, difficulty swallowing, fever, smelly breath, and, sometimes tummy ache. The glands in the neck may be tender and swollen. Tonsillitis can be caused by bacteria and viruses, and may occur as part of a cold. It usually gets better on its own, but if your child's tonsils are covered in pus or she is very unwell, penicillin may be prescribed.

What you can do:

■ Give paracetamol and/or ibuprofen for pain relief and to bring down a fever (see page 259).
■ Encourage her to drink plenty of fluids.

See a doctor if:

■ Your child is having difficulty swallowing.
■ You can see white pus on her tonsils.
■ You can't control her fever.
■ She has severe tummy ache.
■ She has a sore, red tongue and bright red rash, suggestive of scarlet fever.

Bronchiolitis

Every few years in the autumn and winter many of us become infected with a bug called respiratory syncytial virus (RSV). In most of us it causes a cold, but in babies under one it can cause bronchiolitis, an inflammation of the smaller airways. The symptoms are a nasty cough, wheezing, difficulty breathing, and sometimes difficulty feeding.

There is no specific treatment for bronchiolitis and almost all babies make a full recovery, although some may develop a tendency to wheeze with subsequent viral infections. Some babies need to be admitted to hospital for oxygen therapy and nasogastric feeds (where a tube goes up the baby's nose and into the tummy), or they may be put on a drip. A baby with bronchiolitis may need to stay in hospital for 5–10 days and the cough usually continues for several weeks. The most susceptible are the very young, babies who have been born prematurely, and those with other medical problems, such as heart disease.

See a doctor if:

■ Your baby is having difficulty breathing.
■ He has problems feeding.
■ He seems lethargic.
■ He looks bluish in colour.

What you can do:

■ Don't worry about feeding an older baby solids, but make sure he drinks plenty of liquids.
■ Watch his breathing pattern so you can quickly spot if his condition is worsening.

Pneumonia

The word pneumonia often creates images of 19th-century heroines dying of "double pneumonia", and this infection of the lung tissue can be fatal in the elderly, but it is usually easily treatable in children. The symptoms include a cough, high fever, rapid breathing, and, sometimes, chest pain or tummy ache.

The diagnosis is usually made by a doctor listening to the chest and is often confirmed by an X–ray. If your child is not admitted to hospital, keep a close lookout for worsening symptoms. Treatment is usually with antibiotics, which may need to be given intravenously. Children tend to recover from pneumonia rapidly with no long-term problems. The latest vaccine, now given to all babies, is called pneumovax and protects against the commonest cause of pneumonia.

See a doctor if:

■ You are worried that your child's temperature hasn't settled within 48 hours.
■ She has difficulty breathing, or has fast, shallow breathing.
■ She becomes blue.
■ She becomes lethargic.

What you can do:

■ Give your child plenty of fluids and keep her temperature down (see page 259).

Ear infection

A middle ear infection – otitis media – affects the part of the ear behind the drum and often occurs as part of, or after, a cold. It can be caused by viruses or bacteria.

Symptoms are a high fever (see page 259) and earache. The pain is due to pressure building up behind the eardrum, and there may be discharge from the ear, indicating that the drum has burst; this usually brings relief from the pain. If the drum bursts it will heal and the child will get better quickly. Most ear infections do not need to be treated with antibiotics.

What you can do:

- Give pain and fever relief regularly.
- Apply a warm or cool compress, such as a flannel, over your child's ear.
- Encourage him to drink lots of fluids.

See a doctor if:

- Your child seems very unwell.
- To confirm your child has an ear infection.

Outer ear infection

This infection, known as otitis externa, develops in the outer ear canal. It is rare in babies, but common in children with eczema or those who swim a lot. The symptoms are pain and discharge from the ear. It is treated with ear drops.

Glue ear

Sometimes ear infections lead to the build-up of a sticky glue-like substance in the middle ear, which causes deafness and may result in delayed speech. Nose drops can help the middle ear to drain, but some children with persistent deafness over many months may benefit from the insertion of grommets. These are tiny tubes inserted in the eardrums, under general anaesthetic, to equalize the pressure between the middle and outer ear, so allowing the ear to dry out. Grommets do not need to be removed as they usually drop out of the ears by themselves.

Conjunctivitis

The conjunctiva is the layer of tissue that covers the white part of the eyeball and lines the eyelids. It can become infected by either a virus or bacteria, and become red, sore, and may produce pus. One or both eyes may be affected and appear crusty in the mornings.

Mild conjunctivitis will get better by itself, but your doctor may prescribe antibiotic drops or ointment, to be applied several times a day, if it is persistent.

What you can do:

- Wipe the eyes, from the nose to the outside, using separate cotton wool balls soaked in cooled, boiled water.
- Always wash your hands thoroughly, and don't share towels and face cloths.

See a doctor if:

- Your baby's eyelids are swollen or red.
- The eyes need cleaning more than twice daily.

Urinary tract infections

These are infections, usually bacterial, of the urine in the bladder and sometimes the kidneys. Symptoms include pain on passing urine and passing urine frequently, tummy ache, smelly urine, and fever. A baby often has no specific symptoms but may be unwell with a high fever and irritability. Accurate diagnosis and treatment is essential, and you will need to take a sample of your child's urine by collecting it in a sterile pot. One complication is reflux, where the urine travels back up to the kidneys from the bladder. Reflux usually corrects itself but in the meantime antibiotics will be needed.

See a doctor if:

- You suspect a UTI.
- Your child is very unwell.
- She has a fever with no obvious cause.

What you can do:

- Give your child plenty of fluids to drink.
- Treat any fever (see page 259).

Balanitis

This infection of the foreskin is usually caused by bacteria or thrush and causes redness, soreness, and pain on urinating. It usually heals completely but if a baby has recurrent attacks, this may narrow the opening of the foreskin (phimosis) to the extent that the stream of urine becomes poor. Balanitis is treated with antibiotic cream or medicine, or anti-fungal cream. A circumcision is sometimes necessary after repeated infections, but most surgeons recommend gradually stretching the foreskin by easing it back in the bath a little more each day.

See a doctor if:

- You suspect balanitis or phimosis.
- Your baby is unable to wee properly.

What you can do:

- Bath your child gently and give pain relief.
- Don't pull back your child's foreskin while it is infected.

Circumcision

There is no medical benefit for this surgical removal of the foreskin in boys soon after birth, but many parents request it for religious reasons. Until recently the operation was routinely offered in America and when my first son was born there the nurse thought I'd made a mistake as I hadn't signed the circumcision consent form. I explained that I didn't want my son to have an unnecessary operation for which he was unable to give consent.

If your baby is being circumcised as part of your faith, find a highly recommended doctor or Rabbi who does several every week. Give your baby paracetamol beforehand and four hours afterwards, together with lots of cuddles. As a doctor I do see complications, such as infection and serious blood loss, so do remember that, although most babies will come to no harm, no operation is without risk.

Infectious diseases

If you have had or have been immunized against the common infectious diseases, your baby will probably have antibodies from you that will last until he is around six months old. For this reason, the following diseases are much more common after this age.

Chickenpox

This is a very common viral infection that causes crops of itchy, red spots, mainly on the chest and back but also on the limbs and sometimes in the mouth and genital area. These spots turn into blisters that look like water droplets before crusting over to become scabs. Your child will usually be unwell before the rash develops. The illness is variable in severity; all children will itch, but while some will only have one or two spots and feel fine, others will be covered and feel unwell.

The incubation period is 14–21 days and the disease is highly infectious. When chickenpox is about, parents sometimes decide to get the disease over and done with by holding parties where infected and non-infected children mingle. In some countries, children are immunized against chickenpox.

There are some possible complications of chickenpox: infected spots, which need antibiotics; chickenpox pneumonia (although this is rare); encephalitis, or inflammation of the brain (very rare); and shingles (months or years after having chickenpox). Chickenpox can affect a baby in the womb if contracted during pregnancy or around the time of birth. For this reason children with chickenpox should be kept away from GP surgeries or other places where they may come into contact with a pregnant woman, or a person with a weak immune system. If you haven't had chickenpox and are planning a pregnancy, tell your doctor so you can be immunized against it.

See a doctor if:

- Your child seems particularly unwell.
- He refuses fluids.
- He has blisters near the eyes.
- The spots look infected (there is a spreading red area around any of them).
- You can't control the fever.

What you can do:

- Keep your child cool – an experiment carried out by two doctors on their own son showed that the side of his body they dressed in shorts and a T-shirt had far fewer spots than the side they wrapped in trousers and a jumper.
- Clip your child's fingernails short to reduce any harm from scratching.
- Apply calamine lotion to help relieve itching.
- Give appropriate pain and fever relief.

Meningitis

This infection of the membranes that cover the brain (the meninges) can be caused by viruses or bacteria. Viral meningitis is mild, needs no specific treatment and is usually not serious. Bacterial meningitis, most common in babies, can cause long-term problems, such as deafness or cerebral palsy, if it is not treated promptly, and even death, but the vast majority of children make a complete recovery. The initial symptoms are described below (see box). It is diagnosed with a lumbar puncture, which involves taking drops of cerebral spinal fluid. The infection is caused by three different bacteria –

■ **Meningococcus:** this is the most common type in the UK and, if treated early, usually has a good outcome. However, the same bacteria can also cause septicaemia (blood poisoning). This infection often causes a non-blanching rash (see tumbler test, below), which looks like bruises or tiny, burst blood vessels. There are three types: A, B, and C. Babies in the UK are immunized against type C, and a vaccine to protect against type B is being developed.

■ **Haemophilus B (Hib):** there has been a dramatic fall in Hib infections since the vaccine was introduced (see page 93).

■ **Pneumococcus:** fortunately this is rare and should soon disappear now the pneumococcal vaccine is being offered to all babies.

What you can do:

■ If you suspect meningitis, don't wait for a rash to appear before seeking help. Take your child to your GP or emergency department. Trust your instincts – you know your baby best.

■ If your child has a rash, place a glass tumbler firmly against the skin (see box, below), and if the rash doesn't disappear, dial 999. Be aware that sometimes there is no rash or a mild rash that disappears with the tumbler test.

Spot the signs of meningitis

Symptoms in a baby
▸ High-pitched or weak cry
▸ Bulging fontanelle (see page 42)
▸ Vomiting
▸ Irritability, drowsiness and floppiness
▸ Rash or blotchy, clammy skin. The characteristic non-blanching rash of dark pink spots appears late in the illness or not at all.

Symptoms in a child or adult
▸ Severe headache
▸ Stiff neck
▸ Vomiting
▸ Rash
▸ Fever
▸ Drowsiness
▸ Irritability
▸ Photophobia (aversion to light).

TUMBLER TEST *Press a glass against the affected area. If the rash doesn't fade (non-blanching), it may be associated with meningitis.*

Kawasaki disease

No, this has nothing to do with Japanese motorbikes (although it was first identified in Japan). This infectious disease, for which the cause has yet to be found, usually affects the under-twos. The symptoms are dramatic and evolve over several days and will make your baby miserable; they are often mistaken for symptoms of other illnesses, such as measles.

There is no diagnostic test, but the symptoms are a fever (see page 259) for at least five days; a measles-like rash on the trunk and limbs; swollen glands in the neck; a very sore, cracked mouth; conjunctivitis; and swelling, then peeling, of the hands and feet. Officially, a child needs at least five of these symptoms to be diagnosed, but hospital treatment may be started if Kawasaki is suspected to prevent any long-term problems. Treatment includes intravenous immunoglobulin and aspirin to prevent long-term damage to the heart.

See a doctor if:

■ You suspect your child has Kawasaki disease as hospital treatment is essential.

What you can do:

■ Offer plenty of fluids.
■ Keep your child's fever under control.

Measles

Measles is highly infectious and caused by a virus that spreads via droplets in the air. All babies can be spared the disease by having the MMR immunization (see page 93).

The incubation period for measles is 10–14 days. It starts with a high fever and cold-like symptoms, then after four days a red rash first appears on the face, before spreading to the trunk. As the rash fades it becomes brown. Your child will probably have very sore eyes and a cough and feel extremely unwell. She may also have earache.

There are many possible complications of measles, including ear infection, febrile convulsions, squint, and pneumonia. It can also cause sub-acute sclerosing pan-encephalitis, which is a very rare brain disease that can develop years later.

See a doctor if:

■ You suspect measles – it is a notifiable disease, which means that information is collected on all cases for public health reasons.
■ Your child appears to be becoming more unwell, lethargic, has difficulty in breathing or refuses to drink anything.
■ You are worried – trust your judgement.

What you can do:

■ Encourage your child to drink plenty of fluids.
■ Keep your child's temperature down if she has a fever (see page 259).
■ Give her lots of TLC.
■ Keep her away from any unimmunized child or adult.

Hand, foot, and mouth

This viral infection isn't particularly infectious and has nothing to do with foot and mouth disease in cattle. It lasts about a week and causes spots and blisters on the palms and soles, and sometimes the fingers and toes, and in the mouth. It may not affect all these areas. The spots are not itchy, but there may be a fever.

See a doctor if:

- You are unsure of the diagnosis.
- Your child isn't drinking anything.

What you can do:

- If your child's mouth is sore, try sloppy, bland foods and let him drink from a straw.

Mumps

A viral infection spread by droplets in the air and direct contact, mumps is a relatively mild illness that causes fever, headache, and loss of appetite. It also leads to painful swelling of the salivary glands, most notably the parotids, which are in front of the ears. This makes the child look like a chipmunk. A child who has the MMR vaccine is immunized against mumps.

Possible complications are viral meningitis which, although usually mild, may cause deafness; and inflammation of the testes, which may cause sterility in older boys and men.

See a doctor if:

- You suspect mumps (it is a notifiable disease).
- You can't control your child's fever.
- He becomes drowsy.
- He refuses fluids.

What you can do:

- Treat any fever (see page 259) and give small, frequent drinks through a straw. Avoid citrus drinks as acid stimulates saliva production and causes pain in the salivary glands.
- Give your child sloppy food to eat.

RECOGNIZING A RASH

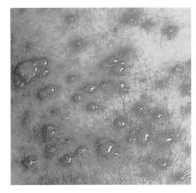

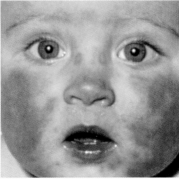

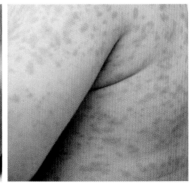

CHICKENPOX *Itchy red spots that turn to blisters and then scab over.*

SLAPPED CHEEK DISEASE *The rash fits its description and spreads to the body.*

MEASLES *Small red spots that start on the face and spread to the trunk.*

Roseola

Common in babies from six months to two years, this virus causes a high fever for 3–5 days with cold-like symptoms and irritability. When the child is improving, a spotty, red rash appears that makes the diagnosis obvious. Sometimes babies with roseola appear so unwell that they are admitted to hospital to rule out meningitis.

See a doctor if:

- Your child is irritable or drowsy.
- She has a febrile convulsion (see page 259).
- She is no better once the rash has appeared.

What you can do:

- Keep your child cool and give fluids.

Rubella

This mild illness, which is also known as German measles, causes a measles-like rash on the first day of the illness. There are often swollen lymph glands at the back of the neck. It is now less common due to immunization as it is included in the MMR vaccine.

Rubella is spread by droplets in the air and has an incubation period of 14–21 days. Although it rarely needs treatment in children it is a worrying illness in pregnant women as it can cause serious birth defects, especially if it is contracted in the early months.

See a doctor if:

- You suspect rubella (it is a notifiable disease).
- You are pregnant and not immune to rubella.
- Your child is not better in four days.

What you can do:

- Give your child plenty of TLC.
- Avoid taking your child to a GP surgery or anywhere he might come into contact with pregnant women.
- If your child also complains of pain in his joints, give him ibuprofen.

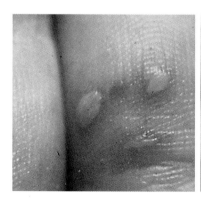

HAND, FOOT, AND MOUTH *There may be blisters on the fingers.*

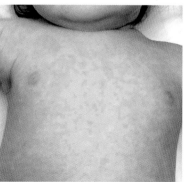

ROSEOLA *This spotty, red rash appears once the child is getting better.*

RUBELLA *A measles-like rash that spreads all over the body.*

Slapped cheek disease

Also known as fifth disease, in most children this is a mild illness caused by a virus called parvovirus, with a bright red rash that first appears on the face. The incubation period is variable, but once the rash appears, the child is no longer infectious.

The rash may just be on the face or can spread to the body. It usually fades in a few days, but sometimes comes and goes over four weeks. Occasionally, children also have joint pains.

Slapped cheek disease may cause anaemia in children with sickle cell disease, which is an inherited blood disorder. In pregnant women there is a small chance of miscarriage as the disease can cause anaemia in the fetus.

Gastroenteritis

This is a highly contagious tummy bug, common in babies and children. There will be a combination of vomiting and diarrhoea that is usually green, watery, and smelly. It can lead to temporary milk intolerance (see page 278).

What you can do:

■ Offer your breastfed baby plenty of feeds and give extra oral rehydration solution (ORS), available from your pharmacist. Don't give your bottle-fed baby milk – offer her small, frequent sips of ORS in a bottle, medicine syringe, or beaker for 24 hours. Give her sips every few minutes to prevent vomiting.
■ Give your toddler ORS to drink and bland solids to eat.
■ Be meticulous about hand-washing.

See a doctor if:

■ There are signs of dehydration (see page 257).

Whooping cough

Also known as pertussis, this is caused by a bacterium that inflames the airways. It starts with cold symptoms, followed by bouts of coughing that include a big breath in, which sounds like a "whoop". There may be vomiting and your child may turn blue or even stop breathing. A vaccine (see page 93) will protect your child against it.

See a doctor if:

■ You suspect whooping cough (it is a notifiable disease).

■ Your child is unable to keep down any fluids.
■ Call an ambulance if your child changes colour (turns blue), stops breathing, or has a febrile convulsion (see page 259).

What you can do:

■ Give your child fluids little and often.
■ Keep him away from babies, particularly those who are not yet immunized.
■ Give paracetamol or ibuprofen to reduce fever.

Gastrointestinal disorders

As a parent, it is highly likely you will have to deal with vomit and diarrhoea in the first two years of your child's life, as tummy troubles are common. Breastfed babies have some protection from antibodies in breast milk. Most gastrointestinal disorders are easy to treat.

Gastro-oesophageal reflux

This is a common condition in young babies, in which the valve at the top of the stomach is leaky, allowing milk to come back up. Mild reflux is simply an inconvenience, as no one likes changing their baby's clothes, and often their own, every couple of hours. It needs no specific treatment, but it can be uncomfortable for your baby as regurgitated stomach acids cause a burning sensation. Reflux almost always gets better in time – starting solids often helps, so the turning point may happen at six months, and most babies are better by one year.

If preventative methods (see right) don't work, your GP or paediatrician may prescribe treatment to block acid production or to help the milk pass through the stomach more rapidly. Some babies have reflux caused by a cow's milk allergy and may benefit from a special, hypoallergenic formula.

What you can do:

■ Consult your GP.
■ Keep your baby propped or held upright after feeds and give her plenty of time lying on her tummy at other times.
■ Thickening milk can help with moderate reflux as can adding infant Gaviscon to bottles. This can be given separately to breastfed babies. Alternatively, you can buy pre-thickened formula milk from a pharmacist.

Pyloric stenosis

This condition occurs when the exit at the bottom of the stomach is too narrow, due to a thickening of the muscle in that area. This causes the baby to vomit with so much force that a regurgitated feed can shoot across the room (known as projectile vomiting). Pyloric stenosis sometimes runs in families and, curiously, is more common in first-born boys.

The vomiting becomes progressively worse. Pyloric stenosis is usually confirmed with blood tests and an ultrasound scan.

Treatment is always with surgery. A small slit is made in the thickened muscle around the stomach exit, which allows milk to pass through once more. The baby usually recovers very quickly afterwards.

Constipation and soiling

One of the most common problems I see in toddlers is constipation. It can cause pain, misery, and embarrassment for a child and become a cause of anxiety for the family. Parents often feel they are the only family suffering because it is a taboo subject.

"Our lives were dominated by our son's constipation for several months. With hindsight, I really wish we had sought medical help much earlier than we did."

EATING FRUIT *Snacking on fruit will help to prevent constipation.*

WHAT IS CONSTIPATION?

Constipation is defined as the infrequent passage of a painful, hard stool. Whether or not your child is regular is not really the main issue. It is normal for some children to pass faeces three times a day while others only pass one every three days. If your baby or toddler simply doesn't poo very often, this doesn't mean she is constipated. It is only a problem if it causes pain and distress.

Constipation often starts after a child passes a very hard poo that causes a split, known as a fissure, just inside the bottom. This is painful and the child understandably starts to hold in the poo in rather than going through the pain of letting it out. Stools then build up and become increasingly difficult to pass. Eventually, runny poo from further up the bowel leaks out around the hard "rocks" inside the child's bottom and causes soiling, which is especially distressing for a potty-trained toddler. As the backlog of poo accumulates, the child becomes miserable, pale, withdrawn and off her food. Family life becomes dominated by this and parents try tactics to encourage their child to poo.

The child often has a severe tummy ache and may be brought to casualty. Eventually she does a poo to the relief of everyone and all is well until the backlog accumulates again.

Babies may become relatively constipated when switching from breast milk to formula or when starting solids. It is unusual for a fully breastfed baby to be truly constipated.

DIET

There are some children who are constipated despite a good diet but these are rare. Constipation can be prevented to a large extent by a diet with plenty of fibre, fluid, and five portions of fruit and vegetables every day. This is easier said than done, but there are many ways in which you can increase your child's intake of fruit and vegetables (see box, right).

FLUIDS

A constipated baby of less than three or four months old usually responds to some extra cooled, boiled water in her diet. If she is bottle-fed, make sure you are not adding heaped scoops to her bottle as concentrated formula can cause constipation. Once your baby is weaned, ensure that she gets plenty of fruit, vegetables, and water.

HOW IS IT TREATED?

The most important part of treatment is to start early, as the longer this problem continues the harder it becomes to treat. If your baby has been constipated for a few days, simple laxatives, such as lactulose, are useful together with increasing the fluid and fibre in her diet. However, after the "rocks" have built up and the problem is chronic, a more powerful combination of laxatives is often needed. This is the stage at which you should take your child to see a GP. You should always seek the advice of a pharmacist before buying any laxatives for a baby or toddler.

Suppositories are rarely helpful and children with already painful bottoms won't thank you for using them. Many parents are concerned that their child will become dependent upon laxatives. It is true that children with severe constipation will need treatment often for two years or more. However, while she is having this treatment, your child will usually be symptom free. This is an enormous relief to those parents who have suffered their child's screaming, soiling, and misery and whose family life revolves around whether or not she has finally managed to do a poo.

Gradually, you will be able to reduce the medicine under the guidance of a doctor, and your child will eventually be laxative-free. Please ignore any "helpful" advice from relatives or friends to stop laxatives, as this will usually set your child right back to where she started. If you feel that the treatment you are giving your child is not working, talk to your GP. Your child may need a referral to a paediatrician if the problem is becoming severe.

THE IMPORTANCE OF SEEKING HELP

Once constipation and soiling become a chronic problem they are difficult to treat. Even in the best clinics only 50 per cent of children are cured after two years of treatment.

I run a specialist constipation and soiling clinic and have listened to the suffering constipation causes to children and their parents for many years. My first son has always eaten a very healthy diet and I was brought into the real world when my daughter came along with her very limited diet, which was particularly low on fruit and vegetables. The day she became severely constipated our lives were turned upside down. The pain and screaming were so alarming that it was hard to believe she didn't have a more serious problem. It took two stressful weeks of high dose laxatives to bring it under control. I can only imagine what parents go through if the problem is only partially treated and drags on for years, so do persevere with treatment.

EATING FRUIT AND VEGETABLES

It isn't always easy to get babies and young children to eat the recommended amount of fruit and vegetables. Here are some ways in which you can increase their intake:

▶ Remember that a cup of juice can count as one portion of fruit.

▶ Low-salt baked beans count as a portion of vegetables.

▶ Lots of toddlers who refuse fresh fruit and vegetables are willing to eat dried fruit, so try raisins. Do, however, brush her teeth well afterwards because they have a high sugar content.

▶ Grapes (cut in half to reduce the risk of choking) are a great snack and finger food.

▶ Try adding vegetables such as leeks, carrots, courgettes, and sweet peppers to a tomato-based pasta sauce and whizz it up in the blender – most toddlers won't spot the difference, especially if you build up the extra veggies bit by bit, so that it doesn't suddenly taste very different.

▶ A smoothie made with fruit, as a drink or frozen in lolly moulds, will also go down well with toddlers.

Intussusception

In this condition one bit of the intestine slips inside another, causing a blockage. It is more common in babies, leads to bouts of crying due to severe tummy ache and should not be confused with colic. The baby lies still as movement is painful. She may look pale, vomit, and pass bright red poo. It is diagnosed by ultrasound or an enema and usually treated by gently pumping air into the bottom, forcing the intestine into position. Most babies don't need surgery and there are usually no complications. See your doctor if you suspect intussusception.

Chronic diarrhoea

To understand diarrhoea it is important to have a picture of what is normal. After the meconium stage has passed (see page 34), babies can have a huge range of normal poos. The colour can range from yellow, to orange, to green and brown, and the consistency from runny to firm. White or putty-coloured poo can be a sign of malabsorption. The change in the smell, colour, and consistency of poos when a baby is weaned often causes parents to worry.

Some babies develop diarrhoea that does not appear to be due to infection and lasts for weeks. If your baby is also not gaining weight as expected, or seems to have tummy ache, some form of malabsorption or food intolerance may be the cause (see box, below). It is useful to keep a food diary before seeing your doctor as you may be able to document which, if any, foods cause the diarrhoea.

If your toddler has loose, frequent poos but is otherwise well and gaining weight, she may have toddler diarrhoea. Toddlers with this condition often have visible food, such as peas and carrots, in their poo. This is due to a rapid transit of food through the gut and is not a problem. Given time, it gets better on its own.

Food intolerance

The most common form of food intolerance is an allergy to cow's milk protein. This may lead to blood in the poo and eczema. It is vastly improved by removing milk from the diet and usually gets better by the age of two.

Some babies are unable to absorb lactose, which is the sugar in milk. A few babies are born with lactose intolerance but more commonly acquire the problem after a bout of gastroenteritis. Treatment includes removing lactose from your baby's diet for a few days or weeks until it settles down. The best way to do this is by replacing her usual milk with formula milk that does not contain lactose.

Coeliac disease is an inability to absorb gluten in foods such as bread and cereals. Like other intolerances it is treated by removing that particular food from the diet, but always under medical supervision.

Allergies

An allergy occurs when the immune system reacts inappropriately to a substance that is either eaten, inhaled, or comes into contact with the skin. Symptoms include wheezing, rashes, diarrhoea, and a stuffy nose. Some severe allergies cause anaphylaxis (see page 280).

Asthma

In this common condition the airways narrow, leading to wheezing, coughing, and difficulty breathing. Asthma is one of a group of atopic (allergic) illnesses that run in families, which also includes eczema and hay fever. Attacks may be triggered by a number of factors, but the most common in young children is a cold. Other triggers include the house dust mite, exercise, cigarette smoke, very cold air, and, in some children, pollen and animal hair. It is impossible to eradicate all triggers, but children must be kept away from smoky atmospheres. As children grow older, their asthma usually becomes easier to control, and many no longer need an inhaler.

Treatment

Mild asthma is treated with a drug called a bronchodilator, which provides instant relief by widening the airways. This is given via an inhaler or nebulizer (a machine that creates a mist which can be breathed in through a mask). Moderate cases of asthma, where your child uses an inhaler daily, require treatment with a preventer, usually an inhaled steroid. A child with severe asthma will need to be under the care of a paediatrician and may require hospital admission.

What you can do:

■ Give any regular treatment prescribed by your doctor, exactly as instructed.
■ Keep dust levels low and use pillows that can be washed regularly.

See a doctor if:

■ Your child is not responding to his inhaler.
■ He is exhausted and you are worried.

TREATING A YOUNG CHILD *A spacer is a long tube that clips to the inhaler, enabling a child to inhale in two steps. For babies and very young children, a face mask also helps.*

Eczema

This atopic skin condition may first appear as red, dry, itchy skin when your baby is a few weeks old. There are plenty of ways to reduce its severity and ease symptoms. A food allergy is sometimes the cause, although allergy testing is rarely helpful. The good news is that eczema improves with age and does not scar.

What you can do:

To help prevent an outbreak:
■ Always dress your child in cotton, rather than wool or synthetic fabrics.
■ Keep her cool with light bedclothes.
■ Use non-biological washing powders, which are gentler on her skin, and use recommended soap substitutes to wash your child.

To treat the rash once it appears:
■ Apply emollients to dry skin at least twice a day to prevent itching. Use steroid creams on red patches of eczema only. Using weak steroids may prevent the need for more powerful ones later.
■ Bathe your child in special eczema products and pat her dry.

See a doctor if:
■ Your child's skin is very red, crusty (possibly yellow), and weepy, as it may be infected.

Anaphylaxis

Foods such as peanuts and seafood, as well as wasp and bee stings, can cause a severe allergic reaction, called anaphylaxis, in some children. This is a life-threatening sudden onset of facial swelling, particularly of the eyes, lips, and tongue, and breathing difficulties. It is treated with steroids and antihistamine, and epinephrine (adrenaline). If your child has a severe allergy you will be given epinephrine in a pre-loaded syringe to use at the first sign of an attack.

What you can do:
■ Administer your child's epinephrine and call an ambulance if you suspect an attack.
■ Inform anyone who cares for your child about what to avoid and what to do in an emergency.

Urticaria

This was my first medical word. I learnt it at the age of five when I woke up covered in a bumpy, red, very itchy rash and my mother (a doctor, naturally) wrote it on the blackboard for me. This allergic rash looks like nettle rash and can be caused by a reaction to food, drugs, or viruses. In children a cause is rarely found.

What you can do
■ Give your child antihistamine syrup.
■ Smother him in calamine lotion.

See a doctor if:
■ You think he is reacting to a drug.
■ He has frequent attacks of urticaria.

Nursery nasties

You are unlikely to escape the pleasures of head lice, worms, impetigo, or conjunctivitis – especially once your toddler starts mixing with other children. If you have a second baby, these common conditions are likely to occur even earlier.

Head lice

This bane of every parent's life rarely affects babies, but is often contracted by toddlers once they are mixing with other children. Head lice are tiny insects that live on or close to the scalp. They can't fly and therefore can only spread from head to head by direct contact. They lay tiny eggs close to the scalp, which are extremely hard to spot and remove, and can survive for several weeks.

Head lice cause itching, so you may notice your child scratching his head a lot. However, you'll probably discover them before symptoms occur because a note is likely to be sent home from the nursery announcing a case of head lice and asking everyone to check their children.

What you can do:

■ Systematically check your child's hair by parting it carefully all over and looking for live lice (hard to spot as they move fast) or eggs (nits) "glued" to individual hairs.
■ Treat your child's hair by applying a recommended lotion – check with your GP, health visitor, or pharmacist before buying one as these can vary in effectiveness as lice become resistant to them.

■ Alternatively, wash the hair and apply lots of conditioner so that it is slippery. Then comb your child's hair thoroughly with a fine-toothed nit comb, wiping it on a kitchen roll or dipping it in water each time you pull it through his hair.
■ Repeat every 3 to 4 days for two weeks, then at least weekly, to help prevent reinfestation.
■ Check other members of your household for infestation and inform anyone that has been in contact with your child recently.

REMOVING HEAD LICE *Check your child's scalp thoroughly using a special head lice comb. After each stroke, remove the comb and wipe any lice on to a tissue.*

Impetigo

This common skin infection mainly affects children. The red, yellow, and crusty rash spreads rapidly and is contagious. It can occur anywhere but is most common on the face. It is usually caused by a bacterium called staphylococcus (staph), which is often carried quite harmlessly in our noses but can enter the skin through a cracked, dry area. For this reason impetigo is more common in children with eczema. It is treated with antibiotic cream or ointment if it is mild, and oral antibiotics if it is more severe. Rarely it will need treatment in hospital by intravenous antibiotics.

See a doctor if:

■ You suspect impetigo.
■ It is spreading despite treatment.
■ Your child appears unwell.

What you can do:

■ As impetigo spreads by direct contact, your child should not share towels or face cloths and should avoid skin-to-skin contact with other members of the family, where possible.
■ Try to prevent your child from picking the rash (not easy) and apply creams as instructed.

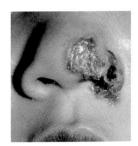

SCABS *Do not cover the scabs as air helps them to heal. Trim your child's nails to minimize scratching. Once there is no crusting over the sores, your child is no longer contagious.*

Cold sores

This viral skin infection, caught from coming into contact with someone with a cold sore, is caused by the herpes simplex virus (HSV1). It causes a tingling and then a painful cluster of unsightly blisters, usually on the lip. It can be distressing the first time your child is infected because she may have extensive blisters all around and in her mouth. Cold sores will make her miserable and she may refuse all food and drink, in which case she will need admission to hospital for fluids and treatment with an antiviral drug called aciclovir. Once infected, the virus remains dormant in your child and reappears as a cold sore from time to time due to stress, cold weather, or being unwell.

What you can do:

■ If your child is older, you may learn to recognize when she is getting a cold sore. She may tell you her lip is tingling – usually the first sign. Apply aciclovir cream at this stage because it won't work once the blister appears.
■ Keep your child away from other children until the sore has fully scabbed over.
■ Encourage her to keep eating and drinking.

See a doctor if:

■ It is a first attack.
■ The sore is near her eye.
■ She refuses to eat and drink.
■ It is not healing as expected.

Worms

Threadworms, the most common type of worm to affect children, are a minor inconvenience but not harmful. They are spread when a child ingests eggs that are passed on by direct hand-to-hand contact. Threadworms cause itching around the bottom, often at night when the threadworms emerge to lay eggs. These are then trapped under the fingernails when the child scratches, and the cycle continues.

Worms can be hard to diagnose unless you actually see them in your child's poo or anus, and while it is possible to trap the eggs on clear sticky tape to clinch the diagnosis, I've yet to meet a parent who has done this.

What you can do:

■ If you suspect that your child has threadworms, you can buy medicine at the pharmacy or ask your GP to prescribe it. Under-twos are given a single dose, which will need to be repeated after two weeks.
■ All family members over the age of two need a one-off dose of a different medicine to prevent them getting threadworms.
■ Wash all clothes and bedclothes thoroughly, cut fingernails short and ensure everyone in the family is scrupulous about hand-washing.
■ Scrub under your child's nails, especially after she has used the toilet.

Thrush

This is a common fungal infection that is caused by an overgrowth of Candida albicans, a yeast that is naturally present in the body. It is often passed to a baby during the birth. It is most common in babies aged two months and younger, but it can appear in older babies, too.

If you notice white patches inside your baby's mouth, which look like milk curds but are difficult to remove, she may have oral thrush. Thrush won't normally make your baby unwell but it might make her mouth sore and may affect her ability to feed. It is also a common cause of severe nappy rash and can be treated with anti-fungal creams.

See a doctor if:

■ You suspect your baby has thrush.
■ If it isn't getting better, despite treatment.

What you can do:

■ Use the anti-fungal drops or gel prescribed by your GP.
■ If you are breastfeeding and your baby has thrush, your GP can prescribe a safe anti-fungal cream for you to rub on your nipples. This cream will prevent the spread of infection. If thrush spreads to your breasts, it may make them itchy.
■ Treat your baby's nappy rash (see page 94).

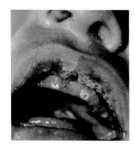

RECOGNIZING THRUSH
Look for white spots in the mouth, which might be slightly raised. Although it can look unsightly, there is normally no pain associated with the spots.

Your baby in hospital

Babies and young children will only need to stay overnight in hospital if they require treatment or special observation around the clock provided by doctors and nurses. Otherwise we doctors do everything we can to keep children at home.

THE HOSPITAL WARD

The whole experience of staying in hospital with your baby has improved enormously in recent years. Children's wards are usually bright, full of toys, and quite informal. Parents are encouraged to stay in with their baby and can visit at any time, day and night. Babies and young children need their parents even more when they are ill and hospitals usually provide camp beds for parents to sleep on, next to the cot.

Play specialists are on hand to entertain your child and the range of electronic equipment available for older children is so extensive that they often tell me they don't want to go home when they are better. The average length of a hospital stay for children is one to two days, but some children with life-threatening or chronic conditions may need to stay longer. It is easy for parents to develop cabin fever in hospital and it is

important, if possible, to share the night shifts because time off is important for you both.

The day usually starts with a ward round, when junior doctors, nurses and often a consultant will check on your baby, answer questions, and decide on her ongoing treatment. You may find it useful to write down questions that you want to ask, but there should be doctors and nurses on hand to answer queries. Never be afraid to ask a question, even if it seems silly.

When it is time to go home, make sure you understand the discharge

plan and know where to seek help if necessary. If you are expecting test results, find out how and when they will be given to you.

WHAT YOU CAN DO

▶ Bring in any special toys, comfort objects, and blankets that will make your baby feel more at home.
▶ Give her lots of reassurance, and expect her to be very clingy.
▶ While siblings are always welcome during the day, try to find someone else to look after them at night while you are at the hospital.

BEING INFORMED *Don't be afraid to ask questions. Understanding the treatment your child is being given will prevent unnecessary anxiety.*

First aid

This section covers basic first aid for a few key emergencies plus tips on how to give effective help in common first-aid situations with babies and children. However, all parents should consider taking a course in first aid because it is a practical skill that is greatly enhanced by expert training. For advice on how to find a course local to you, see the resource list on pages 312.

Action in an emergency

In an emergency, you need to remember four logical steps –

■ **Assess the situation:** ask what happened; how it happened; is more than one child injured; is there any continuing danger; do you need an ambulance?

■ **Think of safety:** do not risk injuring yourself while you try to help; remove any source of danger from your child; move your child, if you must, for her safety but do so very carefully.

■ **Treat serious injuries first:** the two conditions that threaten life are inability to breathe (see unconsciousness, page 286) and serious bleeding (see page 291).

■ **Get help:** shout for help and ask others to make the area safe; seek medical advice or call an ambulance; ask others to help with first aid and to help move a child to safety, if necessary.

When to go to hospital

Use this list as a guide to decide whether your child needs to go to hospital. In a real emergency – for example, if your child has stopped breathing – call an ambulance. Follow the advice in this section while you wait for help to arrive. In less urgent cases where your child still needs medical treatment, go to your hospital emergency department. Always get your child to hospital if she has:

▶ Lost consciousness.

▶ Stopped breathing or has difficulty breathing.

▶ Sustained a deep wound or a serious or large burn.

▶ Symptoms of meningitis (see page 270).

▶ A serious head injury, with vomiting, drowsiness, or loss of consciousness.

▶ A suspected broken bone.

▶ Eaten a poisonous substance.

▶ A foreign object lodged in her ear, nose, or eye.

▶ A snake, animal, or insect bite if there is a family. history of allergic reactions (see anaphylaxis, page 280).

Unconsciousness

If your child is unconscious, assess him before calling for help. If you are alone and he is not breathing follow the instructions for rescue breaths and chest compressions. Some alternative steps are given for a child over one year.

Check for response

1 *Call your baby's name to see if he responds to your voice, or tap his foot gently. Never shake him.*

OR

FOR A CHILD OVER 1 YEAR

Call his name to see if he responds, or tap his shoulder gently. Never shake him.

2 *If there is no response, go to open the airway.*

3 *If there is a response, seek medical advice.*

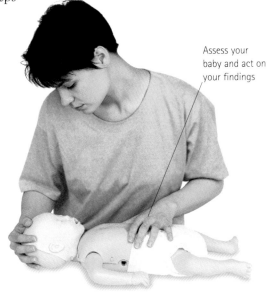

Assess your baby and act on your findings

Open the airway

1 *Lay your baby or child on a flat surface and put one hand on his forehead and gently tilt his head.*

2 *Place one finger of your other hand on the point of your baby's chin and lift it.*

DO NOT *press on the soft part of the neck as it can block the airway.*

OR

FOR A CHILD OVER 1 YEAR

Place one finger of your other hand on the point of his chin and lift it.

DO NOT *press on the soft part of the neck as it can block the airway. Lift your child's chin.*

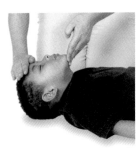

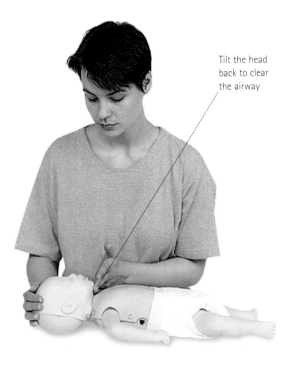

Tilt the head back to clear the airway

Check for breathing for up to 10 seconds

1 *Look, listen, and feel for breathing. Look along his chest for movement, listen for sounds of normal breathing, and feel for breaths against your cheek.*

2 *Send a helper to call an ambulance.*

3 *If he is breathing hold your baby with his head tilted down or put your child in the recovery position (see box, below) and wait for help to arrive.*

4 *If he is not breathing, give rescue breaths (see below).*

Rescue breaths

This is to be used on an unconscious baby who is not breathing. Always give five initial rescue breaths before beginning chest compressions.

1 *Make sure your baby or child is on a firm surface and open his airway (see left).*

2 *Pick out any visible obstructions in the mouth or nose.* **DO NOT** *do a finger sweep of the mouth.*

3 *Take a breath and seal your lips tightly round your baby's nose and mouth. Blow gently into the lungs until the chest rises. Remove your mouth and watch the chest fall back.*

OR

FOR A CHILD OVER 1 YEAR

Pinch his nostrils closed. Take a breath and seal your lips tightly round his mouth. Blow into his mouth for one second until the chest rises. Remove your mouth. Watch the chest fall back.

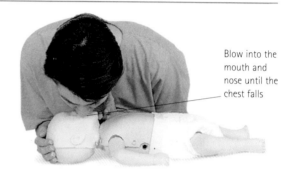

Blow into the mouth and nose until the chest falls

4 *Give your baby five rescue breaths. If you can't achieve a rescue breath, recheck the airway and mouth and make sure you have a tight seal around his mouth and nose.*

OR

FOR A CHILD OVER 1 YEAR

Give your child five rescue breaths. Keep the nostrils pinched. If your child's chest does not rise, check his mouth again and adjust the position of his head.

5 *After five attempts at rescue breaths, begin chest compressions (see next page). If breathing returns, place your baby or child in the recovery position (see box).*

Recovery position

Hold a baby with her head lower than her body or turn a child on to her side (as shown). This keeps the airway open and allows vomit or fluids to drain from the mouth.

FOR A BABY

FOR A CHILD

Chest compressions and rescue breaths (CPR)

CPR is a combination of chest compressions and rescue breaths. If you are alone, give CPR for a full minute before you call an ambulance.

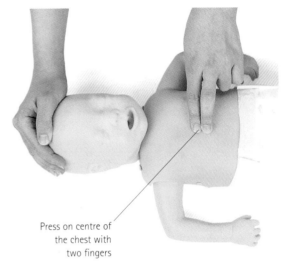

Press on centre of the chest with two fingers

1 *Place your baby or child on his back on a firm surface. Place the tips of two fingers on the centre of his chest.*

OR

FOR A CHILD OVER 1 YEAR
Place the heel of your hand on the centre of the child's chest. Lean forwards over the child so your shoulder is above your hand.

2 *Press down by one-third of the depth of the chest. Release the pressure but don't remove your fingers or hand. Allow the chest to come back up fully. Repeat to give 30 compressions at a rate of 100 per minute.*

3 *Give two rescue breaths as on previous page.*

4 *Continue the cycle of 30 chest compressions to two rescue breaths for one minute.*

5 *Call an ambulance if this has not been done. Continue the cycle as above until help arrives, your baby or child starts breathing, or you are too exhausted to continue.*

6 *If breathing returns, place your baby or child in the recovery position (see page 287) and call an ambulance if this has not been done already. Monitor your child until the ambulance arrives.*

Resuscitation summary

The sequence for treating an unconscious baby or child is summed up below. It is worth trying to learn it by heart so that you know exactly what to do in an emergency.

OPEN AIRWAY
▼
CHECK BREATHING
▼
NO BREATHING
▼
SEND HELPER TO CALL AN AMBULANCE
▼
GIVE FIVE INITIAL RESCUE BREATHS
▼

BEGIN CHEST COMPRESSIONS WITH RESCUE BREATHS
▼
REPEAT FOR 1 MINUTE
▼
IF NOT ALREADY DONE, CALL AN AMBULANCE
▼
CONTINUE CPR UNTIL HELP ARRIVES

Choking

Children can easily choke on food or small objects which may get stuck at the back of the throat and block the windpipe. Your priority is to remove the obstruction quickly and clear the airway. Instructions for a child over one year are given on the next page.

For a baby (under 12 months)

If the choking is mild, a baby will still be able to cough. If the blockage is severe, a baby will be unable to cry, cough, or breathe.

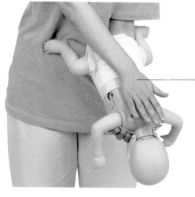

Give five sharp blows on his back with heel of hand

1 *If your baby is unable to cough or breathe, lay him face down, head low along your forearm. Support his head and shoulders with your hand and give five sharp blows to the upper part of his back with the heel of your hand.*

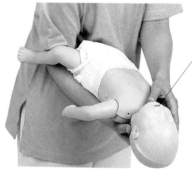

Look in mouth and remove visible object

2 *Turn his face up along your other arm. Look inside his mouth and pick out any visible obstruction from the mouth or nose with your forefinger and thumb.*

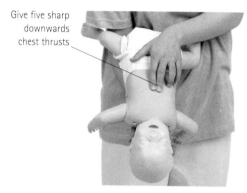

Give five sharp downwards chest thrusts

3 *If back blows fail, give chest thrusts. Place two fingers on the lower half of the breastbone and give five sharp downwards thrusts at a rate of one every three seconds. Then check the baby's mouth.*

4 *If the blockage has not cleared, repeat steps 1-3 three times. Call an ambulance.*

5 *Continue cycles of back blows and chest thrusts until help arrives, the obstruction clears, or the baby loses consciousness.*

6 *If the baby loses consciousness (see page 286) and you can't achieve rescue breaths, give 30 chest compressions to try to clear the obstruction and then try 2 breaths again.*

IMPORTANT

▸ DO NOT shake a baby.

▸ DO NOT feel blindly down your baby's throat to try to clear the obstruction.

▸ Any baby who has been given chest thrusts must be seen by a doctor.

For a child over 1 year

If the blockage is mild, your child will be able
to speak, cough, and breathe. If it is severe, he
will not be able to speak, cough, or breathe.

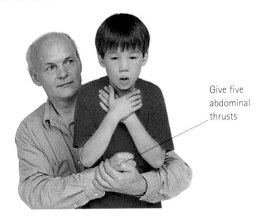

Give five
abdominal
thrusts

1 If your child can cough, encourage him to do so to
remove the object.

2 If your child cannot talk, cough, or breathe, help him
to bend forwards. Give him five sharp slaps between the
shoulder blades with the heel of your hand. Check his
mouth. Remove any object you can see.

3 If the back blows fail, give abdominal thrusts. Place one
fist in the middle of his upper abdomen, just below his rib
cage. Cover your fist with your other hand. Give five
upwards thrusts. Check your child's mouth.

4 If the abdominal thrusts fail, repeat steps 2 and 3 three
times. If this is unsuccessful, call an ambulance.

5 Continue cycles of back blows and abdominal thrusts
until help arrives, the obstruction clears, or the child loses
consciousness. If your child loses consciousness, see step 6
for a choking baby on previous page.

IMPORTANT

▸ DO NOT feel blindly down your child's throat to try
to clear the obstruction.

▸ Any child who has been given abdominal thrusts
must be seen by a doctor.

Burns and scalds

You must seek medical advice for all burns on children. A child with a large
burn must be taken to hospital. It is very important to cool the burn as
quickly as possible to minimize damage.

1 Cool the affected area
immediately. Hold it under
cool, running water for at
least 10 minutes. Pour
water over or shower a
large burn but don't immerse
the child in cold water as this may cause hypothermia.

2 Once cooled, remove any clothing from the burned area.
If pain persists, cool again. Cut round material that is stuck
to the skin. Remove tight clothing in case swelling occurs.

Cover burns
with a clean
plastic bag

3 Cover the burn with a sterile dressing or clean, non-
fluffy material. Use a pillowcase for a large burn or put
a clean plastic bag over a burned hand or foot. Keep your
child warm. Take her to hospital. Never put fat or ointment
on a burn or scald. Do not give your child anything to eat
or drink. Watch for signs of shock (see right).

Serious bleeding

Heavy bleeding is both serious and distressing and should be dealt with as an emergency. If too much blood is lost, shock and loss of consciousness can result.

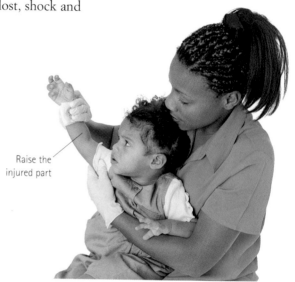

Raise the injured part

1 *Apply pressure directly over the injured area using your fingers or the palm of your hand or by placing a clean pad over the wound and pressing firmly to stop the bleeding.*
2 *Raise the injury above the level of your child's heart. Cover it with a clean, non-fluffy dressing and keep the injury raised.*
3 *Secure the dressing with a bandage tied firmly but not so tight as to reduce blood supply.*
4 *Lay your child down, still keeping the injured area raised and get her to hospital as soon as possible as she may need to have the wound stitched.*

Shock

The most likely cause of shock is serious bleeding or severe burns or scalds. Early signs are pale, cold, sweaty skin, tinged with grey; a rapid pulse becoming weaker; and shallow, fast breathing. As it develops, the child may become restless, start yawning and sighing, have a severe thirst, and then become unconscious.

1 Lay your child on a blanket or rug if possible and raise her legs higher than her heart by supporting them on cushions, a pile of books, or a chair. Call an ambulance.
2 Loosen any tight clothing at the neck, chest, and waist.
3 Cover her with a blanket to keep her warm but do NOT give her a hot-water bottle or any other direct source of heat.
4 Monitor her pulse, breathing, and level of consciousness by talking to her. If she loses consciousness, put her in the recovery position (see page 287) and wait for help to arrive.

Raise and support her legs

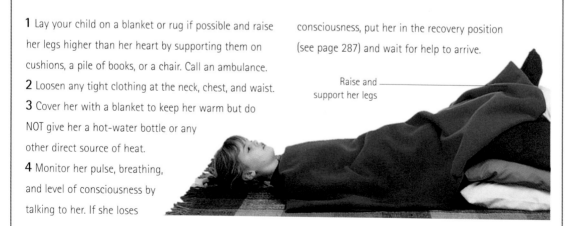

Leg, arm, and hand injuries

It can be difficult to tell the difference between broken bones and muscle sprains or strains. Always treat such an injury as a possible broken bone, which needs prompt treatment by a doctor and X-rays or a scan in hospital.

Leg injury

1 *Keep your child as still as possible while an ambulance is called. She will need a stretcher so don't try to take her to hospital yourself. Your child could go into shock (see page 291), especially if the thigh bone is broken.*
2 *Sit or lay your child down and encourage her to stay still. Hold the joints above the injured area to prevent any movement. Support her leg with cushions or a blanket and call an ambulance.*

Support leg at joints above and below injury

Arm or hand injury

A fall on to an outstretched hand can injure collarbones and shoulders, while a direct blow to the arm can cause a break or a greenstick fracture, in which the bone bends and splits but does not break.

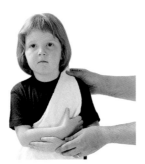 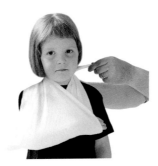 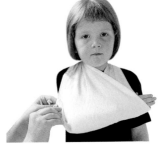

1 Hold your child's injured arm across her chest. Slide a triangular bandage between her arm and chest so that the longest edge of the bandage is parallel to her uninjured arm.

2 Bring the lower half of the bandage up over the injured arm and take the point round the back of your child's neck. Tie the ends together in a knot behind her neck or over the hollow above her collarbone.

3 Tuck the two ends of the bandage under the knot and then fold the bandage over your child's elbow and fix it in place with a safety pin. Once the sling is in place, take your child to hospital.

Basic first-aid tips

This chart offers basic first-aid tips that will help you act quickly and safely in a
range of common emergency situations with babies and children. If you are in any
doubt about the treatment your child needs, seek medical advice.

INJURY	WHAT TO DO	MEDICAL HELP?
▶ Object in nose	Don't try to remove a small object even if you can see it. Ask your child if she has put something in her nose.	Reassure her and take her to hospital.
▶ Object in eye	Sit your child on your lap, separate her eyelids and ask child to look left, right, up, and down. If you can see the speck, tilt her head and pour water into the inner corner of her eye or lift the speck away with a damp swab or the corner of a handkerchief. If the object is under her eyelid, lift her upper eyelid over her lower one.	If you suspect a scratch to your child's eye, take her to hospital.
▶ Object in ear	Reassure your child. Don't try to remove the object.	
▶ Swallowed object	Reassure your child and try to find out what she has swallowed. Most objects pass through the digestive system. If the object is small and smooth, such as a pebble or coin, there is little danger. Small batteries are dangerous as they contain corrosive chemicals.	Seek medical advice. If your child has swallowed a battery, or a sharp or large object, take her to hospital.
▶ Insect sting	If the sting is in the skin, brush or scrape it off sideways using a plastic credit card or your fingernail. Don't use tweezers as you will inject poison into the skin. Cool the area with a cold compress for 10 minutes.	If you have a family history of allergic reactions to stings take your child to hospital.
▶ Poisoning	If your child is conscious, find out what she has drunk (look for containers nearby). Do not make your child sick as this can cause further harm. If she falls asleep try to rouse her. If she falls unconscious, go to page 286.	Call an ambulance and tell control staff what your child has swallowed.
▶ Swallowed chemicals	Find out what she has swallowed, wipe any remaining chemical from around her mouth and give frequent sips of cold water or milk if her lips are burned. Do not make your child sick as this can cause further harm. If she falls asleep, try to rouse her. If she falls unconscious, go to page 286.	Call an ambulance and tell control staff what your child has swallowed.
▶ Knocked-out tooth	If the socket is bleeding, rinse her mouth with water and place a wad of tissue or gauze in the socket. Ask your child to bite down to stop bleeding. Do not try to replace the tooth; it will be replaced eventually by a permanent tooth.	See a dentist if your child has lost more than one tooth or a chipped tooth has a sharp edge.

Developmental concerns

Most parents worry about their child's development at some stage – it is especially difficult when it is your first baby because you don't know what to expect. But rest assured that "normal" development is very varied in the first two years.

While babies develop at different rates, most milestones are achieved in a predictable order although there are some exceptions. For example, babies who get around by "bottom-shuffling" instead of crawling often learn to walk late, by which time they may be quite chatty. Others may be walking at nine months, but not starting to talk until the age of two. If your baby is desperate to be on the move, he may not spend as much time on fine motor or language skills as the baby next door because he is busy concentrating on finding a way to get across the room. Equally, if your toddler is fascinated by books and little toy people and animals, he may be quite happy to sit on the floor playing with them for now and will put his energies into running around in a few months' time.

"We endured agonies over our daughter's late talking. Then when she was two, she finished her dinner and said, 'All gone!' Now she never stops."

A number of factors affect rate of development, including the position of the child in the family and the sex of the child. It is only natural to compare your baby with others but it is more useful to look at the general timespan for when a skill develops – see the chart on the following page. On the other hand, you should seek advice if you do have concerns, in case there is a specific cause that needs to be addressed. Talk to your health visitor or GP who will be able to put your mind at rest or will carry out the necessary checks. If it does turn out that your child has a developmental delay or disability, try to stay positive and, above all, enjoy whatever stage of development he happens to be at.

Developmental milestones

There is a broad timespan of development for most skills, and this chart gives an approximate guide to the age ranges in which most milestones occur. There is no need to worry unless your child is very late in acquiring a skill. Always seek advice from your GP or health visitor if you have any concerns about any aspect of your baby's development.

KEY

1st Year
2nd Year

MONTHS	1	2	3	4	5	6	7	8	9	10

MOBILITY

BEARS WEIGHT ON LEGS

CRUISES AROUND FURNITURE

DEVELOPS HEAD CONTROL

SITS UNSUPPORTED

STARTS TO CRAWL

WALKS ALONE

ROLLS FROM BACK ON TO SIDE

PULLS UP TO STANDING POSITION

ROLLS ONTO FRONT

DEXTERITY

DROPS OBJECTS DELIBERATELY

DISCOVERS HANDS

PLAYS WITH FEET

USES PINCER GRIP

PASSES OBJECTS FROM ONE HAND TO THE OTHER

BEGINS TO GRIP OBJECTS

REACHES FOR OBJECTS ACCURATELY

POINTS, CLAPS AND WAVES

HEARING / LANGUAGE

STARTLED BY LOUD NOISES

TURNS TO SOUNDS ACROSS THE ROOM

EARLY BABBLING

BEGINS TO COMBINE SOUNDS

MAKES COOING SOUNDS

MAKES LONG AND SHORT SOUNDS

RECOGNIZES OWN NAME

SOCIAL SKILLS

BEGINS TO COPY ACTIONS AND SOUNDS

ENJOYS GAMES SUCH AS PEEK-A-BOO

BEGINS TO SMILE

GURGLES AND LAUGHS

WRIGGLES WITH EXCITEMENT

WHEN TO WORRY

- ▸ Not following face with eyes by six weeks.
- ▸ Not starting to smile by eight weeks.
- ▸ Not turning to quiet noise by seven months.
- ▸ Not sitting by eight months.
- ▸ Not walking by 18 months.
- ▸ No words by two years.

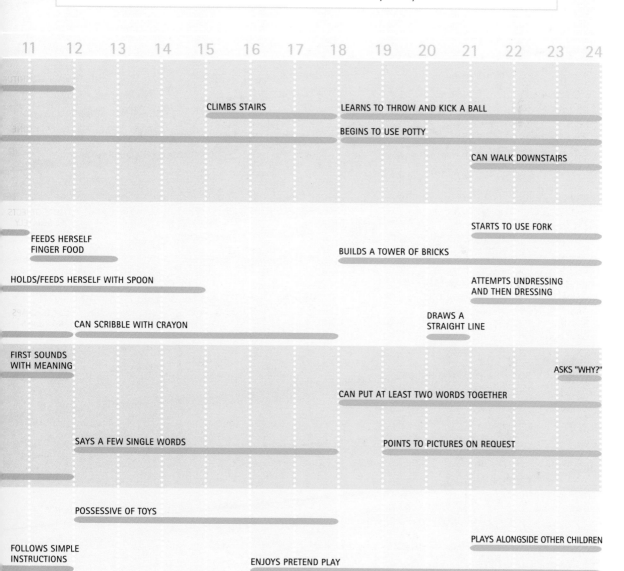

| 11 | 12 | 13 | 14 | 15 | 16 | 17 | 18 | 19 | 20 | 21 | 22 | 23 | 24 |

CLIMBS STAIRS

LEARNS TO THROW AND KICK A BALL

BEGINS TO USE POTTY

CAN WALK DOWNSTAIRS

STARTS TO USE FORK

FEEDS HERSELF FINGER FOOD

BUILDS A TOWER OF BRICKS

HOLDS/FEEDS HERSELF WITH SPOON

ATTEMPTS UNDRESSING AND THEN DRESSING

DRAWS A STRAIGHT LINE

CAN SCRIBBLE WITH CRAYON

FIRST SOUNDS WITH MEANING

ASKS "WHY?"

CAN PUT AT LEAST TWO WORDS TOGETHER

SAYS A FEW SINGLE WORDS

POINTS TO PICTURES ON REQUEST

POSSESSIVE OF TOYS

PLAYS ALONGSIDE OTHER CHILDREN

FOLLOWS SIMPLE INSTRUCTIONS

ENJOYS PRETEND PLAY

SHY WITH STRANGERS

Detecting problems

You know your child better than anyone, and if you have a concern you should expect to be taken seriously. If your toddler is not interacting or behaving as you would expect, or as other children his age seem to behave, your first port of call will probably be your health visitor or GP, who will discuss your concerns with you and assess your child.

It can be difficult to formally diagnose problems in babies and young children, but an intervention programme to help a child's development will do no harm whatsoever – even if it turns out that there is not a problem.

Vision and hearing

Problems with vision are usually detected early. If your baby doesn't fix his gaze on a face or object and follow it with his eyes, he will probably be referred to an ophthalmologist (a doctor who specializes in diagnosing and treating eye problems). Hearing problems are far harder to detect, which is why the newborn hearing test (see page 27) is so important, and your baby will be referred to a specialist if there is any concern. The first sign of deafness may be speech delay and if your toddler doesn't have any words by the age of two he should have a hearing test.

Even if no problems were found in his newborn hearing test, conditions such as glue ear (see page 267) may mean he no longer hears as well as he should.

Motor skills

This area of development is divided into gross motor skills, such as sitting and walking, and fine motor skills, such as picking up small objects. Any delays may become more obvious

Squint

Newborn babies' eyes are sometimes not well coordinated and it is normal for one or both of your baby's eyes to "drift", making him look rather cross-eyed. If after the age of three months, you notice that your baby or toddler's eyes sometimes move in different directions, talk to your health visitor or GP, as he may have a squint. It is important to get this checked out to avoid double vision.

If your child has a squint, his brain will learn to recognize the image from his dominant eye, while ignoring images from the weaker eye. This can result in the weaker eye eventually losing vision, known as amblyopia.

Treatment involves giving your child's eyes a thorough check, then the following options may be considered, depending on the reason for his squint:

▶ Covering up the good eye for periods of time each day to encourage the bad eye to work.
▶ Prescribing glasses for your child if the eye that drifts is weaker visually. Glasses may need to be combined with a patch.
▶ Dilating the pupil in the good eye with drops, which has the same effect as using a patch.
▶ Surgery is sometimes necessary.

as your baby grows. Many babies who are late walkers will catch up, but if there is significant delay, such as not sitting unsupported by nine months or not walking by 18 months, your GP will usually refer you to a paediatrician who will carry out further tests.

Social and communication skills

This type of delayed development can be more subtle than late motor skills, but you may be concerned that your baby doesn't seem to be as interactive or socially aware as other babies. For example, he may not smile readily or be keen to make eye contact. Or you may notice that he doesn't learn to play in the same way as other babies. These can be signs of social and communication problems, which may either improve or become more apparent as your baby grows. Communication difficulties may be due to a disability such as an autistic spectrum disorder (see page 300), or could be due to impaired hearing or your child simply needing more one-to-one stimulation (see below).

Possible causes

Children born prematurely and those who have had long periods of illness or have special needs, may have developmental problems. An important and correctable cause of delayed development is lack of stimulation. An example

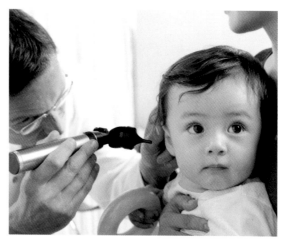

HEARING TEST *Problems with hearing may be detected if a child's speech is delayed. Your health visitor or GP will refer your baby to a specialist for further tests.*

of this is the children found in Eastern European orphanages, whose development had been affected by the lack of care and attention they had received in the early years. Under-stimulated children adopted after the age of one may never attain their full potential. Unfortunately, I also see cases of slow development in neglected children at my UK hospital.

Babies whose mothers suffer from severe postnatal depression (see page 101) may suffer in a similar way if there isn't another adult around to interact with the baby. This is why it is so important to talk to your GP. PND is a treatable illness and your doctor can ensure you have the treatment and support you need.

"I use my internet support group when things are difficult with my baby, who is disabled. It is an invaluable source of advice from other parents in the same situation as me."

What happens next?

If your baby does have a problem you may be a referred to a paediatrician who specializes in child development, who will make a more detailed assessment. You may also need to see a specialist – for instance, an audiologist, if there is concern about your baby's hearing.

In some instances, your baby may need tests such as an X–ray, blood test, and scans to help reach a diagnosis and establish the cause of the problem, although with certain conditions, such as cerebral palsy, no cause may be found despite many tests. Your paediatrician will arrange for you to meet other professionals, such as physiotherapists, speech therapists, and occupational health therapists, who can help your child and offer advice about his treatment. Your paediatrician will also be able to advise you about your child's future education and discuss playgroups, pre-school programmes, and specific support that can help to give your child the best chance of fulfilling his full potential.

There is a huge amount of information and support available for families who have a child with developmental problems and if you are not able to get out to meet other parents and children, the internet is a wonderful resource.

Autistic spectrum disorders (ASDs)

Autism is a developmental disability that encompasses a very wide range of behaviour and there are broad differences in the degree to which a child is affected – hence the term autistic "spectrum". An ASD may be suspected if a child has a "triad" of difficulties: social interaction, communication, and imagination. Autistic children are also very resistant to change, find routine and rituals soothing, and many develop inexplicable fears. The problem with diagnosing ASDs in under-twos is that the above could be observed in pretty much any "normal" toddler. Therefore, experts are reluctant to diagnose a child too early.

Nevertheless, if you have any concerns about your child's social, emotional, and behavioural development – even if it is just a gut instinct that something is wrong but you can't put your finger on what it is – do seek help. ASDs affect more boys than girls, and experts believe this may be due to physical factors affecting brain development, which may have a genetic cause.

The world can be a bewildering, scary place for an autistic child because he won't have the developing social awareness and love of interaction that characterize this stage of development. He may be hypersensitive to sound, smell, taste, texture, or touch, making ordinary family life extraordinarily difficult for him and for you. Tantrums or withdrawal are common in autistic toddlers, as life may be simply too much for them to cope with.

If you, or anyone working with your child, suspect that he may be on the autistic spectrum, there is plenty of help and information available, including early intervention programmes, parent education, support groups, and dietary advice.

While there is no cure for autism, there are various programmes that can be very effective for some young children: it is often a case of trial and error to see what suits each individual. Intensive behaviour intervention, where a child is taught to interact and play by parents and volunteers at home for several hours a day, is thought to work particularly well with very young children. Other programmes aim to help parents to understand and communicate with their pre-school autistic child and some offer continued feedback and support.

Contact the National Autistic Society for more information (see page 312).

"My baby didn't make eye contact and as he grew he seemed different from other children, but I couldn't understand why. When he was diagnosed with Asperger's Syndrome, it was a relief as we were able to start finding ways to help him."

Attention deficit disorders (ADD and ADHD)

Most toddlers are impulsive, have short attention spans, and a tendency to be restless and very active. If, however, these qualities seem to be more pronounced in your child than in other children his age, talk to your health visitor or GP. Your toddler may be referred to a paediatrician or a child psychiatrist, although these disorders are extremely difficult to diagnose at this age.

ADD is also sometimes known as attention deficit hyperactivity disorder (ADHD), although hyperactivity is not always a feature of this problem in older children and adults. As with ASDs, these disorders can range from relatively mild to severe, and children who are diagnosed with ADD may struggle with low self-esteem as they grow older because of the way people respond to their behaviour. There are many strategies that can make life easier for you all as a family, and sympathetic, specialist support in school and at home can help a child with ADD to reach his full potential.

ADD and ADHD affect more boys than girls, seem to run in families, and are caused by physical factors affecting the brain. It is essential to remember that the very difficult behaviour that often characterizes these disorders is neither your fault nor your toddler's. Although drug therapy is sometimes beneficial for children with ADHD, this is not usually an option for toddlers. Treatment for very young children is based around managing difficult behaviour, understanding how to create an environment that will help your child stay calm and, in some cases, modifying his diet if what he eats seems to have an adverse effect on his behaviour.

Contact ADDISS, the Attention Deficit Disorder Information and Support Service (see page 312).

Special children

We all hope for a perfect baby and during pregnancy have tests
to check for and in some cases prepare for problems. An unborn
baby's development is complex and it is always surprising to me that
more babies aren't born with abnormalities.

How you come to terms with your baby being
born with a disability will depend on many
factors, including the severity of the disorder,
whether or not it is life threatening, the way
in which you are told about it, your religious
beliefs, and the support and treatment options
that you are offered.

Some parents are overwhelmed with grief
over a relatively minor problem, such as their
baby being born with an extra finger, while
others are better able to accept conditions such
as Down's syndrome (see page 307), which have
long-term implications for their child's future.

You may be told during pregnancy that there is
a possible problem with your baby, in which
case your birth plan can include giving birth in
a specialist centre that deals with that particular
problem. In these circumstances, you will
probably find it easier to cope emotionally than
if you have had no prior warning of difficulties,
and your baby's abnormality comes as a shock.

If you are told your baby has a disorder,
you will want as much information as possible.
Make sure you ask all the questions you can
think of (it may help to write them down
beforehand) but don't be surprised if you can't
remember the answers. It is a good idea to take
along a friend, who is less emotionally involved
and more able to absorb what is being said.
Also try to get written information. There are
support organizations (see page 312) that can
put you in touch with other families in the same
situation, who are now getting on with their
lives and enjoying their children.

DOWN'S SYNDROME *It is all too easy to make
generalizations about a child who has a disability,
but children with Down's syndrome, for instance,
have a range of IQ and abilities, and are just as
much individuals as any other children.*

Loving your special baby

If your newborn baby is not the perfect baby you were expecting, the shock and grief may be overwhelming at first. The good news is that the bond between you will ensure that you will love her just as much.

Don't worry or feel guilty if bonding takes time, as this is very common even when a baby does not have a health problem. There is no relationship that compares to the one between you and your child, and there will be a great deal of specialist support available to help you get through the difficult times.

About 10 per cent of all babies have to go to the neonatal unit (NNU) when they are born, but there are still ways that you can bond with your baby (see pages 36–37).

What is a congenital disorder?

About 1 per cent of babies are born with a congenital disorder, which is an abnormality that is present at birth. This can vary from something as minor as a skin tag or an extra toe to something life threatening, such as heart disease. Disorders can be broadly divided into several areas –

■ **Structural problems:** conditions include cleft lip and palate, hypospadias, and undescended testes (see pages 304–305).

■ **Problems with the way a baby's body functions:** conditions include hypothyroidism, in which the thyroid gland doesn't produce enough of the hormones that affect the function of all the body's organs.

■ **Problems of both structure and function:** conditions include duodenal atresia (in which the intestine is closed off so nothing passes through the digestive system), congenital heart disease (see page 306), and spina bifida (see page 309).

■ **Chromosomal problems:** conditions include Down's syndrome (see page 307), and Edwards syndrome.

Treatment

Many congenital abnormalities, such as cleft lip and hypospadias, are completely correctable by surgery and have no long-term implications. If your baby needs an operation, though, however minor, this can be a time of tremendous anxiety.

Operations on small babies are always performed by specialist paediatric surgeons and anaesthetists and most carry a low risk. Some rare problems, such as a blocked bladder exit, can be treated before birth in the womb.

"I was devastated about my newborn baby's cleft lip, but soon grew to accept it and actually felt quite strange after it had been repaired."

Common congenital disorders

Fortunately, some congenital disorders are becoming less common due to antenatal screening and the use of folic acid supplements in early pregnancy to prevent spina bifida and cleft lip and palate. However, screening tests aren't foolproof as they can miss serious problems or detect apparent abnormalities which turn out to be nothing to worry about.

Cleft lip and palate

In this condition the two halves of a baby's face don't join up properly while she is growing in the womb, leaving a gap either in the top lip, or the palate (the roof of her mouth), or, more commonly, both. Cleft lip and palate is sometimes diagnosed on an antenatal scan. You will meet a member of the cleft palate team soon after the birth and a series of operations may be needed to correct the problem. This surgical treatment gives remarkable results. The main problem initially is with feeding your baby because she can't suck, but a series of special teats have been designed to help with this.

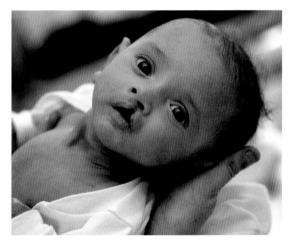

TREATMENT *Cleft lip and palate can be corrected with surgery. This is usually carried out when the baby is three months old, with a further operation at six months.*

Congenital dislocation of the hip (CDH)

This is a condition in which a baby's hip isn't properly formed so the ball part of the hip joint slips easily out of the socket. It affects around one in 1,000 babies and is more common in girls than boys. All babies are tested for CDH at birth during the newborn examination (see page 27) and, if it is suspected, your baby may have an ultrasound scan of the hip. Babies at risk include those with a family history of CDH, breech deliveries, and babies with club foot (see page 305). A splint will be needed to keep the hip in the correct position and encourage the socket to develop normally, but CDH causes no long-term problems.

Club foot

Some babies are born with feet that turn downwards and inwards (see page 22), a condition described as positional talipes or club foot. It is correctable by massaging and stretching your baby's ankle; a physiotherapist can show you how to do it. With early treatment there should be no problems as your child grows. Rarely, talipes is more severe and the baby's foot is twisted in a way that cannot be corrected simply by holding it in the right position. If your baby has this form of talipes she will need surgical treatment to lengthen her tendons, but again, the long-term outlook is usually excellent.

Hypospadias

This condition, which affects boys, is where the opening of the urethra (the tube that goes through the penis) is not at the tip of the penis. Instead it can be anywhere along the underside of the penis (though it may not be possible to spot where it is until you see urine coming out of it). Hypospadias is quite common, occurring in around 1 in 300 boys, and is treated with surgery to extend the urethra to the tip of his penis. The operation is normally carried out before the age of two. The foreskin is the perfect tissue for this task and it is therefore vital that babies with hypospadias are not circumcised before having their operation.

If hypospadias is severe, more than one operation may be necessary, but the outlook is generally very good. The condition is sometimes associated with kidney abnormalities, so babies with hypospadias will usually be given a kidney scan as a precaution.

Undescended testes

Your unborn baby boy's testes are formed in his abdomen and by the time he is born, both of them should have descended to his scrotum. However, sometimes this doesn't happen and one, or both, gets stuck en route. This is usually detected when your baby is examined as a newborn, although he will be checked again during his six-week assessment (see page 80).

The testes are a very sensitive part of the body and have a habit of popping up into the inguinal canal (just above the scrotum) if they are being examined. Therefore, if they can't be felt, this may not mean that there is a problem – they may simply be a bit "shy". If they are both felt in the scrotum, even on only one occasion, they are not "undescended".

Testes that are properly undescended do need an operation to pull them into the scrotum and fix them there. This should be done within the first year of life as testes that are left in the abdomen may result in infertility and an increased risk of cancer. Rest assured that the procedure is quick and easy, and it won't cause your baby any pain or discomfort.

Hydrocele

This is another very common problem and again, one that only affects boys. A hydrocele is a fluid-filled sac in the scrotum around the testes, which is usually harmless and disappears by the age of one, if not before.

A hydrocele rarely needs surgery or causes any problems, but it is sometimes confused with a hernia, which is where a piece of bowel slips down into the scrotum. This is potentially far more serious and nearly always needs an operation to correct it. If a hernia gets stuck, both the bowel and the testes risk a loss of oxygen supply, with serious consequences. For this reason, if your baby has a painless swelling in his scrotum, see your doctor. If the swelling is painful, or you see a new swelling that doesn't disappear when your child lies down, seek urgent medical advice.

Congenital heart disease

This occurs when there is an abnormality in the structure and/or function of a baby's heart. Before birth, your baby receives all his oxygen via the placenta, but when he takes his first breath, his heart starts to receive oxygen-laden blood from his lungs. For this to happen, a duct (the ductus arteriosus) between two major blood vessels, and an opening (the foramen ovale) between two chambers of his heart, have to close. His heart then pumps the oxygenated blood around his body. To do this, blood must pass in the correct sequence through the four chambers of his heart, which are connected by valves.

Congenital abnormalities can involve the valves connecting the chambers; a hole between two or more chambers; or a misconnection between the chambers and the arteries or veins. If your baby looks pink at first, then becomes blue after a few days, this may be because the open duct may initially have allowed some oxygen to get around his body. The most worrying problem is cyanotic heart disease, in which a baby is blue at birth or becomes blue within the first few days and does not become pink when given oxygen.

Diagnosis and treatment

Congenital heart disease is often picked up on an antenatal ultrasound scan and the baby's delivery is planned accordingly. Sometimes a baby is fine at the birth but becomes blue later, and may have difficulty breathing or feeding. A blue (cyanosed) baby is an emergency and will need to be transferred to a specialist unit for surgery.

Far more common is the situation where your baby is very well and a doctor hears a heart murmur during a developmental check. This is usually nothing to worry about, and is simply the sound of blood flowing through the heart, in which case the murmur is referred to as "innocent". Your doctor may arrange a chest X-ray and other tests. Even if a small hole in the heart is found, most close spontaneously so try not to worry.

Genetic and other disorders

Some conditions have a known genetic cause. This may be a problem with a whole chromosome, resulting in a condition such as Down's syndrome or with one or more genes, as in cystic fibrosis. Other conditions, such as cerebral palsy, rarely have a genetic cause.

Down's syndrome

This is probably the most well-known chromosomal abnormality, affecting boys and girls equally, and occurring when a baby has an extra chromosome (see box, below). It results in a range of characteristics. A Down's syndrome child may have –

■ **Floppy muscle tone at birth: this** improves as a baby grows, but she will tend to be late reaching physical milestones.

■ **Particular facial features:** these include eyes that appear to slant due to an extra fold of skin on her eyelids, although she will still have a strong family resemblance.

■ **Particular physical characteristics:** the head may be rather flat at the back and there may be a thickened fold of skin at the back of the neck (the "nuchal fold", which is what is checked for by a scan in early pregnancy), as well as various other physical characteristics, such as a low hairline.

■ An increased risk of congenital conditions: these include heart abnormalities (which are present in around 50 per cent of Down's babies) and duodenal atresia (see page 303).

■ **Learning difficulties:** the degree of this varies from child to child. She is likely to go to a mainstream primary school, but will usually need specialist secondary education.

Your baby's chromosomes

In every cell of the body there are 46 chromosomes. These are arranged in 23 pairs, each pair being made up of one chromosome from the mother and one from the father. Babies with Down's syndrome usually have an extra chromosome on the 21st pair (trisomy 21), making 47 chromosomes in total, although a very few have 47 chromosomes in only some of their cells (mosaicism). A small percentage of Down's babies have a chromosomal translocation, in which a bit of chromosome 21 gets stuck to another chromosome pair. This type of abnormality can be inherited, although it doesn't always cause Down's. If you have a baby with a chromosomal translocation you can be tested to assess the risk of your next baby having the same condition.

While the risk of having a baby with Down's syndrome increases with maternal age, many more Down's babies are born to young women because older mums are more likely to be screened for chromosomal abnormalities. If you discover that your baby has Down's syndrome, the hardest part of coming to terms with her disability may be coping with the shock and grief of not having the baby you expected. There is also the worry that she may have life-threatening heart disease and other problems that require careful monitoring and treatment. Feeding may be slow to begin with and growth will be plotted on a special chart as Down's children are smaller than other children. Most children with Down's syndrome will grow up to lead full and happy lives. Surgery for heart problems is now more effective and life expectancy is longer. Seek support from the Down's Syndrome Association (see page 312).

Cerebral palsy (CP)

This affects around 1 in 500 babies and encompasses a wide spectrum of conditions where the brain has suffered damage. It is similar to a stroke in an adult and can lead to weakness of one or more limbs, learning difficulties, epilepsy, and problems with vision and hearing.

If your baby is diagnosed with cerebral palsy, doctors may not be able to tell you what has caused it. In many instances CP is due to something that took place during pregnancy or delivery, and an increasingly common cause is extreme prematurity. Certain conditions after a baby is born, such as a brain haemorrhage, severe jaundice (see page 35), or infection, can also cause CP.

Mild CP is quite common and can be helped enormously by physiotherapy and occupational therapy. A child with mild CP will probably be of normal intelligence and able to thrive in mainstream education, but she may need some help with getting around. If she has severe CP, she is likely to need more help, including physiotherapy, occupational therapy and speech therapy, and intensive educational support as she grows. She is likely to need a wheelchair and may have difficulty communicating.

Helping your child:

■ Stiff limbs need regular stretching to prevent contractures (permanent tightenings) forming.
■ Lots of stimulation through play and chatting will help your child's development and it is important to take her out, stimulate all her senses including touch and smell, and include her in as many of your activities as possible.
■ Your child will understand you but if she has speech difficulties, you will need to help her communicate.
■ Get support, although this can be difficult due to high demand and depends on where you live, too. If your local services are uncoordinated, it will help to keep a folder with copies of all your child's records. Your GP will be able to help you find the right support.
■ Seek support from Scope (see page 312).

Cystic fibrosis (CF)

In this genetically inherited condition, a defective gene causes the production of abnormal thick, sticky secretions from different glands. This leads to a range of problems including chronic lung disease and failure to thrive. Cystic fibrosis does not affect children's intelligence or abilities, but eventually most will develop diabetes and cirrhosis of the liver, and males become infertile. Life expectancy is shortened for cystic fibrosis sufferers.

A successful heart-lung transplant can give a new lease of life, but this is only an option for a few. However, the outlook for children born now is better than ever and there is hope that in the future, gene therapy will improve the prognosis still further.

CF may be diagnosed by a screening test at birth, depending on where you live. Sometimes a diagnosis is made at birth if a baby suffers from a bowel blockage. Some babies are diagnosed because they don't gain weight or have recurrent lung infections. Eventually, the lungs develop cysts and thickened areas. Occasionally, children have mild symptoms that are not diagnosed until they are in their teens.

Helping your child:

■ Your child needs physiotherapy every day to help clear her lungs, as well as medicines to help her absorb food and provide supplements.
■ Seek support from the Cystic Fibrosis Trust (see page 312).

Spina bifida

In this condition, the tube of protective bones that make up a baby's spine do not close fully around the spinal cord, which can bulge out and become damaged. Spina bifida develops in a fetus in early pregnancy, and there is evidence to show that a diet high in folic acid can reduce the risk. For this reason, supplements are prescribed. The condition is usually picked up on an antenatal scan, but if is isn't and is very severe, parents and doctors may decide together that treatment is not in the baby's best interest.

Babies with spina bifida may have a range of problems from a mild defect over the lower spine which requires surgery to close it, or may even be left to heal on its own, to severe problems with bladder and bowel control,

inability to walk, and delayed development. Along with this there is often hydrocephalus, when the fluid in your baby's brain doesn't circulate properly. Hydrocephalus may cause a variety of problems, such as epilepsy and learning difficulties. A shunt is usually inserted to drain the excess fluid from the brain.

Fortunately, the outlook for most children with spina bifida has improved enormously over the last 30 years.

Helping your child:

■ If you know your baby has spina bifida before she is born, find out as much as you can from the Association for Spina Bifida and Hydrocephalus (ASBAH) (see page 312).

Epilepsy

If your child has convulsions that are not due to a fever (see page 259) or illness, she may be diagnosed with epilepsy. During a convulsion, a child's limbs may jerk violently and go stiff; she may look blank and drop to the ground.

Single convulsions are very common, so if your child has just one she won't be diagnosed with epilepsy. If, however, it happens again, she will need tests and a discussion with a specialist about whether to start treatment. Usually, daily medication is prescribed for about two years, which can be slowly reduced if your child has no further convulsions.

The good news is that most children outgrow epilepsy and there are usually no associated learning difficulties.

Helping your child:

■ If your child is having a convulsion, place her in the recovery position (see page 287).

■ Don't put your finger in her mouth. She won't choke on her tongue if her head is on one side.

■ If it is her first convulsion, call an ambulance. If she has had them before, make sure you know what to do if it lasts for more than a few minutes and when to call for help.

■ Never leave a child who has epilepsy unattended in a bath, as she could drown even in very shallow water if she has a convulsion.

■ You may be given medication as suppositories, or to put beside her gum to stop a convulsion.

■ Seek support from the Epilepsy Association (see page 312).

Hearing impairment

If your baby is deaf, her hearing impairment will be one of two kinds, or a combination of both. Conductive deafness is when the passage of sound through the middle ear is impeded, and this is usually due to a common and reversible condition called glue ear (see page 267). Five to 10 per cent of all children may suffer from this type of deafness, which is usually transitory and needs no treatment.

Sensori-neural deafness affects 1–2 in every 1,000 children. In this condition, the mechanism that carries sound from the inner ear to the brain doesn't work properly, and the resulting loss of hearing can be profound. The sooner this is detected, the better for the child's language and communication skills.

Profound deafness should be picked up by the newborn screening test (see page 27). Sometimes deafness can be inherited, in isolation or as part of a syndrome that has other associated problems. It may also occur after a severe illness, such as meningitis (see page 270).

If your child has a hearing impairment, she will want to keep you in sight at all times as she doesn't have the security of hearing that you are nearby. She will lack many of the clues to understanding her environment that hearing babies have, such as the sounds of dinner being prepared, so she will be shut off from a great deal of family activity if you are not aware that she can't hear. Because of this, undetected deafness can severely affect a child's development.

Depending on the kind of deafness your child has, she may be offered a hearing aid that amplifies sound, or a cochlear implant. The latter is a small electronic device that can help to provide a sense of sound to a person who is profoundly deaf, and although it can't restore hearing, it can help your child to understand speech and other sounds in her environment.

Helping your child:

■ If you think your baby cannot hear, tell your health visitor or GP. If your hearing child appears to be ignoring you, she may have glue ear so if the problem persists see your GP. It is common for children to ignore their parents so try offering her a chocolate biscuit – you will soon discover whether she can hear you!
■ If your child is diagnosed as deaf, you can learn how best to help her maximize her communication skills, and there are many

professionals who can help. You will be given advice about signing.
■ You will need to work closely with a range of therapists to help your child. The National Deaf Children's Society (NDCS) has lots of helpful information and advice (see page 312).

COMMUNICATION *If your child is deaf, the whole family may need to learn to sign and everyone she meets will need instructions on how to communicate with her.*

Sight impairment

If your baby doesn't fix on you and follow you with her eyes by six weeks there may be a problem. Some newborn babies who appear not to see well have a condition called delayed visual maturation. They may not "fix and follow" even at around three or four months, but otherwise have normal development. By 6–12 months this usually corrects itself without treatment.

Severe visual problems are rare. Children who are at particular risk include children with cerebral palsy (see page 308) and those born very early. A family history of blindness or squint (see page 298) is also an important factor.

Helping your child:

■ Bond by giving your child lots of cuddles and talking and singing to her. As she grows, talk to her constantly to help her understand what is happening around her and encourage her to use touch to explore her surroundings.
■ Make sure you have access to the many experts who can help and advise on treatment and strategies to help your child to achieve her full potential.
■ Seek support for your child and your family from the Royal National Institute for the Blind (RNIB) (see page 312).

Resources

ADDISS (The National Attention Deficit Disorder Information and Support Service)
www.addiss.co.uk
Tel: 020 8952 2800

The Anaphylaxis Campaign
www.anaphylaxis.org.uk
Tel: 01252 542029

ASBAH (The Association for Spina Bifida and Hydrocephalus)
www.asbah.org
Tel: 0845 450 7755

Association of Breastfeeding Mothers
www.abm.me.uk
Tel: 0870 401 7711

Asthma UK
www.asthma.org.uk
Tel: 08457 010203

Babycentre
www.babycentre.co.uk

The Breastfeeding Network
www.breastfeedingnetwork.org.uk
Tel: 0870 900 8787

British Red Cross
www.redcross.org.uk
Tel: 0870 170 7000

The Child Bereavement Trust
www.childbereavement.org.uk
Tel: 0845 357 1000

Contact a Family
www.cafamily.org.uk
Tel: 0808 808 3555

Cry-sis
www.cry-sis.org.uk
Tel: 08451 228 669

Cystic Fibrosis Trust
www.cftrust.org.uk
Tel: 0845 859 1000

Down's Syndrome Association
www.downs-syndrome.org.uk
Tel: 0845 230 0372

Epilepsy Action
www.epilepsy.org.uk
Tel: 0808 800 5050

The Family Fund
www.familyfund.org.uk
Tel: 0845 130 4542

FSID (The Foundation for the Study of Infant Deaths)
www.fsid.org.uk
Tel: 020 7233 2090

Gingerbread
www.gingerbread.org.uk
Tel: 020 7403 9500

The Hyperactive Children's Support Group
www.hacsg.org.uk
Tel: 01243 539966

La Leche League
www.laleche.org.uk
Tel: 0845 120 2918

The Meningitis Trust
www.meningitis-trust.org
Tel: 01453 768000

Mumsnet
www.mumsnet.com

The National Autistic Society
www.nas.org.uk
Tel: 0845 070 4004

NCT (National Childbirth Trust)
www.nct.org.uk
Tel: 0870 444 8708

The National Deaf Children's Society
www.ndcs.org.uk
Tel: 0808 800 8880

NHS Direct
www.nhsdirect.nhs.uk
Tel: 0845 4647

National Domestic Violence Helpline
www.nationaldomesticviolencehelpline.org.uk
Tel: 0808 2000 247

National Eczema Society
www.eczema.org
Tel: 0870 241 3604

NSPCC
www.nspcc.org.uk
Tel: 0808 800 5000

ParentlinePlus
www.parentlineplus.org.uk
Tel: 0808 800 2222

St John Ambulance
www.sja.org.uk
Tel: 08700 104950

RoSPA (Royal Society for the Prevention of Accidents)
www.rospa.org.uk
Tel: 0121 248 2000

RNIB (Royal National Institute of the Blind)
www.rnib.org.uk
Tel: 0845 766 9999

Scope
www.scope.org.uk
Tel: 0808 800 3333

STARS (Syncope Trust and Reflex Anoxic Seizures)
www.stars.org.uk
Tel: 0800 0286 362

TAMBA (The Twin and Multiple Birth Association)
www.tamba.org.uk
Tel: 0800 138 0509

The Vegetarian Society
www.vegsoc.org
Tel: 0161 925 2000

Women's Aid
www.womensaid.org.uk
Tel: 0117 944 4411

Index

Acknowledgments

Authors' acknowledgments
We would like to thank our editor, Esther Ripley, for taking a
chance on unknown writers; Maya Isaaks for her enthusiasm
for the project from the start and her expertise as a mother and
writer; Dawn Bates for her skilful role as sub-editor (which
involved playing piggy in the middle at times); Emma Forge
for doing a fantastic job of designing the book; Sally Watkin
for reading through endless drafts; our patients and their
parents from whom we've learned so much; and our friends
and colleagues who've encouraged us to write and whose
quotes are used throughout the book. We'd particularly like to
highlight the contribution of Kate Barker and Banu Mawjee to
the section on the issues surrounding adoption. We'd also like
to thank Leon Hawthorne, Chief Executive of The Baby
Channel for encouraging Su to broadcast her ideas about child
health and then to write about them.

Finally, and most importantly, we want to thank our
children Alex, Emily, and Eddie for introducing us to the
reality and fun of parenting and for putting up with being
ignored while we wrote and rewrote this book.

Publisher's acknowledgments
DK would like to thank first-aid consultant, Viv Armstrong,
Andi Sisodia for proofreading, Sue Bosanko for compiling the
index, Romaine Werblow, the picture librarian, Debbie Maizels
for the illustrations, Lottie Sveas for assistance at the photoshoot
and all the families who took part in our photoshoot.

Picture credits
The publisher would like to thank the following for their kind
permission to reproduce their photographs:
(Key: a-above; b-below/bottom; c-centre; l-left; r-right; t-top)
41 Alamy Images: Picture Partners. **58 Alamy Images:** Janine
Wiedel Photolibrary. **60 Mother & Baby Picture Library. 61**

PunchStock: BananaStock. **70 Alamy Images:** thislife pictures.
73 Photolibrary: Philippe Dannic. **80 Mother & Baby Picture
Library. 89 Photolibrary:** GYSSELS. **90 PunchStock:** Corbis.
91 Mother & Baby Picture Library. 96 Alamy Images: Peter
Griffin (br). **100 Getty Images:** Lena Granefelt. **116 Mother &
Baby Picture Library. 117 PunchStock:** digitalvision. **123
Bubbles:** (tr). **Mother & Baby Picture Library:** (br). **146
Mother & Baby Picture Library. 147 Mother & Baby Picture
Library. 158 PunchStock:** Brand X Pictures (bl). **165
PunchStock:** BananaStock. **191 Alamy Images:** Luca DiCecco.
206 PunchStock: BananaStock. **220 Getty Images:** Elizabeth
Young. **260 PunchStock:** Brand X Pictures. **261 Mother &
Baby Picture Library. 264 Mother & Baby Picture Library.
265 Bubbles:** Bubbles. **270 National Meningitis Trust** www.
meningitis-trust.org. **272 Biophoto Associates:** (bl). **Science
Photo Library:** Lowell Georgia (br); Dr H. C. Robinson (bc).
273 Biophoto Associates: (bl). Kate Cronan: (bc). Science
Photo Library: Dr P. Marazzi (br). **276 PunchStock:**
BananaStock. **279 Bubbles. 281 Mother & Baby Picture
Library. 282 Science Photo Library:** Dr P. Marazzi. **283
Science Photo Library:** Dr P. Marazzi. **284 Mother & Baby
Picture Library:** EMAP. **294 PunchStock:** Digital Vision. **299
Science Photo Library:** Adam Gault. **302 Science Photo
Library:** Lauren Shear. **304 Alamy Images:** Shout. **311 Alamy
Images: Christina Kennedy**
Growth Charts: adapted from charts provided by the Child
Growth Foundation, London
Jacket images: Front: **Getty Images:** Iconica/Jamie Grill bc;
Taxi/Darren Robb t. Spine: **Getty Images:** Iconica/Stretch

All other images © Dorling Kindersley
For further information see: **www.dkimages.com**